CHANGE

THE
BUSINESS
PROCESS
IMPROVEMENT
MANUAL

OR

DIE

CHANGE OR DIE

THE BUSINESS PROCESS IMPROVEMENT MANUAL

MAXINE ATTONG AND TERRENCE METZ

CRC Press
Taylor & Francis Group
Boca Raton London New York

CRC Press is an imprint of the
Taylor & Francis Group, an **informa** business

A PRODUCTIVITY PRESS BOOK

CRC Press
Taylor & Francis Group
6000 Broken Sound Parkway NW, Suite 300
Boca Raton, FL 33487-2742

Printed in the United States of America on acid-free paper
Version Date: 20120618

International Standard Book Number: 978-1-4665-1251-1 (Hardback)

Visit the Taylor & Francis Web site at
http://www.taylorandfrancis.com

and the CRC Press Web site at
http://www.crcpress.com

This book is dedicated to Maxine's nephews, Devon, Andrew, Yohan, and Omari, and to Terrence's father, Thomas Carl Metz, whom in Terrence's eyes, grew taller in stature every day of his life.

Contents

Preface

Welcome

We are going on a journey together—a business trip of change, transformation, and improvement.

Chapter Structure

Our business process improvement (BPI) method promotes the use of facilitator-led workshops to assist the team to make decisions during the project. The appendices are jam-packed with more than 70 pages of workshop tools, agendas, and activities.

Each of the six stages of the BPI method comprises several chapters. At the start of each chapter, the objectives and deliverables are identified. Real-life examples are modified from companies that we have worked with and have been reshaped around a fictitious company called URHere, an illustrative manufacturer of location devices and proximity solutions.

Activities, questionnaires, and examples are used to walk you through the BPI method and to ensure that your team achieves each deliverable. Stages of the BPI conclude with a self-assessment tool to measure the team's progress and its readiness for the next stage and to readily identify any gaps in the team's performance.

Most of the activities and templates are available to download electronically to increase your team's organizational abilities and to promote successful completion of your project. Your team can also use the supplemental activities and tools provided for experiential learning to ease each participant's journey.

Have fun with your BPI project. Your leadership success depends on clarifying and simplifying complex problems with a positive outlook.

Our style eases reference, note taking, and quick scanning. Conventions include the following

■ Large-type headers identify a new section. Each header may contain many topics.
■ Within sections, you may find topical headings. Headings are identified by bold font.
■ We strive to serve a worldwide audience. Most of the world (compared with American English standards) uses fewer periods (ie, full stops). Therefore, and intentionally to save space and keep the eye moving, we subscribe to the global view and do not add periods when deemed unnecessary (using *eg*, and not *e.g.*).

About the Authors

Maxine Attong

Maxine Attong is passionate about writing, facilitation, and business process improvement. Her strong belief in the power of facilitated teams, the creativity of human beings, and the need for alignment between strategy and process has served as impetus to document her thoughts and experiences in the business process improvements field.

Maxine is a graduate of the University of the West Indies (BSc., Accounting) and a Certified Management Accountant (Society of Management Accountants, Ontario). She is also a Certified Manager of Quality with the American Society for Quality, and a life and business coach.

Maxine is the chief executive officer of eink Global Company Limited. The company exists to "enhance vision—one process at a time."

Terrence Metz

Since the end of 1999, Terrence Metz has been a founding principal partner and vice president at Morgan Madison and Company. For more than 20 years, through professional and academic endeavors, Terrence has focused on teaching people *how to* think rather than *what* to think. His experience has proven that the two most important components to high-quality decision making are

1. Nobody is smarter than everybody.
2. There is usually more than one right answer.

Terrence is passionate about using and teaching facilitation so that people become more collaborative. He is the lead instructor and primary curriculum developer for MG Rush Performance Learning and introduced the concept of holism to the field of structured facilitation as a method for keeping meetings on target and aligning objectives across an entire organization.

With a BS from Northwestern University (NWU, Evanston, Illinois) and an MBA from NWU's Kellogg School of Management, his experience also includes a Six Sigma Green Belt from Motorola University and additional graduate work in intercultural decision making at Marquette University.

Acknowledgments

Maxine Attong

Writing a book can be a lonely, internal journey. I am grateful to Terrence Metz, the co-author of this book, for taking this journey with me. Terrence taught me how to facilitate and actually did not laugh when I told his class that I was going to write a book. We met most Tuesdays for more than two years. Terrence has been very patient with me, helping me to clarify my thoughts and challenging me to break the ideas down to levels that anyone can understand. His love for visual displays added a new dimension to the book and led me to develop the tables, questionnaires, and report summaries. Terrence has been the custodian of the document and undertook the tedious task of preparing the tome to the publisher's specifications.

I am grateful to my coach, Connie Kadansky, who helped me get "my ask in gear" during the construction and determination of the direction of the book.

Jack Hilty and Ivor Telamaque challenged me to find my voice and use examples from my actual client experiences to make the book my own.

My cheerleaders during the process were my sisters, Leslie, Carolyn, and Darlene; my mom, Janet; and my aunt Barbera. Other members of the squad were Leah De Souza, Akosua Dardaine, Lorijo Metz, Vicki de Freitas, and Dale Trotman.

Terrence Metz

Our dynamic world of holistic thoughts, words, and deeds supports claims that through the *butterfly effect* (also known as interdependent reciprocities), my acknowledgments are virtually limitless. There are three individuals in particular who need to be acknowledged as special for helping this material come to you.

First, Maxine should be adored for her spirit, passion, and experience that laid the foundation, built the framework, and applied the fabric for the content. She is naturally a clear thinker, and clear thinking leads to clear writing. Maxine is a classy professional, but more important, a wonderful and caring person. Not enough can be said about her, for this book would never have left the ground without her inspiration and perspiration.

Next, my wife and best friend, Lorijo Metz, provided continuous support, guidance, and understanding. As a published author herself, her experience and insight were invaluable. It is the twinkle in her eye, however, coupled with the uplifting resonation of her voice, that made this one's efforts easier and more confident. She is a facilitator in her own right, although her efforts usually change lives one at a time.

Finally, to Kevin Booth, my business partner and mentor for more than 15 years. Kevin taught me by challenging my "psychobabble" (see the first sentence in my acknowledgments) with impeccable logic, well-supported articulation, and the ability to cut through my crappy writing—teaching me, at a minimum, to never again say *precipitation concentration* when the word *dew* works fine. Some people in your life make a lifelong impression and you think about them daily, and Kevin is one of those special people.

Chapter 1

Case Study: URHere Co.

In late March 20xx, executives of the URHere Co. of Santiago, Chile, were reviewing the marketing plans for their three main divisions before adjusting their corporate plans for the following year. The three main divisions for this multinational manufacturer of GPS (global positioning systems) included the following:

1. Government and military
2. Industrial and large commercial
3. Residential and light commercial

Of key interest to the executives were questions such as—

- What can we do to drive our competencies?
- How can we increase profitability—drive costs down, increase efficiencies?
- What new processes should be developed to take advantage of the newest technologies and our partnerships?

Company Background

URHere was founded in 1967 by Owen Trikum, who built and tested his first device with an approved Chilean government satellite linkage. Previous electro-mechanical equipment was potentially less reliable, bulkier, and less accurate than the solid-state mechanism designed by the entrepreneurial engineer Trikum.

By 20xx, company sales were divided approximately as follows:

■ Government (eg, traffic control), 27 percent
■ Military (eg, equipment tracking), 22 percent
■ Industrial (eg, drilling support), 19 percent
■ Large commercial (eg, cargo tracking), 16 percent
■ Residential (eg, hand-held devices), 12 percent
■ Light commercial (eg, in-store product tracking), 4 percent

Selected financial data are shown in Tables 1.1 and 1.2 as millions of Chilean pesos.

Table 1.1 URHere Select Financial Data

Selected Financial Data from Annual Consolidated Statements for URHere Co. (CLP $000,000)	Year Ending March 31	
	20xx	20xx (–1 yr)
Net sales	$322,249	$293,245
Other income	434	547
Total Income	322,683	293,792
Expenses		
Manufacturing and engineering	$194,223	$175,976
Depreciation and amortization	2,345	1,567
Sales and administration	11,238	9,462
Taxes other than federal income	3,786	2,957
Interest	956	679
Total Expenses	212,548	190,641
Earnings	$110,135	$103,151
Provision for federal income taxes	21,486	16,875
Net Earnings	88,649	86,276

Table 1.2 URHere Annual Data

	20xx (–2 yr)	20xx (–3 yr)	20xx (–4 yr)	20xx (–5 yr)	20xx (–6 yr)	20xx (–7 yr)	20xx (–8 yr)
Net sales	267, 529	239,855	201,496	188,469	174,877	171,405	159,603

The GPS Industry

The global positioning industry grew into one of the fastest-growing manufacturing industries by the turn of the millennium. Various estimates placed the total quantity of GPS receivers that are operational worldwide at more than one billion units.

At least seven companies manufactured global positioning systems equipment worldwide, including two major US competitors and one significant European competitor.

Given its early adaptor advantage and strong technology focus, URHere Co. managed to remain number one in market share, but profits and share had been eroding. The company was very reliant on traditional processes, focused on building the next best "widget," and failed to keep up with the competition with its nonengineering- or nonmanufacturing-related activities. Thus, its inefficiency elsewhere in the organization (accounting, customer service, shipping, etc) caused it to bear increasing costs and become far less profitable than its nearby competitors. A summary of financial capacity is shown in Table 1.1.

With manufacturing, support equipment, and geo services, URHere can be found on every continent, including Antarctica. However, its recent financial erosion was generating a very cold shoulder among existing and potential investors. Something had to change.

Strategy Map

The strategy map displayed in Figure 1.1 was built during an off-site strategic planning session. It captures the primary components that drive the unique aspects of their industry and corporate personality.

Scenario

In reviewing current operations, URHere executives decided to allocate additional resources to improve nonmanufacturing- and nonengineering-related functions and activities. They hoped to solicit the voice of employees and customers to help them become more effective with ancillary support and services and more efficient with typical operations. With a solid product and an energetic sales and marketing group, the company realized that they could grow further by strengthening their infrastructure. They feared losing customers to nonproduct-related issues, knowing that it was a lot more expensive to obtain a new customer than to keep an existing customer delighted. They realized that

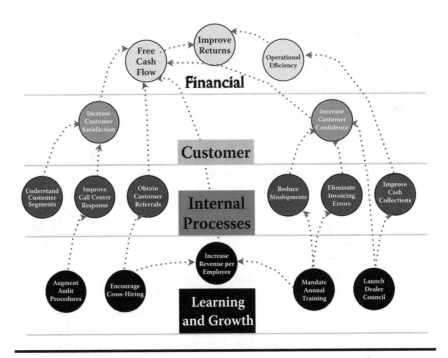

Figure 1.1 URHere strategy map.

they had become the perfect candidate for improved policies, methods, procedures, and activities—known by many as business process improvement.

Structure of URHere

The following groups and their relationships are referred to throughout the book. The purpose here is to provide a graphic reference. Narrative discussions are found in various topics of the workbook that may refer to Figures 1.2, 1.3, 1.4, 1.5, 1.6, or 1.7.

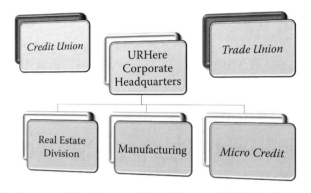

Figure 1.2   Enterprise view.

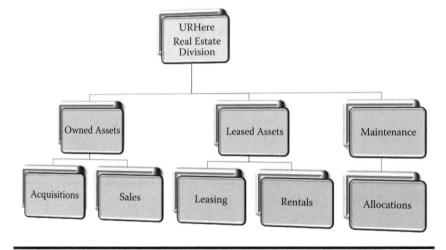

Figure 1.3   Real estate view.

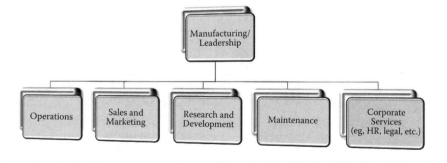

Figure 1.4   Manufacturing view.

Figure 1.5 Micro credit view.

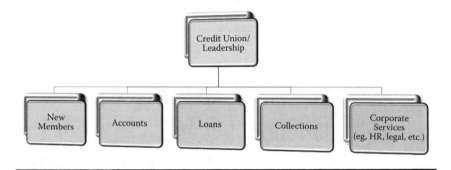

Figure 1.6 Credit union view.

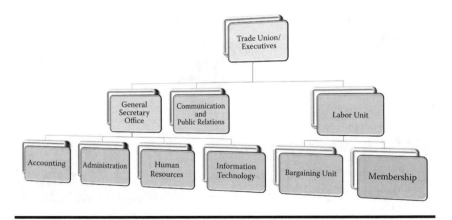

Figure 1.7 Trade union view.

Chapter 2

Vision and Goals

Build or Validate the Vision

> Where there is no vision, the people perish.
>
> **—Proverbs 29:18**

> The world to a blind man is his touch. The world to a stupid man is his mouth. The world to a great man is his vision.
>
> **—Paul Harvey**

When learning to read, many start with the Roman alphabet—ABC. When engaging an organization, we start with the review or development of vision, goals, and objectives. Business process improvement (BPI) takes place within an organization and must be cemented within that context. At the end of this chapter, the team will be able to review or develop the organization's vision, goals, objectives; perform a gap analysis; and develop an action plan for the organization.

At times, we become engaged as life coaches. People come to us when they feel stymied with their career choices and want "more out of life." It is painful to watch clients beat themselves up as they drift from self-doubt to self-pity to self-hate—all because they cannot figure out what to do next with their livelihoods.

We met with the Latin American micro credit manager of URHere who was unsure of her next career move. She worked with URHere for more than 10 years and felt that she had gone as far as she could. One Sunday, we met and got down to the practical details.

We asked her to dream up her perfect work life, detailing the kind of work she would be doing, how and where she would be working, and with whom. She was encouraged to go for it, no holds barred, no expense spared—and she did. She was clear about what her ideal work life should look like, the work she would be doing, with whom, and where she would be working.

When the manager completed her dream, she took some time to enjoy the picture and ensure that she was satisfied with it. The three things she wanted most were job excellence, a specific career path, and to work at an overseas asset.

Clients are usually very clear about the life they want to live. Their dreams are usually rooted in a deep practicality that reflects the inner desire to achieve all that they can.

The Challenge

The URHere manager made a list of all the things that she could do—technical skills, hobbies, and competencies. We then assessed the talents she possessed to determine if they were adequate to achieve the things she wanted. The answers were not always positive.

The final output of her visioning sessions was a detailed five-year plan that outlined ways she would develop the skills she lacked and hone existing skills. At the end of day, the URHere manager firmly established a vision, goals, objectives, and an action plan for going forward.

State the Vision

Just because a man lacks the use of his eyes does not mean he lacks vision.

—Stevie Wonder

Is there anything worse than being blind? Yes, a man with sight and no vision.

—Helen Keller

An organization's vision is like the client's dream. It is how the organization views itself when it is running at full steam, without constraints. The vision statement conveys the reason that the organization exists and what it strives to attain on a daily basis—hence the reason that a vision is so important.

URHere's micro credit business unit provides investment capital for micro entrepreneurs in rural and impoverished regions. Its vision is "To be the leading micro credit financial institution in the region, alleviating poverty, encouraging savings and personal development throughout the organization, thus ensuring client satisfaction." The elements of the vision are broken down as follows:

- To be the leading micro credit financial institution in the region
- To alleviate poverty and encourage savings among customers by realizing the financial benefits of a global positioning system (GPS)
- To ensure the personal and professional development of human capital
- To maintain a 12 percent delinquency rate on its loan portfolio
- To maintain a comparable annual rate of return for its funders

The micro credit unit shared its vision on all its promotional and customer-related materials and held regular staff meetings to help employees relate to the organization's vision. The staff was encouraged to use the vision as a guide to daily business life and choices.

Creating Vision

> The empires of the future are the empires of the mind.
>
> **—Winston Churchill**

The business process improvement team can use the following questions to assist with the development or review of the organization's vision:

- How do you envision a perfect day in the life of your organization—no holds barred?
- To what extent does the current vision give an idea of what this perfect day will be like?
- Is the vision understood by most members of the organization?
- How easily can this statement be translated by the employees?
- How can we make this statement more tangible for employees?
- Is the vision communicated to every member of the organization?

Set Goals

> Define your goals clearly so that others can see them.
>
> **—George F. Burns**

When the manager identified the three things she wanted, she was setting goals. Goals must be aligned to support the vision; they must therefore make sense and add value by enabling measurement toward the vision. Goals are the stepping-stones or milestones that support the *what* of the vision.

Start thinking about goals by answering these questions:

- What are the three to five things that you want the organization to achieve in the next two years, three years, or five years?
- What will be different when we achieve our goals?
- How will we know that we have achieved our goals?
- How do these achievements relate to the organization's vision?

More specifically, goals answer the question, "What will it look like as we begin to realize and approach the vision?" The credit manager may have asked, "What will it look like when URHere is the leading micro credit financial institution?" The simple answer might be, URHere will have increased membership and higher revenues.

Other questions that may assist in developing goals include the following:

Question (Q): What will be different when URHere is the leading micro credit financial institution?
Answer (A): We will have low delinquency rates.
Q: What tells us that we have achieved being the leading micro credit financial institution?
A: Our funders will be satisfied and the finances of the micro credit will reflect strong profits.

From the answers above, the micro credit unit's goals evolved as follows:

- To increase membership usage and corporate revenues
- To retain funding capacity and partners
- To maintain a low delinquency rate
- To ensure timely and accurate reporting

Perform Gap Analysis

The gap analysis is a critical step that may yield an uncomfortable exposure of an organization's weaknesses. It also identifies the existing skills, competencies, and resources within the organization that will lead to goal achievement. Teams that do not perform a gap analysis run the risk of not attaining goals in a satisfactory manner, as they may be unaware that they do not possess the skills or resources necessary to achieve the stated goals.

An honest assessment will align existing skill sets, resources, and competencies of the people, processes, and technologies with the goals. If the skills and resources are absent, the organization needs to determine how they will be obtained—either externally through outsourcing or internally by developing existing resources.

To perform a gap analysis, a skills analysis is completed and then the gaps are identified.

Perform Skills Analysis

Ask the following questions of each goal:

- What skills are needed to achieve the goals (of the organization)?
- How will these skills assist in goal achievement?
- Which of these skills currently exist in the organization?
- What resources are needed to achieve the goals—time, people, and money?
- How can the organization get the skills and resources needed to achieve the goal?

The analysis may look something like the following:

Q: What skills and resources does URHere need to increase membership usage and corporate revenue?
A: (1) Field officers to visit existing members and recruit new members (resources). (2) Proper accounting methods to maintain membership records (resources). (3) Accountant to maintain the membership records (skill).
Q: How will the skill assist in achieving the goals of increasing membership usage and corporate revenue?
A: The field members will meet with the members to increase visibility, early problem detection, and problem solving.
Q: What resources are needed to achieve the goal of increasing visits by field offices?
A: Accounting resources are needed. Field officers need to increase outreach to members.

Perform Gap Analysis

For each skill and resource that is identified as missing or absent from the organization, ask the following questions:

- What are the skills and resources that the organization does not have?
- How can the organization get the skills and resources needed to achieve the goal?
- How can we obtain these skills?

Illustration

Q: What are the skills and resources that URHere does not have to achieve the goal of increasing membership usage?
A: Accounting skills, accountant.
Q: How can URHere get the accounting skills?
A: Outsource the function or develop it internally.
Q: How will the lack of the accounting skills affect the organization?
A: The increase in membership will not be correctly or completely measured. Revenues may not be properly accounted for and members' accounts improperly maintained.

Table 2.1 shows the results of the gap analysis. URHere's micro credit unit has identified the ways that goals will be achieved and which skills and resources are needed. More important, the unit knows what skills are missing and can devise a plan to secure new skills and talents.

SMART Objectives

Management by objectives works if you first think through your objectives. Ninety percent of the time you haven't.

—Peter Drucker

We find no real satisfaction or happiness in life without obstacles to conquer and goals to achieve.

—Maxwell Maltz

When we identify *how* we are going to measure our progress toward reaching the goals, we are setting objectives. Objectives further detail goals and provide

Table 2.1   Skills and Resources Gap Analysis

Goals	How to Achieve the Goals	Skills/Resources Needed
To increase membership usage and corporate revenues	Visit members Promote for new members Maintain low delinquency rates for loans	Field officers *Proper accounting methods* *Outreach programs*
To retain funding capacity and partners To maintain a low delinquency rate	Meet regularly with partners Visit clients regularly Develop relationships with clients Proper and regular reports	*Reports to funders* *Employee retention* *Membership database system*
Ensure timely and accurate reporting	Improve the accounting process Internally maintain and upgrade the system	*Accounting skills* *Accounting software* *Reporting system*

Note: Skills and resources shown in italics are lacking by URHere's micro credit business unit.

a way forward to clarify the shortcomings identified in the gap analysis. Some objectives will be created around the missing skills, competencies, and resources, and others will leverage what already exists to advance goals.

Objectives are narrow and focused statements that identify with additional precision the general or directional goal statements. To develop the objectives we ask, How do we measure the gap being filled? How do we ensure that the gap no longer exists?

Most literature about objectives state that they must be SMART.

■ **S**—specific. Set significant and specific objectives that will challenge the team to go for them. Objectives must hang together; when combined they must not present conflicts or compete for the organization's limited resources. Objectives should be logical and methodical regarding what and how they are going to help measure achievement toward the organization's vision.

■ **M**—measurable. Objectives should be measurable in terms of value: dollar, time, percentage, or otherwise. Specificity makes the objective meaningful and easily remembered by all. There should be a stretch value component so that when achieved the feeling is magical.

■ **A**—achievable and adjustable. The stakeholders being held responsible should agree on the objectives and the way they will be achieved. Responsibility for the achievement of the objectives should be clearly assigned and the people in charge held accountable for the outcomes. Objectives are also adjustable, recognizing that the organization exists in an ever-changing environment.

■ **R**—realistic and relevant. The organization's limited resources need to be spent on activities that will bring it closer to its vision. Objectives should therefore be realistic, set within the context of the organization and its capability. The focus must be on results, because objectives may act as tie breakers when things get confusing. All measurement and evaluation of objectives should be rooted in the facts of the matter. Achievement of the objectives needs to resonate with the organization's goals and vision.

■ **T**—timely. Objectives are set to be achieved within a particular time frame. The outcome must be timely to maintain the momentum and progress toward the organization's vision and goals.

The questions below help to convert goals into SMART objectives illustrated in Table 2.2.

■ What are the specific things the organization needs to realize as it achieves its goals?
■ When are these to be achieved?
■ How will we know when they are achieved?
■ Are we going to fill gaps and hone skills?

From Table 2.2 the company's objectives were identified as follows:

■ Short-term objectives—these were set to be completed with a one-year time frame:
  – Develop an efficient accounting system by the end of year.
  – Hire an accountant by the end of the year.
■ Medium-term objectives—to be achieved within a two-year time frame:
  – Train managers in basic managerial and accounting skills.
  – Develop a pension scheme and benefit plan.
■ Long-term objectives—achieved in two to five years:
  – Visit each client once a quarter.
  – Achieve a delinquency rate of 12 percent.
  – Maintain a minimum of 800 borrowers each year.
  – Increase profits by 15 percent each year.

Table 2.2 Objectives Gap Analysis

Skills/ Resources Needed	*Objectives Related to Gaps*	*Objectives Related to Existing Skills/Resources*
Field officers		Visit each client once a quarter
Proper accounting methods Accounting skills Accounting software	Develop an efficient accounting system by the end of the year Hire an accountant by the end of the year Each manager to be trained in managerial/ basic accounting skills within two years	Reduce the processing time for members' applications by 50 percent
Accounting skills	Hire an accountant by the end of the year	Achieve a delinquency rate of 12 percent Maintain a minimum of 800 borrowers each year Increase profits by 15 percent each year
Accounting software	Develop a pension scheme and benefit plan by the end of the following year	Maintain a minimum of 800 borrowers each year

Check for Alignment

Objectives provide a breakdown of goals, and the goals are used to guide the efforts and actions required to reach the vision. Therefore, the three should be aligned and make sense.

Complete a table similar to that shown in Table 2.3, which was created for URHere's micro credit business unit to match the vision, goals, and objectives. Match each objective to the corresponding goal. Each goal should have at least one objective. Each objective should help in measuring progress toward at least one goal.

Develop Action Plan

A detailed action plan, illustrated in Table 2.4, codifies the systematic activities that will lead to the achievement of objectives. A solid plan will include time frames, resources, and assigned responsibilities.

Table 2.3   Matching Vision, Goals, and Objectives

Vision	Goals	Objectives
To be the leading micro credit financial institution in the region, alleviate poverty, encourage savings and personal development throughout the organization, thus ensuring client satisfaction	To increase membership and revenues	Visit each client once a quarter
		Develop an efficient accounting system by the end of the year
		Hire an accountant by the end of the year
		Each manager to be trained in managerial/ basic accounting skills by the end of the year
	To retain funders	Maintain a minimum of 800 borrowers each year
		Increase profits by 15 percent each year
	To maintain a low delinquency rate	Develop a pension scheme and benefit plan by the end of the following year
		Achieve a delinquency rate of 12 percent

Create an action plan for each objective to show how and when it will be achieved. Identify the person responsible and, where appropriate, generate a budget for the item to be completed. Establish the monitoring points and how the action will be evaluated on completion.

- What actions are to be taken to achieve the goal?
- What resources are required to achieve the goal?
- Who, what, when, and how will the actions be performed?
- What is the desired outcome of each action in the plan?
- How will we monitor the achievement of each outcome?
- How will we evaluate the outcomes?

The action plan is a template that gives a stepped approach for the daily progress toward objectives and goals.

Objective: Hire an accountant by year end.
Evaluation: Do we have an accountant by the end of the year?
Monitoring: The deadlines and cost help to monitor progress.

Table 2.4 Action Plan

	Action Items	Options	Responsibility	Cost	Deadline
1	Develop a scope of work for the accountant	Ask partners for the scope of work used within their companies Develop a scope of work Ask auditor to develop a scope of work	Micro credit manager	No out-of-pocket cost	March 20xx
2	Advertise the position	Advertise within the company Advertise externally Advertise among stakeholders	Human resources	No cost $XX,000 No cost	May 20xx
3	Host interviews	Select candidates for the interview	Micro credit manager and human resources	No cost	June–July 20xx
4	Select candidate	Use the URHere/ partners' selection process to select the candidate Micro credit to develop its own matrix to select the candidate	Micro credit manager and human resources	No cost	August 20xx
5	Recruit the candidate	Human resources to finalize recruitment	Micro credit manager and human resources	$XX,000 per year	September 20xx

Complete the action plan with your team to develop its vision, goals, and objectives. If your organization has already defined its vision, goals, and objectives, then review them to ensure satisfaction and ownership.

Relevancy to Business Process Improvement

> The difference between what we do and what we are capable of doing would suffice to solve most of the world's problems.
>
> **—Mohandas K. Ghandi**

All activities in an organization should contribute toward the achievement of a business objective or goal aligned with the organization's vision and ultimately with the longevity of the organization. The business process improvement project should be no different. It should begin with goals and objectives and progress through detailed action plans as it moves toward full implementation.

URHere's micro credit unit set one objective as, "Increasing membership usage." Management identified the lengthy membership application process as a serious constraint to goal achievement. In response, the unit established a short-term objective: "To reduce the processing time for members' applications by 50 percent."

To realize the objective, the application process needed to be improved. The process was scrutinized and recommendations were made to reduce the processing time for new members. On acceptance of the recommendations, a detailed action plan was developed to fully implement the recommendations.

When the actions were completed, the objective was achieved and the processing time for members' applications was reduced by 50 percent. Management could now pursue its goal of increasing membership because the application process was no longer a constraint. The micro credit unit was one step closer to its overall vision of being the leading micro credit institution in the region.

Chapter 3

Change Management

Background

As an organization moves forward to achieve its vision and goals, it plans, prioritizes, and affects actions. Some old ways will no longer serve the new purpose. Existing resources may need to be bolstered or replaced to drive the new efforts. Changes will be made to the things that are done, how they are done, and ultimately who does them. Humans are not indifferent to change; we react or go numb. The business process improvement (BPI) team needs to anticipate and manage the reactions and numbness that the staff may have around the proposed changes. This chapter equips the team with the tools that will help them minimize the associated risks that change brings.

> Change is the process by which the future invades our lives.
>
> **—Alvin Toffler**

> A process cannot be understood by stopping it. Understanding must move with the flow of the process, must join it and flow with it.
>
> **—Frank Herbert**

> You must be the change you want to see in the world.
>
> **—Mohandas K. Ghandi**

With a membership of more than 50,000, United Front, the trade union that represents URHere workers is one of the largest and oldest in South America. Through the fiery 1970s and the economic hardship of the '80s, United Front fought in favor of minimum wages for daily paid and unskilled workers, and its membership grew. By the start of the new millennium, the firebrands of the '70s and '80s, retired, and younger people felt less need to join the union as most countries' economies dramatically improved. As a result, the union's revenues began to decline, as its operations were funded primarily through members' monthly subscriptions.

The union's leadership traditionally enjoyed access to large pools of money and saw little need for monthly financial reports. As the union's economic situation changed, leadership quickly understood the need for accurate and timely reports and wanted an immediate implementation of a system that could deliver.

The finance system was substantially improved within six months—accounting software was upgraded, manual processes were automated, and new workflow and procedures were developed. However, complete implementation of the new processes and activities to support the changes spanned a two-year period. As improvements developed, employees were trained to use the new software and processes, fears of job loss were allayed, and staff were convinced that the new system would improve work life and bring real benefit to the union.

Younger staff members embraced the changes. Many of them were computer-literate and enjoyed the challenge of learning new, transferable skills.

Long-standing staff members, who were close to retirement, saw no personal benefit in learning new methods. They found the improved process disrespectful of traditional work habits and resented that information that was previously the sole domain of senior members could now be accessed by staff with less tenure. As younger members grasped and excelled at new applications, the senior members became even more uncomfortable as they anticipated a shift in the cultural power base. Eventually, the finance team separated into two groups that were self-named Goldies and Just Come—and the groups almost came to blows.

Within the finance department, the old ways of performing were no longer suitable, and the heroes of yesteryear were left behind.

Introduction

> Design is directed toward human beings. To design is to solve human problems by identifying them and executing the best solution.
>
> **—Ivan Chermayeff**

You are about to embark on a BPI project that will change the way your business operates and the way that people interact in your organization. Your project

Figure 3.1   Six stages of a business process improvement project.

will have supporters and naysayers—people who may have something to lose from the introduction through successful completion of the project. Some of the loss may be only perceived loss, but to these people it is very real. It is never too early to think of a change management plan, as a project may be derailed from the onset because of poor public relations or communication. All the information needed to effectively put a change management plan in place may not be immediately available during the Examine stage (see Figure 3.1) of the project. However, it is worthwhile to start setting the framework for effective change management over the course of the project. The tools identified later in this chapter will assist in the anticipation of problems that the project team may face and, more important, encourage proactive thinking about mitigation actions to limit the negative impact on the project.

The change management tools are dynamic and have a life that will outlive the project. The content prompted by the tools needs to be refreshed monthly (or frequently), as well as every time the project moves from one stage to the next, throughout the six stages of our life cycle as identified in Figure 3.1.

Exercise 1

Think of a time when you faced or watched others face unwanted change. If it is your own experience, think of your feelings at that point and some of the things you said to yourself and to others. Answer the questions below and share them with your team members.

- What was the reason for the change?
- What did I/they do?
- What did I/they say?
- What was my/their attitude to the change?
- How did it worsen or assist the situation?
- What were the reasons for resistance?
- What helped me/them to manage the change?
- Who and what made it better?
- Why did that make it better?
- If I/they had to do it again, I would …
- If I/they had to do it again, I would not …

People Fear Change

> Change is the law of life. And those who look only to the past or the present are certain to miss the future.
>
> **—John F. Kennedy**

We are often afraid of the unknown. Remember the mice in *Who Moved My Cheese?* (or as we prefer to consider it, *Who Melted My Cheese?*)—they preferred to starve rather than take the unknown paths to look for new cheese. All of us have had moments in our personal lives and careers when we had to change to experience something new. New relationships, marriage, divorce, and illness are some of the personal issues that we go through to emerge on the other side.

People often resist change because of the following factors:

- Fear—fear of the unknown. Asking me to get out of my comfort zone is an awful suggestion. My comfort zone may be smelly, broken, or too small for me; but hey, I spray air freshener, avoid the holes, and curl up to fit. I am uncertain what the new place looks like, I do not know the holes, and my air freshener may not work.
- Feeling powerless—comfort brings a feeling of power. I may not be the one with the final authority in the current situation, but I am familiar with the players, what they want, and how I fit in with them. Moving into a new environment means new negotiations with all the factors that currently work for me.
- Too much effort or pain involved—to change implies that physically, emotionally, and mentally, I will need to make some adjustments before I can comfortably settle into the new routine.
- Absence of self-interest—change is frequently not the choice of the individual, but something the individual is asked to accept for the greater good. I am more likely to embrace change that stems from personal decisions related to self-improvement or achievement.

The responsibility of the project team is to manage the innate resistance to change and lessen the negative impact that it may have on the organization's ability to embrace the outcome of the BPI project.

Culture

> Never doubt that a small group of thoughtful committed people can change the world: indeed it's the only thing that ever has.
>
> **—Margaret Mead**

An organization's culture is its personality and character—what makes it unique. Culture governs the intangibles of the organization—the way people work, the things they say, what is valued, the way they behave, the dress code, the traditions, and the privileges they enjoy.

The trade union's unwritten motto was, "Money is no problem." Its pockets were deep and it spent funds with little accountability or constraint. Except for industrial activities, the organization had no urgency and no deadlines.

Within the finance department, the culture was manifested in prolonged and unapproved absences by senior staff, hefty overtime claims, and inaccurate and late reports. Senior staff believed that their many years of service and dedication entitled them to do whatever they wanted, whenever they wanted. The department's strict hierarchy governed seating arrangements and, of course, who had access to all of the information. The junior staff were kept in tight check to ensure that they understood and respected the status quo. Senior members resisted proposed changes because the new approach called for equal access to data, timely and accurate data entry, and daily accountability and responsibility.

Business Unusual

Change your thoughts and you change the world.

—Norman Vincent Peale

God, give us grace to accept with serenity the things that cannot be changed, courage to change the things which should be changed, and the wisdom to distinguish the one from the other.

—Reinhold Niebuhr

The union's general secretary coined the term *business unusual* and declared herself the champion for change. She made an open and undisguised threat that anyone who did not want to embrace the changes could and should leave immediately.

After her initial salvo, she met with smaller groups, explaining the link between the BPI project and the union's ongoing financial stability and viability. To staff members she explained that in the long term, the union may not be able to meet its monthly administrative payroll. To the executives she explained that privileges like attendance at international conferences were unlikely to continue. Moreover, to the shop stewards she explained the reduced ability to service membership as they had been accustomed. She acknowledged that some minor pain and suffering would be felt, but guaranteed that better days were ahead—that the business process improvement project was one of the stepping stones. Everyone understood what she was saying. Her promises and the staff's acceptance of the need for change gave the BPI team its admission ticket to begin to make the necessary changes.

Fear

We have all been afraid of something—the dark, being laughed at, bugs, and other things. We believe that feared things will hurt and bring us pain. When hurt, most people react with inertia, anger, or resentment as they try to cope with suffering and feeling powerless.

The BPI project promises to change the way that things are done, and not everyone will be able to live with the discomfort of the unfamiliar. The threat of punishment was effective in the union's culture; however, it is unacceptable in most business environments.

The BPI team needs to mitigate the root cause of the resistance to change. Are the staff fearful because the situation is new? Have they gone through a similar situation before? Do they fear the loss of jobs? Some fears are real—there may be job loss or reassignments, new requirements, and change in status quo. The BPI team cannot guarantee outcomes but can only alleviate fears in the short term by showing compassion, walking in the staff's shoes, listening and empathizing with the staff, and building trust. There is little other choice.

Throughout the trade union's BPI project, the BPI team upheld a practice of open and honest communication. Staff were encouraged to ask questions and participate actively over the course of the plan's development. Troublemakers were listened too closely so that the reasons behind their behavior could be understood. All rumors were met head on and denied the chance to grow due to erroneous assumptions. The entire organization was regularly updated through internal newsletters and meetings.

Change Management

> It is not the strongest of the species that survives, nor the most intelligent, but the one most responsive to change.
>
> **—Charles Darwin**

Significant change results in a cultural shift among the organization and its members. The BPI project changed the trade union's structure, reporting relationships, roles, policies, and procedures. The project outcome challenged traditions and called for its members to adapt different core values.

Where the prevailing culture does not support the recommended changes, resistance will solidify. The level of resistance can be gauged by the amount of "newness" that the improvements bring—more newness equals more resistance. Resistance is quantified by what is going to change—people (roles, jobs), their activities, and technology—because of the improvement efforts. The business process improvement team needs to understand resistance as a risk that can be mitigated and managed. Change resistance should be included in the *risk register* (see Chapter 9). The *project plan* (also Chapter 9) identifies when the changes will occur and gives the team a planning horizon for the stakeholder reaction.

At the onset, the team should identify and engage a change champion, someone who has the power to make a difference and is viewed as credible and, most importantly, trustworthy. Formal and informal leaders also need to be encouraged to make positive contributions to the plan.

Change Management Defined

Change management captures the mitigation of stakeholders' fears of the unknown impact of the soon-to-be improved process. The project team needs to be compassionate by working to identify and understand *why* each fear exists. It is only through dispelling the fears that the team can hope to win over the stakeholders.

Managing Change

> The universe is transformation; our life is what our thoughts make it.
>
> **—Marcus Aurelius**

Since you now understand why people resist change, you can begin to mitigate the risks by providing information about the Five E's to positively lead change efforts.

■ Enticement—enticements can be positive and negative. People can be rewarded for varying levels of contributions they make to the project and to the successful implementation of the project. Negative enticements do not always work and may even backfire, but they can be used in small doses to dissuade stubborn, negative behaviors.

■ Evidence—fear often finds root and thrives among the unknown and uncertain. Rumors replace facts and stories grow wilder, evoking more fear. The team needs to take charge of what is said about the project to ensure that the story that needs to be told is the only one repeated. Posters, intranets, social sites, Wikis, and other forms of regular communication will support the organization to keep up to date with what is happening in the project. Caveat: Be careful about what you sell, for if the staff or other stakeholders lose trust in your communiqués, they will lose trust in the project. The need for honest, open communication cannot be overstressed.

■ Explanation—the project team must be willing to provide one-on-one sessions with closely affected staff members, ensuring that each person understands what is happening and will change in their lives. The team may also have to challenge people who are rumored to be giving incorrect information about the project.

■ Essence—stakeholders should develop a sense of urgency, leaning toward the belief that the organization cannot survive without the improvement program. The project essentials reflect the following:

  - What the change aims to achieve—why the improvement project is important needs to be clearly stated, preferably quantified regarding its impact on costs, assets, and labor hours. Tie the project to a higher purpose that relates to the organization's vision and objectives. For example, the project is about not only efficiency and effectiveness, but also getting the organization to increase market share by 20 percent within the next five years. Use the following tool to capture the purpose of the project: "The purpose of improving the process is to … so that …"

  - Why the changes are necessary—after the purpose is codified, it is easier to see why the changes are necessary. Again, relate the articulated purpose directly to the vision and goals of the organization.

  - Consequences of the changes to the organization and the individuals— state the positive effects, results, and benefits for the organizations and its stakeholders. It is useful to state the negative effects that will be eliminated when the project is completed and successfully implemented.

■ Engagement—the team alone cannot make the project successful. The team's role is to lead and guide the effort with the understanding that they cannot create success without the support of stakeholders. The more that staff members are involved in the approach, the more they feel a part of the solution, and then the more likely they will own and embrace the improvement project. Change management is about mitigating fear and making the project and its outcome more familiar to the other staff members.

Develop Components

A successful change management program includes the following:

1. A detailed stakeholder project plan (see also Chapter 9). The plan must consider and address the following:
   - Who will be involved—the target audience as well as other stakeholders who will affect the plan need to be identified.
   - What is going to change—identify and quantify (where possible) the people (roles, jobs), the activities, and the systems that will change, resulting from the improvement efforts. Identification assists in defining the target audience and refining project scope.
   - What new information will be required—start with the information you have to define the gaps. As the project proceeds, new information needs will surface.
   - What new deliverables are expected—the changes will influence the new expected state or condition of the organization.
   - How the change affects each stakeholder—what does each need to learn to deal with the proposed changes?
   - Selection of key personnel for the program—the team will determine the necessary roles that must exist for the plan to succeed. The different types of leaders in the organization and the ways that each leader could contribute to the change plan should be identified.
   - Clear understanding of the change impact on strategy, culture, roles, activities, and adjustments for the business process improvement project.
2. Detailed communications plan.
   - Stakeholders (internal and external) have a stake in the project and its outcome. Each stakeholder should be identified and an examination made of the impact the project outcome will have on the stakeholder and his or her power base. It is necessary to think about how project completion will affect each stakeholder's status quo and comfort zone.
   - The communications plan is critical and best done at the onset because it identifies the stakeholders of the project and their importance to the project's success.
   - The communication plan will be continually updated over the life of the project.

It is best to use the protocols and terminology that are established within your organization when developing a communications plan. The plan addresses the following:

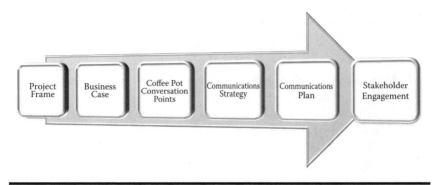

Figure 3.2 Stakeholder engagement.

- Who—the plan identifies the stakeholders or stakeholder groups that need directed communications.
- What—the specific message for each stakeholder group will be addressed.
- When—the time frame for the communication. The time component does not have to be a specific date but could reflect an interval.
- How—the method for the communications—one-on-one, meeting, presentation, and so forth.

The plan is simplified and shown in Figure 3.2.

Conclusion

Your project will encounter some resistance; it cannot all be avoided. However, you can limit the amount of resistance by preparing a change management plan from the onset and regularly refreshing and updating the communication plan throughout the project life. The communication plan provides a major strategic tool for your change management plan.

Chapter 4

Stakeholder Analysis

Stakeholders may include external or internal people, groups, systems, and other organizations that interact with the organizational group or a specific process.

Monthly dues that United Front, the trade union, members paid for representation contributed more than 90 percent of the trade union's income. As the trade union's fortunes dwindled, the shortcomings of the revenue collections—how revenue was collected and what was done with it—became a major issue for the union. Trade union members became more knowledgeable and demanded far more effective use of the paid dues, as well as transparency and accountability for those responsible.

The business process improvement (BPI) changed the requirements of the internal process—the activities performed and by whom; and the external interactions with the banks, the employees, and the supervisors and managers at URHere. Stakeholders needed to be satisfied that the new collection process would give them what they needed before they were willing to accept the changes. The BPI team needed to implement a strategy for each discrete stakeholder group that would encourage support of the new collection process. At the end of this chapter, the team will be able to develop a strategy for managing stakeholders.

Define Organizational Stakeholders

Stakeholders are identified by examining the way that they interact with the organization in providing or receiving services or benefits. The trade union's stakeholders are identified in Table 4.1.

Table 4.1   Stakeholders

Internal	*External*
Employees	Banks
Union executives	Employers
Trade union members	Trade union members
	Industrial courts
	Vendors
	Other trade unions
	Country as a whole

Each stakeholder is affected, directly or indirectly, by the decisions that the trade union makes. When the trade union participates in legal action against an employer, the result sets a precedent for the representation of all workers in the trade union. The decision to change the collections process affects each of the stakeholders differently, as shown in Tables 4.2 and 4.3.

Process Stakeholders

Process stakeholders are identified by examining contributions to the process (inputs) and their benefits or what they receive from the process (outputs). The three-step approach below helps identify the stakeholders of the trade union's collection process.

Step 1: Identify inputs

1. *What are the inputs* to the collection process, or, what goes into your process? Examples are a members' list, checks, and bank notices of remittances. A members' list is a list of the names and the amounts that are being paid to the trade union on a monthly basis by the employer.
2. *Who provides each input* identified in activity #1 (above). Associate the source(s) of each input. Employers provide checks, bank remittances, and members list. Members provide the money and checks.
3. *How is the input used?* Describe the activities and how each is performed. A manual receipt is generated in duplicate for each check and bank notice received. The receipts are used to update the revenue collection system. The members' lists are used to update the members' status within the database (new members, retired, etc).

Table 4.2   Internal Stakeholders

Interests	Employees	Shop Stewards	Union Executives
Interest in process	Sustained payment of benefits, salaries, and allowances Union's ability to make postretirement commitments	Representation in court of workers Knowledge of members' status	Continuity of union as a going concern Ability to meet financial commitments Benefits and allowances Conferences and perks
If process fails	Job loss Loss of postretirement benefits	No worker representation Job loss Ignorance of members' status	Loss of power Loss of status Derision from other unions
If process succeeds	Better pay and benefits Improved health postretirement benefits	More personal benefits Greater bargaining power	Better perks More clout with the bank and other financial institutions More status
Ability to impact on changes	High—5	Low—1	High—5
Interest in changes	Medium—3	High—5	High—5

Step 2: Identify outputs

4. *What are the outputs of the process?* These are usually *things* or nouns such as a form, report, or event (such as a deposit); for example, receipts, an updated members' list status, and funds for the union's use.
5. *Who uses or benefits from the output* of the process—associate the client(s) or customer(s) of each output; for example, members, trade union, and employees of the trade union.
6. *How is the output created?* Describe activities that are dependent on the inputs and how each is further transformed into something of value. The members' lists are used to update the members' database. When checks or bank remittances are received, a receipt is generated for the payer.

Table 4.3   External Stakeholders

Interests	Members	Bank	Employers
Interest in process	Adequate representation Payment of benefits	Meet monthly financial commitments—loans and overdraft Continuity as a client	Recognition of monthly funds paid
If process fails	No representation No ability to recoup monies/dues paid over the years Limited bargaining power	Unpaid loans and overdraft Financial exposure Legal proceedings	Greater bargaining power Less monthly commitment
If process succeeds	Better representation Increased bargaining power	Continuity as a client Increased business— loans overdraft	Less bargaining power
Ability to impact on changes	Low—1	Low—1	Low—1
Interest in process	High—5	High—5	High—5

Step 3: Identify stakeholders

7. Each input and output can be linked to one or more stakeholders by one or more activities within the process. A stakeholder relationship shown in Table 4.4 clarifies the relationship between stakeholder, input, output, and activity within the process.

Group Stakeholders

Stakeholders can be grouped together according to how they use or interact with the inputs and outputs. From Table 4.4, members and employers can be grouped together as one stakeholder group called Payers, as they interact with the collection process in the same manner.

Table 4.4   Stakeholders' Relationships

Provider	Input	Action	Output	Used By
Employer	Members' list	Entered in members' system	Updated members' system Accounts receivable	Shop stewards Members
Employer	Checks	Receipts generated Bank deposits	Receipts Bank deposit slips	Employers Management Loans officers (bank)
Members	Cash	Receipts generated Bank deposits	Receipts Bank deposit slips	Members Management Loans officers (bank)

Acknowledge Stakeholder Interests

The motives and needs of the stakeholders determine their interest in the process and indicate how they can either contribute to or derail the success of the project.

As the trade union's frontline representatives, the shop stewards deal with membership on a daily basis. Consequently, they need to have accurate and timely information on the status of its members. Status determines voting rights and access to representation and benefits, such as insurance, saving plans, and worker compensation. Member status can be categorized as follows:

- Financial—all dues have been paid within a specified time frame.
- Nonfinancial—dues are owed.
- Expired—the member is no longer part of the union because of death, retirement, or resignation.
- Canceled—membership has been revoked.

When the stewards understood and believed that an improved collection process would positively affect the accuracy and timeliness of the member data, they immediately championed the process improvement.

Define Stakeholder Strategy Plan

The stakeholder strategy plan (SSP) is a blueprint for the BPI team's interaction with stakeholders. The focus on stakeholder's contribution shows how the team can use the stakeholder's interests to support the project and make it successful.

The SSP identifies the following:

- What the project wants to achieve with each stakeholder
- Stakeholder issues and interests
- How stakeholders will be managed
- The frequency of communication
- The changing content of communication over the life of the project

The plan is dynamic, meaning that it must be constantly updated to reflect changes in stakeholder opinions over the life of the project. The template below supports development of the stakeholder strategy plan.

Develop Stakeholder Strategy Plan

Stakeholder Name: _____

Objective
- The objectives of the strategy plan are ...
- It is important for the project to have a stakeholder plan because ...
- The purpose of the plan is to ... so that ...

Define the stakeholder
- Give a short description of the stakeholder group:
- The members of this stakeholder group are ...
- Describe each group's role in the process:
- Identify inputs the group provides:
- Identify outputs the group uses:

What does the stakeholder think?
- The stakeholder thinks that the current process ...
- The stakeholder thinks this because ...
- The stakeholder's interest in the current process ...
- The stakeholder's power in the current process ...
- The stakeholder thinks that the BPI project ...
- The stakeholder's likely reaction:
- The stakeholder wants ... from an improved process.

Where does the stakeholder need to be?
- It is important for the stakeholder to support the project because …
- Without the stakeholder's support …
- The stakeholder's support …
- The stakeholder can contribute to the success of the project by …
- The stakeholder can hamper the project by …

How will the team move the stakeholder?
- The BPI team wants the stakeholder to …
- The three things that are important to the stakeholder are …
- The team can guarantee …

Communication with stakeholders
- We need to tell the stakeholder …
- We need to tell them because …
- The best way to communicate with this group is to …
- This will cost (prepare a budget) …
- We need to meet with this group because or when …
- At what points in the project is it critical to meet with each stakeholder?

Confidentiality
- How do we deal with confidentiality issues?
- Can each team member be privy to all information?
- Can each stakeholder be privy to all information?
- What is the strategy to ensure that confidential information stays that way?

Define Communication

Each stakeholder group is different and needs to be communicated with in a manner that honors their interests and responses. The team will appoint a stakeholder interface who is responsible for communicating with the stakeholders on an ongoing basis.

Develop a Communications Action Plan

The communications action plan identifies exactly how and when the project team will communicate with each target audience (or stakeholder) over the life of the project. The plan is flexible, as it is updated over the life of the project and recognizes the need for intervention and ad hoc meetings. Match the communications plan with the project milestone and plan outreach to the stakeholders and staff at critical points of the project, as shown in Table 4.5.

Table 4.5 Map Communications Plan

Project Stage	Audience	Message	Type of Communication
Examine— determine the need for BPI	Executive management	We have a problem. BPI can solve it.	Face-to-face meeting Reports
Negotiate the process that is selected	Senior management and process owner	The vision and goals will be best served by improving this process.	Meeting Presentations and findings Reports
Go for it—set goals for the process	Senior management, process owner, key process members	This is what the new process will deliver.	Facilitated workshop—to capture input and concerns
Action— design the process, improve the process	All staff before the design is done	The BPI is launched. We are going to improve the process to give these results.	Official and festive launch—food and drinks
Generate excitement and commitment— implement the new process	All staff, process members	This is the new process. It starts on xx-xx-xxxx date.	Festive presentation Diagrams, intranet Facilitated workshops for stakeholders
Engage staff—audit, procedures, and daily use of the new process	Process members	The new process is in effect. It works!	Intranet message to all staff from process owner Detailed documentation re process Report to executive management

Consider the need for different types of meetings. One-way communications may be appropriate when the team needs to reveal the decisions made and share information. Facilitated workshops can be used for decision making and to encourage participation and ownership. Ad hoc meetings may be held to deal with negative situations and to negotiate among stakeholders. This plan provides significant input for the change management communications plan.

Define Outreach Role

The team can define the outreach role by answering the following questions:

- Who are the stakeholders that the outreach needs to touch?
- What are the responsibilities of the outreach? How is the responsibility different for each stakeholder (internal vs. external stakeholders)?
- Who on the BPI team is responsible?

Select Outreach Member

Communication with stakeholders must be considered critical, as one incorrect statement can wreak havoc on the team's best intentions. The outreach role should be filled by someone on the team who has outreach competence and is viewed as credible and trustworthy by the team and stakeholders.

The following steps will assist the team to select an outreach member:

- What are the characteristics of each stakeholder group?
- What are the traits the outreach should have so as to match those of each stakeholder group?
- Determine the characteristics of your outreach team member—the team needs to identify what characteristics will best describe this member, such as trustworthy, open, good orator.
- Identify the team member who best fits the characteristics above.
- Select a member using Table 4.6. Identify each candidate's strengths and weaknesses. For each weakness, identify a mitigating factor that can lessen the impact of the weakness (mitigation may include training).

The team can recruit an external communications expert to fulfill the outreach role.

Table 4.6   Candidates for Outreach Member

Name	Strength	Weaknesses	Mitigating Factors
MA	Good orator and listener, believes in the process	Impatient, tends to be bossy	Is liked by staff, thought of as credible

Define Stakeholder Analysis

The stakeholder analysis document examines how the proposed changes will affect each stakeholder and their interaction with the process. Upon completion of the document, the team will identify strategies for dealing with each stakeholder. The analysis provides the information for completing and updating the stakeholders' strategy plan.

Determine Stakeholder Risks

The amount of power each stakeholder or stakeholder group enjoys now and the extent to which their power will change are good indicators of the level of resistance the stakeholder will have to the project. The more pain that stakeholders are asked to absorb and the more power or status they lose, the greater the resistance. Figure 4.1 can be used to predict the amount of resistance from the stakeholder group.

The collections staff will resist because they will experience much pain and lose power. Employers will lose little power and suffer little pain and will generally support the change. The team can anticipate where the resistance lies and devise a strategy to reduce the risks.

Define Stakeholder Opportunity

Not all groups will resist the changes. The improved process may reverse the pain that some groups feel with the current process and provide more status, power, and better results. The shop stewards will gain power with little pain and should support the proposed change.

Perform Detailed Stakeholder Analysis

A more detailed analysis can be conducted for each stakeholder to help the team understand resistance and develop ways to engage stakeholder support for the

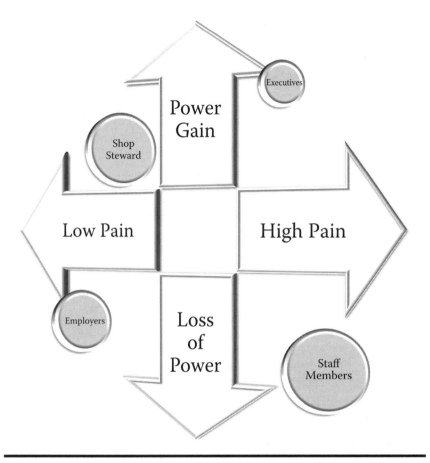

Figure 4.1   Resistance.

project. The stakeholder analysis for the collections supervisor was completed to understand how to alleviate her fears around the improved and updated process.

The collections supervisor was not a supporter of the proposed changes; however, the shop stewards' praises of the improvements enthused her to get involved in the implementation. For stakeholders, provide the impetus that will encourage them to support the process—identify what is in it for each of them.

Mitigate Behavior

From the stakeholder analysis shown in Table 4.7, we can develop an action plan, as illustrated in Table 4.8, to encourage the positive behaviors and limit the negative behaviors.

Table 4.7   Stakeholder Analysis

Name: Mrs. JD	*Position: Collections Supervisor*
Ability to impact project 1 High 1 2 3 4 5 Low (circle position on the line)	View of project commitment 5 Positive 1 2 3 4 5 Negative (circle position on the line)

Risks: *This indicates how the stakeholder may negatively affect the project. Includes behavior, actions, and thoughts. Mitigation strategies can be identified.* The supervisor is a well-respected member of the union and has a lot of influence. If she does not buy into the project, other staff will follow suit. She may also sabotage the efforts of the project team by withholding data.
Help: *Identifies the actions that each stakeholder can perform to assist in the project. These are within the stakeholder's scope but may not be what they are willing to do.* The supervisor can encourage staff to support the project; she can highlight problems with the current process. She can get out of the way.
Power Today: *Identifies what in the current process gives the stakeholder status, recognition from peers, or monetary benefit or defines the stakeholder as successful. This may be real or perceived. It may also reflect the organizational culture.* All the receipts come to her for sign-off. She prepares the bank deposit, knows the bank balances, and determines who gets what information. She is the only person who can generate reports.
Power Tomorrow: *Determines the power or status that the stakeholder may have after the BPI. May involve a loss or gain of power, status, or recognition. A statement needs to be made of what the new role is and how the change will be perceived. May reflect an emerging or new culture.* She is responsible for exceptions in the process; problem solving and ensuring that the process is followed will be her remit. She will not be involved in all daily processes and may perceive the change as a loss of power.
Hinder/ Hurt: *Defines the power that the stakeholder has in the current process and how this power can be leveraged to promote or hinder the BPI project. This includes formal or informal leadership, influence, and control.* She can deny staff permission to attend workshops, withhold information, discourage other people from participating, and not implement solutions.

Table 4.7 (continued)   Stakeholder Analysis

Strengths: *Determines the personal characteristics and the status or the role that the stakeholder plays in the current process, and suggests how these can be used to promote the project. Identifies how the project can leverage these strengths to add to the project's influence.* She can encourage staff to get involved with the project. She can help in the determination of future roles because she knows the strengths and weaknesses of her team. She can pinpoint risks for the implementation.
Weaknesses: *Determines the personal characteristics and the status or the role that the stakeholder plays in the current process, and suggests how these can be used to hamper the project. Identifies how the project can limit or control the weaknesses.* She can sabotage the project. We need to get her on board from the onset, but must make a decision if she is not cooperating.
Benefits: *Proposes the potential rewards in terms of status, power, influence, or other tangible or intangible benefits that the stakeholder can obtain with the successful implementation of the project. This is a selling point for the project.* More influence with the shop stewards as information provided will be current and accurate. Better relations with the banks as deposits will be timely. More scope for negotiation of wages—as she is close to retirement she needs to get better ratings on her annual performance to maximize earnings and get a better pension.
Losses: *Proposes the loss in status, power, influence, or other tangible or intangible benefits that the stakeholder may face with the successful implementation of the project. This must be anticipated so that strategies can be developed to minimize losses.* Lose the power associated with preparing the bank deposits, preparing reports, and being privy to information considered for "her eyes" only.
Losses: *What are the proposals in the new process that may be perceived as negative by the stakeholder in terms of his or her role, organization, personal interests, and loss of power or status? What may bring pain to the stakeholder?* Does not like the fact that the improved process can run effectively without her presence.

Continued

Table 4.7 (continued) Stakeholder Analysis

What actions does the team need to take? *Identify the actions that the BPI team may engage to limit the negative effects of the stakeholder and promote the positive aspects.* See that the clients—shop stewards, banks—see real value in the process. Invite the stakeholders to a meeting where they can articulate their interests in the new process. Demonstrate how the new roles may result in increased earnings or support other objectives. **Time Frame:** *Immediate* **How:** *Meet with shop stewards and supervisor*

Source: Adapted from *Business Process Management: Practical Guidelines to Successful Implementations*, by John Jeston and Johan Nelis. Published by Elsevier Ltd., 2006, Chapter 24, "Project Management," Table 24.2 Individual Stakeholder Analysis and Table 24.3 Stakeholder Analysis Matrix, pages 258 and 259.

Update Analysis

As the project advances, the BPI team will make decisions that threaten current supporters and encourage dissuaders. The stakeholder analysis recognizes the fragility of the human condition and sensitivity to its environment. The BPI team must constantly monitor and evaluate stakeholders' reactions by revisiting the stakeholder analysis at each milestone.

Conclusion

Stakeholders (internal and external) have vested interests in the project and can provide positive support to the project. It is the team's responsibility to identify the contribution each stakeholder can make and to extract it. The project team needs to be aware of the impact the BPI may have on each stakeholder and their power base, and develop strategies that are appropriate for advancing the project.

Table 4.8   Action Plan

No.	Task List	How	Responsibility	Date
1	Identify the ways that the collection process can result in increased wages	Meet with the union's HR function to understand the wage increase process Determine what specific actions the supervisor needs to take to increase her wages via the new collection process	Human resources liaison Project manager	To be completed in the next three months
2	Increase supervisor's "power" with the shop stewards	Host a meeting with the shop stewards and the collection supervisor. The objective is to show that the shop stewards want the new system and to establish this as a power base for the supervisor.	Team communications manager	Within the next four weeks

Continued

Table 4.8 (continued)   Action Plan

No.	Task List	How	Responsibility	Date
3	Get the supervisor to release staff for training and to be part of the project implementation	Use the advantage gained from tasks 1 and 2 to encourage participation. Get the executive in charge to make training mandatory. Work with human resources liaison to have the training as requirement for the job.	Human resources liaison BPI champion BPI sponsor	Within the next three months
4	Teach the supervisor what a supervisory role entails	Retrain the supervisor from "doing" in the process to dealing with exceptions and adding real value in her role.	Human resources liaison Human resources manager May require external training	Over the next six months

Table 4.8 (continued) Action Plan

No.	Task List	How	Responsibility	Date
5	Convince the supervisor that the information is to be accessed by all members	Use the shop stewards to sell that they no longer have to wait on information and can provide a better service to members if they can get the information from anyone and at any time. Maintain the importance of the supervisor as the leader of this new initiative.	Project manager	Over the next three months
6	Nip negative behavior in the bud.	The project team needs to be aware of any negative comments by the supervisor. They need to communicate intentions to all staff and, when necessary, meet with the supervisor and exchange ideas.	All team members BPI sponsor BPI public relations	Ongoing

Chapter 5

Core Process

We need men who can dream of things that never were.

—John F. Kennedy

In this chapter, the core processes within the organization are deliberately identified. We critically examine core processes to ensure that they are functioning optimally when measured by resources consumed and contributions (ie, value added) generated. This analysis includes processes that generate intangible benefits and processes that consume assets of the organizations such as wealth. For example, marketing processes might generate "goodwill" that is viewed as beneficial and yet very difficult or costly to measure.

Over the long term, business process improvement (BPI) should consider all the processes within the organization; the challenge now is where to start. We have found that the core processes are a good place to start.

Focusing on core processes will help maximize the BPI project's contribution to vision and generate a higher rate of return on the resources and monies invested in the project. Additionally, we acknowledge reluctance to interfere with processes that are delivering strong results, especially if the team is new to BPI. The methodology that follows provides a broad definition of all the processes within the organization, core or otherwise. The choice of the process that needs improvement is ultimately a decision that needs to be made by the BPI team with necessary approvals from the management of the organization.

Lisa was assigned to the internal audit department at URHere. As the junior (ie, new hire) in the office, she was assigned mostly to jobs that no one else wanted—copy, file, collate time sheets, and write reports. While her assignments comprised a large part of her daily routine, her annual performance review paid attention to her ability to audit the financial processes of URHere and make suitable recommendations. She was hired and paid to "audit" and "recommend"; the other tasks—copying, filing, and report generation—were supporting activities.

Many of the activities that we conduct on a daily basis are in support of our critical roles. The BPI project typically distinguishes core processes as being critical to the organization's vision.

A Process Is

We embrace a simple definition that *a process is a collection of activities*. We make no distinction between a process and a subprocess because we believe that only the quantity of activities distinguishes the two terms. Processes are the *what*s of the organization and answer the question of *what* is done. For example, What is done when invoices are received? The activities that result refer to the accounts payable process.

Define Core Processes

In each organization, typically fewer than 10 processes intensely affect the achievement of the stated vision. The absence of core processes may limit the organization's ability to serve its customers and its objectives. URHere may ask, Can we serve customers if we eliminate real-time feedback? The obvious answer is no, since precise global positioning system (GPS) locations are critical to their features and customer benefits. Can we outsource this process and not lose any sleep over it? If the answer is no, then you may consider the process to provide a core component toward reaching your vision and objectives.

Can the organization serve its clients if the process is absent? If the answer is yes but evokes uncertainty about the level of customer service and satisfaction, then the process may be critical. If the response is no, then the process may likely be core to the organization's vision.

Is the organization willing to outsource the process? If the answer is no, then the process may be critical to the business and needs to be controlled from beginning to end. Any process seen as noncritical may be outsourced. URHere may be willing to outsource the payroll function since outsourcing payroll will not directly affect its ability to service its clients well.

Commonly, core processes are identified by the significant role they play in the following:

1. Contribution to revenue—the process may make a direct or indirect contribution to the earnings of the organization. Looking at projections of the revenue streams without the process easily identifies revenue contribution.
2. Improved consumption of resources—the process may be a large consumer of resources. Perhaps an indicator that the process needs improving, velocity should not be confused with efficiency. The engineering of GPS components is one of the largest consumers of URHere's resources, but it is widely accepted that there is no business without product innovation, improvement, and development. Our assumption is that the process is not clear and apparent to all the stakeholders and may be so severely mismanaged that it is hemorrhaging resources—because if it is clear to everyone, then you can skip this chapter and get on with the improvement project.
3. Amplification of intangibles such as goodwill—some processes are the soul or backbone of the organization, which sets them apart from their competition. Such processes may not be direct consumers or generators of resources. The marketing that reflects URHere's value proposition has become synonymous with location devices. Its brand comprises part of the intangible goodwill that many companies find invaluable.

Determining Core Processes

With over $850 million in assets, the real estate division of URHere rented, acquired, and sold properties on behalf of its business units worldwide. The division's functional structure, shown in Figure 5.1, is as follows

- Acquisitions—acquiring properties and real estate space for the company and its clients
- Allocations—matching the rental needs of clients with outside or owned properties
- Leasing—rental of owned properties and long-term leases
- Maintenance—maintenance and major repairs of company- and client-owned properties
- Rentals—rental of excess space and client properties
- Sales—sale of properties, both company- and client-owned

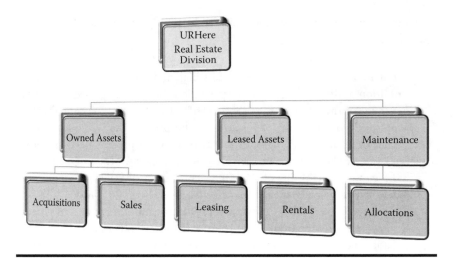

Figure 5.1 Core processes.

Identifying Core Processes

The real-estate division defined its core process by working the following five-step approach:

1. Define the organization's purpose
2. Define what the organization does to support its purpose
3. Identify the processes
4. Define the processes
5. Ask the question—challenge

Step 1: Define the Organization's Purpose

Defining the true purpose of the organization will set the context for process definition and help scope the natural limits of discussion. During workshop activity, the team will complete the following statement to build consensus around the organization's purpose:

> The purpose of the real estate division is to … so that …

URHere's real estate division established its purpose as follows:

> The purpose of our division is to suitably accommodate our clients in environments that meet their requirements so that we can maximize the socioeconomic benefits of real estate and agency-owned assets.

Table 5.1   Action Items

Lease Property	Prepare Contract	Approve Invoices
Acquire property	Collect rent	Generate payments
Rent property	Update client accounts	Approve contracts
Negotiate contracts	Value property	Dispose of property
View property	Survey property	Obtain statutory and regulatory approvals for property
Certify property	Grade/rate property	

Step 2: Determine What the Organization Does to Support Its Purpose

Action items are activities that are performed on a daily, weekly, or annual basis to serve the organization's purpose. Action items are defined by pairing the verb (the doing word) and the noun (person, place, thing, or event upon which value is added). An action item explains the activity performed—just one at a time (ie, in the singular)—on each noun.

Through workshop activity, identify the action items for the entire organization that contribute to the meeting's stated purpose. If you are stuck, identify action items by departments, groups, or individuals to accelerate results.

Make a list of the actions performed by completing a form similar to Table 5.1.

Step 3: Identify the Processes

Many actions may be performed against one noun. In your workshop activity, categorize the action items by common noun. For example, grouping all the property actions shows that the actions of lease, acquire, rent, value, dispose, and view occur to a property during the asset's life cycle.

Step 4: Define the Processes

In your workshop, find the terms that best describe each bundle of verbs and noun. Use the naming convention of a repeating verb or noun plus suffixes ending in *ing*, *tion*, *ble*, or *ment* (ie, verbals). For example, the bundle of action items that refer to the assets of the company called property was labeled *asset disposition*.

Note that the naming convention avoids the use of the terms *process* and *management*—terms that may be viewed as vague, too broad, or uncertain.

Step 5: Ask the Question—Challenge

1. Can the organization provide value to its customers if the process was absent? If the answer is no, then the process may be core.
2. Can we outsource this process and not lose any sleep over it? If the answer is no, then the process may be core.

At the end of this exercise, there will be 3 to 10 main processes (some organizations have more) that directly support the purpose of the organization.

The real estate division decided that they could not live without property processing since this group of activities was the mainstay of their business.

Process View

Three core processes of URHere's real estate division were identified:

1. Asset disposition—activities related to the acquisition and disposal of the property
2. Contracting—activities related to contracting space (leasing, rentals)
3. Maintenance—activities relating to the upkeep of the assets or real property

These three processes were leading indicators about customer satisfaction and could not be trusted to a subcontractor.

Core processes are subject to the organization's purpose and how it achieves it objectives. Organizations within the same industry may identify different core processes that reflect each one's own vision, goals, and objectives. This division felt responsible for the outcome of the maintenance process, even though much of the detail work was outsourced to subcontractors. The real estate function in a different organization might consider maintenance activities as noncritical and exclude maintenance from its core processes.

Define Core Processes

Definitions demystify jargon. Each core process must be defined so that there is shared meaning and intent across the organization. For each core process above, Step 1, Define the Purpose, generated a statement such as, "The purpose of (the core process) is to … so that …"

During workshop activity, the definition should be agreed upon consensually. URHere defined *asset disposition* as follows:

> The purpose of asset disposition is to provide delivery of structurally sound and safe accommodations so that the assets satisfy or exceed client requirements.

Activities

Activities, captured in the verb–noun format, are the simple actions that support the following complex core processes, also illustrated in Figure 5.2:

- Planning—resourcing, coordination, and planning activities for the process. The planning activities for property processing included identifying client needs, evaluating (ie, rating) properties, and selecting properties.
- Acquiring—acquisition activities such as securing inputs from a supplier. Acquiring includes valuing the property, price and mortgage negotiations, and buying/leasing the property.
- Executing—conversion of inputs to outputs. Here are the due diligence activities such as financing, legal, safety, and other reviews or approvals needed to secure the property.
- Controlling—monitoring and evaluation of outcomes. Ongoing activities include evaluation of market rates, lease prices, maintenance expenses, escalation fees, and so forth.

Determine all of the action items (plan, acquire, execute, or control) separately for each core process. Group actions together based on common purpose and determine

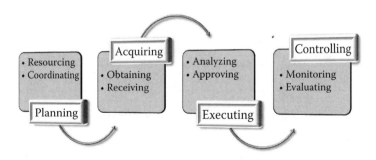

Figure 5.2   Life cycle.

a name for the group of activities (as was done for the core process). Within the core process of asset disposition, the main supporting processes were defined as follows:

- Property acquisition—includes action items as research properties, view properties, value properties, and acquire property.
- Property operations—includes action items such as grade/rate property, evaluate services (property), rent property, and negotiate cost increases.

Tasks

Tasks are the granular set of actions that roll up to complete the activity. They explain *how* something gets done rather than *what* is done. For example, under the activity *acquire property*, you will find the activity *schedule an appointment*. How to acquire property is performed and may include using a calendar scheduler such as that in Microsoft® Outlook.

Process View

The process view can be mapped to the departmental (ie, functional) organizational chart to understand how the two are linked. In Table 5.2, place the core processes as headings in the title row and the departments in the furthest left vertical column. Match each department to the core process to create a visual feedback about core processes that support more than one department.

Table 5.2 Processes and Functional Mapping

	Core Processes		
Departments	*Asset Disposition*	*Contracting*	*Maintenance*
Maintenance		⊗	⊗
Acquisitions	⊗		
Sales	⊗		
Rentals		⊗	⊗
Leasing		⊗	
Allocation		⊗	

The agency's Process and Functional Mapping in Table 5.2 reveals that asset disposition occurs primarily in the acquisitions and sales departments. Contracting occurs across the maintenance, rentals, leasing, and allocation departments. Maintenance occurs in the maintenance and rental departments.

The mapping shows the departments where the processes occur and makes it easier to establish the process owners. It also identifies potential areas of resistance and most of the stakeholders with a vested interest in the project outcome.

Conclusion

Identification of core processes represents a critical milestone for the BPI project. Before going further, the BPI team should discuss and agree on the operational definitions of the core processes with its executive sponsor(s) and champion. Thus, we have a defining moment in the BPI and a good indicator to review and update the change management and strategic plans.

Chapter 6

Business Process Improvement

Design is not just what it looks like and feels like. Design is how it works.

—**Steve Jobs**

This chapter presents an operational definition of the phrase *business process improvement* (BPI) and describes the overall methodology for conducting a BPI project. Definitions remove barriers and level expectations so that all stakeholders are engaged in the same manner during the project. The chapter provides the road map explaining the journey that the BPI team will take and identifies significant landmarks along the way.

At the end of the chapter, the project team will be able to—

- Define the benefits of business process improvement
- Describe the methodology that will be used for the project

Cable television channels host a slew of improvement shows. The HGTV channel focuses on upgrading and updating homes and gardens with such programs as *Ready to Sell*, while the Lifetime channel concentrates on improving the dress styles and looks of men and women with programs such as *Jury for Design* and *What Not to Wear*.

In the program *What Not to Wear*, caring family and friends send a plea to the stylists (Stacy and Clinton) because they believe that the candidate's appearance mismatches their age, status, or profession. Stacy and Clinton ambush the unsuspecting "victims" and apprise them that they have been selected for a makeover. Wardrobes are scrutinized and outfits are tossed in the garbage. The stylists show the clients new and improved looks that flatter their appearance. Each victim gets a $5,000 shopping spree for a new wardrobe based on the tips received. The stylists monitor the purchases and intervene when the client is deviating from the recommended choices. After a professional makeup session and haircut and style, the client's *new* look is revealed to an audience of friends and family, who are reduced to tears and gush that the person has "never looked better."

Improvement shows on television use the same formula: an existing condition is presented, its problems are highlighted, recommendations are made and then implemented (within budget), and the outcome is evaluated.

Our BPI methodology similarly evolved from identifying problems, and then facilitating and supporting implementations wherever we worked. We have read books, brainstormed (ie, "ideated"), tried solutions, failed, started over, and succeeded in making real improvements that reduced delivery time, human effort, and cost. We got the people around us involved and encouraged, cajoled, "bribed" them to support the initiative—to implement and sustain the changes on a daily basis. We did not think in terms of BPI, but we simply aspired, like Stacy and Clinton, to give the client a new look that will better serve their daily purpose.

We did not bandy around the term *BPI*, as business jargon is often viewed as evidence of how out of touch senior management is with the daily concerns of its employees. Instead, we worked to make it relevant and indispensable for their organization.

Think about it. Host a meeting with senior managers and ask, "How do we not obfuscate the processes we work with?" What kind of responses will we get?

Ask an administrative assistant, "How can we simplify or clarify the accounts payables process?" He would probably give a number of solid reasons why improvement needs to be considered and offer up a few solutions.

Definition

> To design is to communicate clearly by whatever means you can control or master.
>
> **—Milton Glaser**

Business process improvement is achieved by examining and understanding the *why*, *what*, and *how* of the process and demystifying the interactions between the people, process, and technology. During the project, people are empowered, activities are simplified, and the use of technology as an enabler of accurate, complex actions is promoted. At the end of the project, each team member will have a similar understanding of the process and its expected results.

To add value, the BPI project must be completed in the context of the organization's vision, goals, and objectives with a focus on issues such as—

- Customer satisfaction
- Flexible systems and processes that can meet the requirements of a changing business environment
- Increase on the returns from every dollar of resources invested or consumed
- Reduction of operational and production cost and time to market
- Retention or surpassing of the organization's standing in the marketplace

The aim of the BPI project is to—

- Simplify—examine the details of what, why, and how we perform on a daily basis within the organization. Interactions within the organization will be demystified and made understandable regardless of the hierarchy.
- Clarify—members will develop a similar level of understanding of the processes and the expected results.

The project deals with—

- People—emphasizes the empowerment of people. Nothing can happen without the consideration of an organization's most valuable resource.
- Processes—all activities and tasks that occur on a daily, monthly, and annual basis to provide the products and services of the organization.
- Technology—enables complex actions to be completed with speed and accuracy. People need to understand the value of technology to reap its promised benefits.
- Organization vision—to add value, all of the above must be completed in the context of the organization's vision, goals, and objectives. The focus is on the following:
  - Customer—ensuring that the customer is satisfied with the outcome (product or service) of the interactions among staff, technology, and processes
  - Flexibility—having systems and processes that are easily maneuvered to meet changes in the business environment
  - Marketplace—retaining the organization's standing in the marketplace, whether as a pioneer, a follower, or the lowest cost producer
  - Profitability—reducing operational and production cost and time to market, to increase the return from every dollar invested or consumed

Beliefs

Our BPI approach is based on a positive belief in human beings and the power of teams. We believe that all individuals are creative; the challenge is to unleash the creativity in a structured manner and on a sustained basis.

We believe that people are resourceful. People take charge, show initiative, solve problems, and make decisions each day in their personal lives. The organization needs to foster an environment in which staff is permitted to make mistakes.

We believe that most people have a dream of doing something extraordinary and making a positive contribution. The organization can provide the permission, the resources, and the support for the risk taking that accompanies extraordinary success.

We believe that your personnel selection process works and that the people engaged for the job are the truly competent. The organization needs to provide keys that help unlock an individual's true promise.

From success with the various projects, we identified four critical factors for successful BPI:

1. Collaboration—a holistic approach plays great homage to the team as an integral part of the project. It promotes the involvement of and communication among team members every step of the way. For the improvement to be effective, they need to buy in and commit to using the new process, in the prescribed manner on a consistent basis, and encourage other operators to support the changes.
2. Facilitation—team members are encouraged to share and argue their thoughts, ideas, and recommendations for improvement. Facilitation harnesses the collective creativity of the team members and creates solutions that everyone can live with.
3. Safety—a safe environment needs to be created for challenging the status quo and expressing a variety of ideas.
4. Limited use of consultants—we reject the notion that only consultants can improve processes. Team members often resent management's willingness to pay consultants who package solutions that include recommendations the team has been promoting for years. A consultant may have an optimal solution that is a logical solution, but how useful is their solution if it is not implemented or sustainable? Many consultant reports gather dust in organizations and the solutions lose support when an exception occurs that forces staff to gently slide into old familiar positions. Your team knows the organization and its culture, and understands the problems they will face during and after implementation. The team will need help

to challenge traditions, discover new solutions, and present ideas in a more formal manner. This approach engages your team in defining problems, creating and implementing solutions, and maintaining the new process.

Teams

Designing your product for monetization first, and people second, will probably leave you with neither.

—Tara Hunt

Our faith in the human spirit led us to develop a team-based BPI approach. We envision engaging a team of staff members in defining problems, creating and implementing solutions, and maintaining the new process.

We promote the use of facilitated workshops to harness the collective creativity of the team, and ensure that stakeholders buy in and commit to decisions made. We encourage the development of safe environments for the sharing and expression of ideas and for the challenging of the status quo.

Your team is best positioned to perform the BPI. Team members often know what is wrong and may have voiced their opinions several times. Staff understands the problems, knows the culture, and can anticipate problems during and after implementation. The team will need the help of a facilitator (or a consultant with a facilitative approach) to challenge traditions, discover new solutions, and aggregate ideas in a formal manner.

The foundation for a robust BPI approach lies in a positive belief in the power of teams and their willingness to have improved activities. We celebrate human beings as—

- Creative—all of us are creative in different ways and possess different talents. We all have dreams (suppressed or not) of being recognized for an exceptional effort. Most times, we do not have permission, the resources, or the courage to go for it.
- Intelligent—organizations select staff based on the results of an intensive selection process. We honor that you selected the best in the lot.

The BPI Approach

Our BPI approach starts with determination of the need for improving a process and concludes with the team's celebration of a successful implementation

Figure 6.1 Six stages.

of the improved process. The method continues after implementation through constant monitoring, evaluation, and tweaking of the newly improved process, illustrated in Figure 6.1.

Engage business process improvement with the following six stages:

Stage 1: Examine the need for process improvement in your organization.
  Determine the process to be improved
  Determine the BPI team and its mandate
  Define the project scope
Stage 2: Negotiate with process stakeholders.
  Change management
  Stakeholder analysis
  Strategy plan
Stage 3: Go for it.
  Define the project goals and objectives
  Roll out the project plan
Stage 4: Action and achieve the dream.
  Improve the process
Stage 5: Generate excitement and commitment to get it together.
  Procedures
  Implementation plan
Stage 6: Engage and excite staff—evaluate improvements on an ongoing basis.
  Audit plans
  Celebration of successes

Conclusion

This BPI approach is a tested and proven methodology that has been used in many industries including the following:

■ Energy companies—streamline processes
■ Financial institutions—reduce the completion time and cost of monthly reports, payroll processing, delinquency rates for loans; increase collections; as well as streamline the operational and administrative procedures and systems.

- Labor and trade unions—change the culture; improve the strategic and managerial planning and implementation processes; introduce new financial, administrative, and operational processes; introduce new technology and provide training
- Manufacturing concerns—improve efficiency, reduce costs, improve inventory management, develop systems for acquisitions, and improve budgeting processes
- Retailers—design new systems for inventory management, credit and hire purchase collections, and accounts receivables collections

Across all industries, the implementation of business process improvement resulted in an average of 20 percent rate of return on the resources consumed during the project. Organizational knowledge bases were increased as new skills were acquired to accompany a deeper appreciation of how organizational decisions were made.

Chapter 7

Facilitation and Business Process Improvement Methodology

Overview

The verb *facilitate* means to make easier. For our purposes, the *facilitator* is the one who leads a group of people and makes it easier for them to make decisions that are more informed.

Ideally, the role of facilitator is to focus on the method (ie, context) and not the solution (ie, content). In most business or organizational situations, groups do not rely on a facilitator true to this definition. This ideal role of the facilitator demands that the person in the role remains a neutral party and leads the group to shared understanding with core skills such as active listening, challenging, asking questions, effectively presenting, and observing (ie, reading nonverbal signals and responses).

People frequently meet or come together in business settings for the following reasons:

- Communicate information
- Gather information
- Gain support
- Solicit new ideas
- Some combination of the above

Our focus remains on specialized workshops and not common meetings. Therefore, we limit our discussion about the role of facilitator to the workshop activities required to support business process improvement (BPI), especially structured ideation, decision making, prioritization, and other activities that support building consensus around complex topics.

Benefits

The primary purpose of meetings, workshops, and other information-gathering activities is sharing and collecting good information—either to build the right product the first time or to make well-informed decisions. Common challenges associated with information gathering include the following:

- Communication—word choice, assumptions, gaps, cost of errors, and omissions
- Consensus—clear agreement and shared knowledge
- Methodologies need help—analytical methodologies, design methodologies, decision-making techniques, and so forth have not addressed the quality of the information or decision
- Power—politics, security, misunderstandings—often occurring not intentionally but because of differing approaches to and definitions about the same problem
- Two heads are better than one—building on ideas, completeness, selective memory

> If we are to achieve a richer culture, rich in contrasting values, we must recognize the whole gamut of human potentialities, and so weave a less arbitrary social fabric, one in which each diverse human gift will find a fitting place.
>
> **—Margaret Mead**

Facilitation serves to mitigate potential conflict and accelerate team performance. Well-tuned workshops rely on structural elements combined with defined roles, proper support, and the appropriate tools. A robust technique necessarily includes the following:

- Assignments and timelines associated with next steps and open items
- Clear purpose; well-prepared annotated agenda; and objectives that are specific, measurable, achievable, relevant, and time-based (SMART)

- Emphasis on appropriate ownership of the facts, implications, and recommendations
- Expert, certified session leader (facilitator) with proven structure, yet remaining flexible
- Information-gathering and decision-making focus as opposed to an unstructured discussion
- Understanding and awareness of group dynamics
- Use and management of conflict as a source of inspiration rather than to eliminate or squelch it
- Well-defined deliverables (outputs) that get created on time
- Workshop environment with rules, tools, and prompts that substantially increase productivity

Facilitated workshops are effective for our BPI approach because of the following:

- Consensus-derived information becomes input to the process
- Groups of tasks combine and finish concurrently
- Ownership is clear and participants "can live with it"
- Participants have well-defined roles, and expectations are managed in advance
- The analysis method is supported by proven methodologies such as structured analysis, information modeling, and process flow diagrams
- The approach is predictable, manageable, well documented, and reusable
- The group reaches mutual understanding about its business needs
- The session leader stimulates participants with a toolkit of visual aids, analytical tools, and group dynamic skills
- Well-defined deliverables create measurable impact
- Workshop structure and group dynamics provide more complete and accurate information

Components

A facilitated workshop often resembles "herding cats." Components of the workshop are—

- neutral guidance through a
  - structured approach where
  - every participant is heard within
  - a community of experts who
  - share skills and insight to
  - achieve consensus.

Group Size

While workshops can be held with groups ranging from less than a handful of people to more than 100 people, empirical evidence suggests that groups of between five and nine people make the highest quality decisions. With a five-participant minimum, there are enough views and diversity to stimulate innovation and yet few enough (ie, not more than nine) that all voices have an opportunity to be thoroughly heard and understood. Our own experience suggests that using breakout groups during workshops becomes important to get more done faster, and a group of nine participants splits effectively into three breakout groups with three people each.

Roles

> Here's to the crazy ones, the misfits, the rebels, the troublemakers, the round pegs in the square holes … the ones who see things differently—they're not fond of rules … You can quote them, disagree with them, glorify or vilify them, but the only thing you can't do is ignore them because they change things … they push the human race forward, and while some may see them as the crazy ones, we see genius, because the ones who are crazy enough to think that they can change the world, are the ones who do.
>
> **—Steve Job**

A role is a function of assigned activities, and one person can function in different roles. The same person who facilitates the workshop frequently reserves the room (the role of coordinator), creates the agenda (the role of methodologist), manages the documentation (the role of documenter or scribe), orders refreshments (the role of coordinator), and handles other duties also.

If the facilitator is also an indispensable subject matter expert (SME), then the role of facilitator should be deferred to someone else. Executive sponsors who want to assume the role of facilitator should remember to stay in that role during the workshop. Role shifting will leave participants confused about the roles and distrustful of the facilitator's neutrality, which is a critical element of being highly effective and completing the workshop deliverable.

Project managers also need to beware and leave behind their role of project manager. When they enter the room to facilitate, they need to remain in that role until they leave the room.

Observers may also witness workshop discussions and activities, but they should be sitting in an area separate from the workshop participants (eg, back of the room). It is critical that they remain absolutely silent (although they can converse with participants during breaks, lunch, etc).

Workshop Life Cycle

As with most techniques, there are at least three separate processes over the life of a workshop:

1. Preparation (ie, get ready)
2. Workshop event (ie, do it)
3. Review and resolution (ie, wrap it up)

Size constraints for this book do not permit us to dive deeply into each of the life-cycle stages. Simply preparing your participants may require interviewing, documentation packages, and risk assessment (among others). Additionally, reading about facilitation is far removed from the learnings you obtain from practicing, so take a good class that offers video feedback and simulated practice sessions. To become a professional facilitator, we highly advise you to take a training class so that you can fully understand all the activities embedded in the three processes mentioned above.

Disciplined Leadership

Context means that you understand the importance of the workshop deliverable, how it supports the project, and why the project is important to the organization. Meeting and workshop time is expensive. With eight people valued at an all-in rate of $150/hour, you are consuming $20 per minute in labor value, not including the real estate and opportunity costs. Practically speaking, workshop failure jeopardizes the project. If the project fails, what is the value to the organization—frequently expressed in monetary units or labor hours (eg, full-time equivalents, or FTEs)?

Workshops, as detailed in the appendixes, need to build upon prior work and harmonize with an organization's purpose, scope, and objectives (frequently called a strategic plan). Be prepared to draw upon the organization's core competency and values to help the group choose among competing options.

Overview

A disciplined workshop pulls together the preparation, tools, and skills of the session leader (ie, facilitator) into one environment (context). When combined with the aspirations, skills, knowledge, and abilities of the workshop participants, the basis for leading groups to make more informed decisions (content) is established.

A facilitator's goal is always win–win, defined as consensus. *Consensus* implies that although the decision may be less than ideal for some participants, it is reasonable enough that they can support it and not lose any sleep over it. *Compromise*, as opposed to consensus, is lose–lose, because both sides give up something. Compromise should be avoided.

We discourage voting, because that method reflects winners and losers. More votes do not necessarily equate to a better answer. See Arrow's impossibility theorem for a separate discussion on the dangers of voting.

Guiding Principles

The role of a facilitator is therefore as follows:

- Channels a diverse set of latent, disorganized, and perhaps chaotic ideas into meaningful action
- Directs the group toward shared purpose and objectives
- Galvanizes consensus about what is known yet also helps manage the uncertainty and other open issues
- Guides the group stages through activities as the group evolves
- Liberates the group to concentrate on the content (answers) rather than the context (questions) or process

Primary Skills

The role of facilitator demands one consistent factor—the ability to remove distractions and keep the group focused on one issue at a time. Facilitators should develop four core skills to improve their effectiveness:

1. Active listening is a tool for building understanding.
2. Neutrality is a tool for establishing balance and integrity.
3. Presentation skills are necessary for effective communication.
4. Questioning is a tool for effective information gathering.

Keep in mind that simply reading and understanding the core skills above does not make somebody proficient—these need to be practiced and rehearsed. Consider professional training to develop the full complement of structured facilitation skills.

Considerations

An effective facilitator learns to use simple word choices; for example, a *bunch* and not a *plethora*. Remember, clear leaders speak clearly.

Get familiar working with Post-it° paper. Part of the active listening process demands reflection, and no method is quicker or more effective than a visual reflection of what somebody has said. To the extent possible, use graphics and slides to explain, define, and stimulate contextual understanding about the content being gathered.

Develop a set of intervention tools that you can pull out of your "hip pocket" to stimulate and challenge groups. For your convenience, we have included dozens of icebreakers, mind warmers, and team-building activities with the supplemental resources.

Get familiar with the personalities involved and some of the sources of potential conflict. The group depends on you to manage disruptive personalities and to protect all of the participants in the room. Above all, remember the importance of removing distractions, including the person who is seriously deterring progress toward the deliverable. Many participant arguments are actually about the project or program and not related to the scope of the workshop deliverable.

People Principles

Following are our "10 commandments" or guiding principles for dealing with people (all based on "Treat others as you wish to be treated"):

1. People are creative if stimulated.
2. People are intelligent.
3. People are intrinsically reasonable.
4. People do not like to be blamed.
5. People have different goals in life.
6. People prefer the positive to the negative.
7. People share similar fears.
8. People want to be recognized.
9. People never want to be embarrassed, especially in public.
10. People want to make a difference.

Ground Rules

Use a set of ground rules to help manage behavior. Some of the ground rules we have found particularly effective include the following:

- Be curious about different perspectives—practice teamwork
- Be here now (ie, turn off electronic leashes)
- Bring a problem, bring a solution
- Consensus means "I can live with it" (and will support it inside and outside)
- Don't beat a dead horse
- Focus on *what* not *how*
- Focus on interests, not positions
- Hard on facts, soft on people
- Make your thinking visible
- No "Yeah, but ..."—make it "Yeah, and ..."
- No big egos or war stories
- One conversation at a time
- Phones on stun, no laptops ("topless meeting")
- Share reasons behind questions and answers (or, Share all relevant information)
- Silence or absence implies consensus
- Team is responsible for outcome

Groups and Conflict

Learn to understand the life cycle of groups and the timing of when to be their process policeman (ie, high tell) and when to be their sounding board (ie, high empathy). See Tuckman's group developmental model for a richer understanding of group performance.

Do not run from conflict. Conflict is arguably the best reason to justify the cost of a face-to-face meeting. Good books and good movies are "good" because they embrace and resolve conflict. They do not ignore conflict or sweep it under the carpet.

Know thyself as well. Some conflict is internal, such as the fear of public speaking. It is not important to get rid of your fears but it is important to be aware of them so they do not allow your performance to become a distraction to yourself or others.

Finally, be prepared to deal with anger. Remember, anger is only one letter short of danger. Your role is critical when tempers flare because someone in the room needs to be listening, and that responsibility is the role of the facilitator.

Chapter 8

The Case for Business Process Improvement

Many criminal defense lawyers, regardless of what you might think about them, are brilliant. These guys (and gals) know the law and look for the smallest of loopholes to build a defense for their clients' innocence and save them from guilty verdicts. In this chapter, we are the defense for the approach. We will build a strong case that the organization will sit up and listen to, a strong case that will firmly and conclusively establish that the organization needs to embark on a business process improvement (BPI) project.

Clients rarely hire us to perform BPI projects. They usually want to fix something that isn't going right—not collecting enough revenue, losing sales, unable to get a handle on accounts payables, and so forth. In response, we meet with staff, work with them to identify and eliminate problems, and put new solutions in place that increase revenue and reduce expenses.

Labels

Business process improvement is a label that needs to be dejargonized (or simplified) and made relevant and tangible for the organization. For BPI to be relevant, managers and staff must understand and appreciate why the project is required. The *why* will provide adequate justification when the staff is asked to collaborate on the project and implement and commit to changes that need to be made.

Why We Need Business Process Improvement

Organisms react to external and internal stimuli, and in this regard companies are no different. When customers change their desires and expectations because of new experiences and knowledge, the organization that has not anticipated change is forced to react. New business models that lower entry costs and split markets into smaller segments that service almost every whim and fantasy of the customer also present threats to organizations that are unwilling to change.

Selling the need for flexible, effective, and efficient processes is easy when the organization faces external threats to profitability, competitiveness, and customers; but what if the threat is not obvious? What if your organization, because of the environment, country, industry, strategic paths, or other factors, is not severely affected by external conditions? How do you sell the need for such a BPI project?

Solid and undeniable proof must be presented to clearly demonstrate that improving the interactions among people, their activities, and the use of technology will help advance the organization toward achievement of its vision, goals, and objectives.

Vision, Goals, and Objectives

Where there is no vision, the people perish.

—Proverbs 29:18

Revisit the organization's vision, goals, and objectives. To what extent will the process improvement assist in achieving them? Determine how the BPI project serves the organization's vision, objective, and goals.

Completing a chart as shown in Table 8.1 immediately puts the project on the management's radar as part of the organization's strategic actions. Here, project #2 might be favored because it is easier to quantify, as shown by its support of objectives that are SMART (specific, measurable, achievable, realistic, time-based) by definition.

Table 8.1 Matching BPI to Vision, Goals, and Objectives

	Vision	Goals	Objectives
BPI project #1	☒	☒	
BPI project #2	☒	☒	☒

BPI candidate #2 has the most impact on achieving the objective of the organization. For URHere's credit union, this translates to supporting the following specific objectives:

- Improve the application process so that applicants are approved within one day
- Increase membership by xx percent

Interactions

An assessment of the interactions between the people, processes, and technology will indicate the type of problems that exist in the organization and how the people, processes, and technology are affected. The reports analysis and the BPI quiz are two exercises to begin an evaluation of the interactions.

Reports Analysis Activity

The reports analysis is a three-step process:

Step 1—identify the reports, spreadsheets, and other documents used in the organization.
Step 2—articulate the reasons why these reports exist within the organization.
Step 3—think about what could be done to eliminate some of these reports.

Step 1: Identify the Reports

Your organization invested in a multimillion-dollar technological solution to process data and generate reports for more effective decision making. Yet, managers and employees throughout the organization generate and maintain independent spreadsheets, text documents, and other smaller database sets that duplicate data entry and retain a similar form as provided by the information technology group, illustrated in Figure 8.1.

Extra reports are a leading indicator that there may be a misalignment of the interactions between the people, processes, and technology involved in the organization. The recommendation is to identify the shortcomings in the interaction and generate solutions.

Invite your colleagues from different departments to complete Table 8.2, Reports Analysis. Count the number of reports that exist by department and the total for the organization.

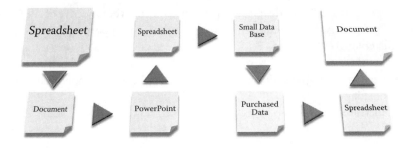

Figure 8.1 Multiple source documents.

Table 8.2 Reports Analysis

Report Used	What It Does	Reason Why I Use or Created It
Invoice register— Excel spreadsheet	Identifies for each vendor:	The system cannot identify the purchase orders that are relevant to my department only
	The purchase orders generated for the department only	The system cannot in real time indicate the invoices received against the purchase order (only after the invoices are processed)
	The invoices that have been received against the purchase orders	Only the accounts payable department can see if the invoice was paid/unpaid, but we do not trust their answers
	The due date of the invoices	The balance left on the purchase order can be calculated by pulling more than one report
	The paid/unpaid status of the invoices	
	The balance left on the purchase order for use	
Total Number of Reports in the Department _____		
Total Number of Reports in the Organization _____		

Complete the Table

In Table 8.2, identify all the worksheets, word processor tables, and database reports that are generated from sources other than by the information technology group.

The URHere research and development department generates and manages its contracts for goods and services. Invoices for these contracts are approved by the research and development (R&D) department, and then sent to the centralized accounts payable department for processing.

The R&D team maintained invoice registers by purchase order for each vendor from whom they procured goods or services. Preparing a report analysis reveals the results shown in Table 8.2.

Step 2: Why the Reports Exist

Now that all the spreadsheets and extra reports are listed, search for the real reasons that they exist, typically related to the following:

■ People—how they perceive and use the existing reports, process information, and interact with other people
■ Process—how information gets into the system and then into the hands of the people that need it
■ Technology—how it helps or hinders, what it can and cannot do, and how it is used

Use Table 8.3 to identify the reasons and lay out the information in one of three categories.

Table 8.3	Reasons for Reports	
Spreadsheet	*Why They Exist*	*Category*
Invoice register	Lack of trust in the accounts payable process	People
	Inability to generate the necessary reports	IT/people
	The manager's belief systems	People
	Difficulty of obtaining the relevant information	Process

Step 3: How to Eliminate the Unnecessary Reports

Brainstorm with your colleagues on ways to solve the problems identified. The project team determined—

- Project employees will be trained to generate the relevant reports.
- Project employees will be given access to banking information that will enable them to determine when an invoice was paid.

For tentative solutions, develop an action list as shown in Table 8.4.

Despite the numerous assurances that the relevant reports could be generated from the information technology group, the R&D manager's attitude remained unchanged; he wanted to maintain the invoice registers (people's perceptions are often the most challenging but critical problems to change).

There was a need to simplify and clarify what the R&D members needed from the accounts payable process to work effectively and efficiently, and this was easily resolved.

Problems that are not easily resolved need further investigation to simplify and clarify the process so that everyone understands the decisions being supported by the information.

The reports analysis alone may not be relevant for your organization or may not have convinced you that there is a problem to address. The quiz below looks at common reasons why organizations implement BPI. Answer yes or no to the questions below and compare your answers to the level of need in your organization for BPI.

Table 8.4 Action List

Problem	Action	Responsibility	Date
Lack of trust	Have weekly meetings and quarterly team builders	Team leaders	Ongoing
Inability to generate reports	Have the software provide a similar report	Information technology department	Six months

BPI QUIZ

Answer the following questions either Yes or No:

1. Do staff work long hours to complete routine tasks and month-end reports?

   ☐ Yes   ☐ No

2. Is there a constant backlog of work?

   ☐ Yes   ☐ No

3. Does the backlog of work decrease and slowly pile up again?

   ☐ Yes   ☐ No

4. Do payroll reports regularly feature overtime hours or payments for routine work?

   ☐ Yes   ☐ No

5. Are temporary staff hired for special assignments that involve clearing up backlogs more than once a year?

   ☐ Yes   ☐ No

6. Does staff complain that there is a problem with the information technology group, such as how work is processed or inadequate reports?

   ☐ Yes   ☐ No

7. Are your managers bogged down by the daily routine activities?

   ☐ Yes   ☐ No

8. Are you satisfied that executives spend 75 percent or more of their time on strategic activities?

   ☐ Yes   ☐ No

9. Are the root causes of problems identified and solved?

   ☐ Yes   ☐ No

10. Are databases separate from your primary technologies group–provided ones being used to collate data, prepare reports, or manage the business?

    ☐ Yes   ☐ No

11. Are measurement systems focused on quantity and not quality?

    ☐ Yes   ☐ No

12. Are the same data being entered more than once (ie, one database)?

    ☐ Yes   ☐ No

13. Is the cost of rework calculated and known?

    ☐ Yes   ☐ No

14. Do staff members take all decisions to the supervisors to be made?

    ☐ Yes   ☐ No

15. Are the costs of processes, activities, and tasks known?

    ☐ Yes   ☐ No

16. Is staff measured on mainly qualitative measures?

    ☐ Yes   ☐ No

17. Does each process team member understand his or her role?

    ☐ Yes   ☐ No

18. Does each process member understand the role of the other people involved in the process?

    ☐ Yes   ☐ No

19. Do customers internal or external complain about the process outcome?

    ☐ Yes   ☐ No

20. Are up-to-date documented procedures written for the process?

    ☐ Yes   ☐ No

21. Is the process owner clearly identified?

    ☐ Yes   ☐ No

22. Do the process stakeholders agree that the process is successful?

    ☐ Yes   ☐ No

23. Are your managers primarily focused on cost and time?

    ☐ Yes   ☐ No

24. Are fewer than 75 percent of projects completed on time, on budget, and with the anticipated rate of return?

    ☐ Yes   ☐ No

25. Are your processes largely focused on internal aspects?

    ☐ Yes   ☐ No

SCORING

Score the following questions 1 if answered Yes:

   1, 2, 3, 4, 5, 6, 7, 10, 11, 12, 14, 16, 19, 23, 24, and 25

Score the following questions 1 if answered No:

   8, 9, 13, 15, 17, 18, 20, 21, and 22

Use the following totals to rank your organization:

   ■ Greater than 20—start the BPI project *now*
   ■ 15 to 19—attention urgently needed
   ■ 10 to 14—focus on specialized processes that have problems
   ■ Less than 9—tolerable

Conclusion

Now there is proof that despite the terrific sales numbers, the satisfied clients, and the overall competitiveness of the organization, there is room for improvement among the internal interactions between people, technology, and processes. The case can be made for how the interactions may affect the organization's long-term ability and flexibility to add value in the marketplace.

Share findings with senior management and get permission and resources to pull a project team together to further investigate initial suspicions. When the results from the report analysis and affirmation from the BPI Quiz are linked to the vision, goals, or objectives of the organization, it becomes easier to understand why the organization needs to engage in a BPI project.

There was a previous Colgate advertisement in which the kids in the classroom chanted, "Good, better, best! Never let them rest until we make our good better and our better best." What better, simpler explanation for BPI does anyone need?

Chapter 9

Tools for Business Process Improvement

Just as the carpenter has tools for his trade, so too must the business process improvement (BPI) teams. This chapter equips the teams with the necessary tools from start to finish for a successful BPI project. The tools for the project presented here include a project plan, risk and opportunity register, lessons-learned register, and documentation discipline.

Each of us has worked on projects—organized a party, built a house, planned and taken a vacation, and many others. We may not have labeled them as projects, but any set of activities that involves planning, sequencing, coordinating, budgeting, and consuming resources to achieve a preset outcome (ie, a deliverable) in a stated time frame is actually a project.

Evaluations generate lessons learned for future project plans and their execution. In hindsight, we can give a general evaluation of the success or failure of the project or a detailed examination of the various aspects of the project. The project was late (time), there were cost overruns (budget), and the results were not as planned (outcome).

Before embarking on the BPI project, it is worthwhile to review past experiences and establish what did and did not work. These lessons will be reflected in the project plan to increase its likelihood of success.

Project Issues

Answer the questions 1 to 6 and complete the sentences 7 to 16. Next, or concurrently, compile a list of answers for lessons learned shown in Table 9.1.

1. Think of a project that you worked on in the past and identify it.
2. What was the desired outcome?
3. What were the resources at hand?
4. What was the specified time frame for completion?
5. Who was in charge of the project and what did they do?
6. Was the desired outcome achieved: time frame, outcome, resource consumption?
7. The challenges for the project were …
8. The challenges existed …
9. The challenges were overcome …
10. The things that worked for the project …
11. These things worked …
12. Every project should always …
13. The project leaders should always …
14. The project team should always …
15. The next project I work on I will …
16. The next project I work on I will not …

After the team discussion, aggregate the findings and complete Table 9.1.

Table 9.1   Lessons Learned

Items	Findings
Role of the team leader	
Common challenges	
Reasons challenges existed	
Actions taken to overcome	
Actions that worked	
Reasons actions worked	
Every project should always	
Project leaders should always	
Project team should always	
I will	
I will not	

Project management professionals cite the prevailing reasons for project failure:

- Ill-defined scope—at least one of the projects was not well defined. This cause of failure includes scope creep and uncontrolled changes in the scope or requirements of the project.
- Lack of engagement by human resources—staff members are usually left to sustain and maintain project outcomes. A project may be successful in the short-term, but without executive buy-in and commitment, the positive results may diminish over time. The staff responsible for owning the process needs to be engaged at the onset of the project.
- Lack of planning—projects involve the coordination and sequencing of activities. The planning process becomes critical for activities that are dependent on the completion of other activities. Consider a thorough planning effort to build the project plan before moving on to analysis or "solving."
- Lack of senior management commitment—senior management sanctions the project and will release the human resources and budget for the project. If they are not involved, then the project is likely doomed.
- Underresourced—reflected by inadequate time allocated to planning activities, inaccurate budgets, or insufficient resources required by the project.

Project Tools

The unspoken remit of every project is to maximize the use of assigned resources and ensure a commonly desired outcome. Four important tools need to be used and maintained throughout the life of the BPI project to increase the likelihood of success:

1. Project plan
2. Risk and opportunity register
3. Lessons learned register
4. Documentation plan

Project Plan

The project plan captures the planned use of resources to complete a thorough planning effort and comprises at least four elements:

1. Project team
2. Team charter
3. Project budget
4. Project timetable

Project Team

> When you're part of a team, you stand up for your teammates. Your loyalty is to them. You protect them through good and bad, because they'd do the same for you.
>
> **—Yogi Berra**

> Players win games, teams win championships.
>
> **—Bill Taylor**

> Individual commitment to a group effort—that is what makes a team work, a company work, a society work, a civilization work.
>
> **—Vince Lombardi**

The initial project team comprises the group of people who have taken on the responsibility for determination of the project scope, execution, completion, and implementation. Team members will rotate over the life of the project as the varying types of expertise about the organization and its processes are needed at the six different phases shown in Figure 9.1 across the life cycle of the project.

The process management team comprised of executive and managerial staff will execute Stage 1, the *Examine* phase, which confirms the need for the improvement process in your organization. This team has developed the strategic plan and is aware of the prevailing market conditions and the challenges that the organization will face. It has an organizational overview that is critical for a successful undertaking and must be convinced internally that the BPI project adds value. Hence, the process management team should select the process for improvement.

The process examination team is responsible for Stages 2 and 3, *Negotiate* with stakeholders and *Go for It*. This team bridges the strategic with the tactical (managerial and operational content). It is engaged in goal setting for the process and the development and approval of the project's strategic plan.

Process owners and a cross-functional team will form the dream team, which is responsible for the Stage 4—*Action* and achieve the dream. Staff that are involved frequently with the process will be engaged for the Action phase, since

Figure 9.1   Six BPI phases.

their buy-in and commitment to the results is critical for the improved process to generate the returns expected. Their daily jobs will be impacted by the changes.

The last two, Stages 5 and 6, are *Generate* excitement and commitment and *Engage* and excite. In these stages the staff are responsible for the implementation of the design, developing the procedures, and preparing audit plans for the results. Here, some members of the project implementation team may be combined with prior members from the dream team. After implementation, the process owners may co-opt an internal audit team or other staff members to assist in the ongoing evaluation and monitoring of the process.

Distinctions between the teams are not hard and fast (rules), as some members may serve all the teams. The teams shown in Table 9.2 are provided names to clearly identify the activities and deliverables they are responsible for and the corresponding milestones or hand-over moments.

We chose to distinguish between the teams in recognition of the fact that not all of the planning or analytical personnel will need to be part of the implementation.

Team Composition

The process management team includes the following support roles:

- Champion—member of the senior management team who is supportive of the team, its efforts, and the project objectives. May be the executive sponsor or another person who is more readily accessible and involved than the executive sponsor.
- Executive sponsor—resides within the executive management team and has accountability for ensuring that the project comes off as proposed. All team members eventually report to the executive sponsor.
- Document controller—maintains, distributes, and archives project documentation.
- Human resources and information technology—experts forming part of the team's support systems. They need to provide inputs at the design, implementation, and auditing phases of the project.
- Gatekeeper—individual who ensures that meetings are kept to time and that deadlines are maintained.
- Process owner—the owner of the process being improved. May not be involved from the onset, but after the process has been selected for improvement, needs to be on board to ensure the 'improved process' owner's commitment and buy-in.
- Scribe—keeps notes during team meetings and provides raw output to the document controller (who may be the same individual).

Table 9.2   Four BPI Teams

Includes	Team	Project Phase	Responsibilities	Deliverables
Executives and managers	Process management team (PMT)	Stage 1: *Examine* the need for improvement	Get executive buy-in for the project Select process for improvement	Team charter Project team Project budget Project timetable Risk and opportunity register Lessons-learned register Documentation discipline
Managers and process owner	Process examination team (PET)	Stage 2: *Negotiate* with process stakeholders Stage 3: *Go for It*	Document the as-is state of the process Determine possible pitfalls for the project Develop the vision, goals, and objectives for the improved process Secure executive approval for the project to continue	As-is process flowcharts Vision, goals, and objectives for the new process Approved strategic plan

Process owner, process staff, and experts from IT and HR	Dream team	Stage 4: *Action* and achieve the dream	Design the improved process	Flow charts of improved process
Process staff and cross-functional experts	Process implementation team (PIT)	Stage 5: *Generate* excitement and commitment Stage 6: *Engage* and excite	Implement the improved process Design new procedures Hand over the improved process to process owner Generate final project reports	Implementation plan Procedures for new process Process organizational chart Roles and responsibilities Final reports
Internal audit process staff		After project	Monitoring and evaluation of process and continuous improvement	

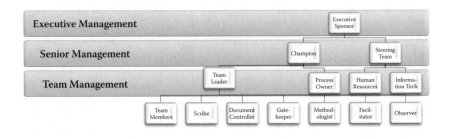

Figure 9.2   Organizational chart for BPI.

- Team leader—assigned the responsibility for the outcome. The leader can be selected either by the team or by the executive team and will likely not be the process owner. This individual has a strong, vested interest in the project's success.
- Team members—other team members will be selected according to the needs of the team during the rotating phases of the project life cycle.

Please note that some team members may perform more than one role at any point in time.

The reporting relationship among the team members is displayed in the organizational chart shown in Figure 9.2.

Team Charter

The team charter outlines the responsibility of each team and its members during the project. At various phases of the project, the team will have rotating members, varying objectives, and discrete deliverables. The team charter needs to be updated for the change that occurs over the life of the project. Each team member should also sign the charter as a visible commitment to its contents.

A team charter is illustrated in Figure 9.3 and may include the following:

- Assumptions—the assumptions that the team has made in developing the other components of the team charter.
- Beneficiaries of the project—stakeholders and how the project will service their purposes.
- Constraints—existing conditions that may limit the achievement of objectives.
- Cost of the project (by line item)—including the project budget.

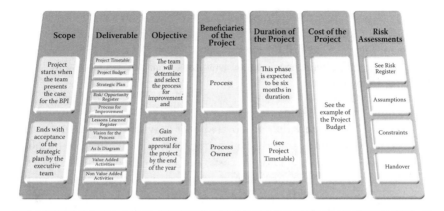

Figure 9.3   Simple team charter.

- Deliverables—define the deliverables for each specific phase of the project. This is an exact statement of what the team should deliver at the end of each phase of the project.
- Duration of the project—number of months that the team will be engaged.
- Handover—when the team relinquishes its role in the project.
- Members—the members of its teams and the roles that they will manage.
- Objectives—over the life of the project the rotating teams will have varying objectives and goals. For example, the goal of the process improvement team may be to redesign the process to achieve increased efficiency with xx percent of time or $xx savings. The objective of the implementation team may be to retain the specified constraints of time and budget.
- Risk assessments—see the risk and opportunity register.
- Scope of the project—the start of the team's responsibility and the end of the responsibility.

Project Budget

The national budget must be balanced. The public debt must be reduced; the arrogance of the authorities must be moderated and controlled. Payments to foreign governments must be reduced, if the nation doesn't want to go bankrupt. People must again learn to work, instead of living on public assistance.

—**Cicero**

The executive team wants to know the cost of the project and its estimated rate of return to justify economic investments for the project. The project budget, shown in Table 9.3, identifies the resources needed for the completion of the project. Team members need to know who does what and when. The focus will be on the following:

- Human resources—internal staff involved in the project may not represent additional cost since they are covered under payroll. However, if there is a need for overtime or to bring in contract staff to fulfill the team members' daily roles, then the additional costs need to be included in the budget.
- Special events—the project team may want to plan special events to engage and excite staff for the project—kickoff, off-site workshops, and celebrations. Estimate costs on the elements of special events and place a budgeted cost on them.
- Tangible items and services—cost of tangible items and services needed, such as external conference rooms, flip board, chart paper, stationery, hosting of workshops, refreshments, binding services, copying, teleconferencing, and so forth. Any extras your team needs should be identified and a dollar value attached to each item.

Include a contingency (eg, 10 percent of the project budget) to cover unexpected costs. Engage the executive sponsor, project champion, and other managers to review and comment on the budget before final presentation. Be ready to be challenged on each projection. Provide context, how this project affects organizational goals, within which the budget will be presented. The context is covered in the strategic plan that is covered in a later chapter.

Budget Justification

The rate of return represents the reward or return on investment. Specifically, it is the change in the process cost (typically a reduction) expressed as a percentage of the total amount of money spent on the process improvement. The calculation is completed in three steps:

1. Calculate the total cost of the project: for example, $22,990
2. Calculate the change in the process cost: $5,000 annual savings
3. Calculate the rate of return: change in process cost ÷ total cost of the project × 100 (5,000 ÷ 22,990 × 100 = 21.74 percent)

In this example, for every dollar spent on the project, 21 cents is returned to the organization annually. Alternatively, the BPI project generates a 21 percent simple annual return on the investment.

Table 9.3   BPI Project Budget

Item	Description	Cost ($)	Total Cost ($)	Comment
1	Company BPI launch		1,800	This is an interactive session to answer any questions and allay fears.
	Hall rental	1,000		
	Guest speaker	300		
	Refreshments	500		
2	BPI team cost		11,000	Team members with clashing holiday schedules will be paid for holidays if they agree. Temporary staff will support the process team.
	Payment in lieu of holidays	5,000		
	Temporary staff to replace staff in routine tasks	6,000		
3	Conduct of BPI		7,000	A facilitator will work with the BPI team.
	Off-site rentals	4,000		Some of the meetings will be off-site.
	Facilitated workshops	3,000		
4	Team costs		1,100	
	Printing and binding	500		
	Stationery	600		
	Total Cost	20,900	20,900	
	Contingency— 10 percent		2,090	
	Grand Total		22,990	

The rate of return is used by many organizations to justify economic spending. The rate can be negative or positive, since the change in project cost can result in a savings or a loss. If the process costs $8,000 before the project and $3,000 after the project, then the savings is $5,000. If after the project the process costs $10,000, then the project has a loss of $2,000 (annually). The loss shows a negative rate of return for the project of -11.4 percent ($-2,000 \div 22,990$), or for every dollar spent on the project, the organization lost 11 cents annually.

Payback Period

The payback period can also be used to justify the outcome of the project. Payback establishes how long the organization has to wait to get the money back it invests in the improved process. For the savings of $5,000, the project payback period is slightly more than four years, calculated as follows:

1. Calculate the total cost of the project: $22,990
2. Calculate the change in the process cost: $5,000 annual savings
3. Calculate the payback period: change in the process cost ÷ the total cost of the project, or $22,900 \div \$5,000 = 4.58$ years

As the project advances, the team will develop better information to calculate the specific change in the cost (ie, savings or losses from the project).

Project Timetable

> If I had to sum up in one word what makes a good manager, I'd say decisiveness. You can use the fanciest computers to gather the numbers, but in the end you have to set a timetable and act.
>
> **—Lee Iacocca**

The project timetable reflects the time frame within which all the activities over the life of the project will be completed. The project start and end dates and duration are clearly defined. The timetable includes the following:

1. Activities—the actions that will occur during the project. Each activity should be decomposed into smaller tasks. For example: the activity check generation will include tasks such as—
   - Confirm vendor balances
   - Generate accounts payable register
   - Generate/write check

- Identify vendors and amounts to be paid
- Procure signatures
- Update database with vendor information
- Update check registers

The type of activity will determine its timing on the schedule. Actions (includes activities and tasks) can be—

- Concurrent—different actions can take place at the same time and not compete for resources; procure signatures (for completed checks) and update registers can be performed at the same time.
- Dependent—some actions are dependent on other actions before they can occur; check generation is dependent on the necessary checks and balances within the process.
- Independent—some actions can happen independently of other actions, or without any other actions being affected. "Update database with vendor information" is independent of any other action and happens on a daily basis whether or not checks are generated.
- Primary—actions that are essential to the entire process and nothing can happen (successfully) without their timely and accurate completion; eg, update check register.
- Secondary—minor tasks that contribute to the completion but are not essential; confirm vendor balances.
- Sequential—some actions can only occur after others have occurred. The accounts payable register can only be accurately generated after the vendor database has been updated.

2. Duration—each activity and task is assigned a specific start and end date with the number of days and hours for the action clearly defined and predetermined.
3. Responsibilities—responsibility and expectations for task completion is clearly outlined and assigned.
4. Updating—the project timetable is constantly updated throughout the life of the project, including—

- Actual completion dates for assigned tasks—early or late completion of primary tasks and activities will compromise the start of dependent activities.
- Company events—organization events and other projects may also impact the set schedules, causing unforeseen adjustments.
- Human resource schedules—vacation time, study leave, and public holidays will impact team members' availability to complete schedules.
- New tasks or activities that may evolve—as the project develops, the team may need to include new activities to adequately reflect findings or discoveries that were not anticipated.

Table 9.4   Activity Types

Sequence of Activities in Check-Generation Process			
Update database with vendor information	░		░
Generate accounts payable register	░		
Confirm vendor balances		░	
Identify vendors and vendors to be paid		░	
Generate/write checks			░
Procure signatures			░
Update check registers			░

Keeping the timetable updated allows the team to predict complications and change the expectations of project stakeholders. Table 9.4 provides an illustration.

Build Project Plan

Luck is what happens when preparation meets opportunity.

—Seneca

The basic project plan can be built using Microsoft® Excel or Microsoft Project or other project management tools that you use. An illustration is provided in Figure 9.4. The earlier you build the plan, the more you begin to understand the project and its possibilities. Update the plan as tasks are completed and calibrations are required.

Risk and Opportunity Registers

The risk and opportunities registers encourage the project team to anticipate the challenges and identify risks and opportunities that may affect or be available for the team. Assign one team member the responsibility for the register's maintenance. Update your registers at least once a month as you capture information from the team's experiences during the project.

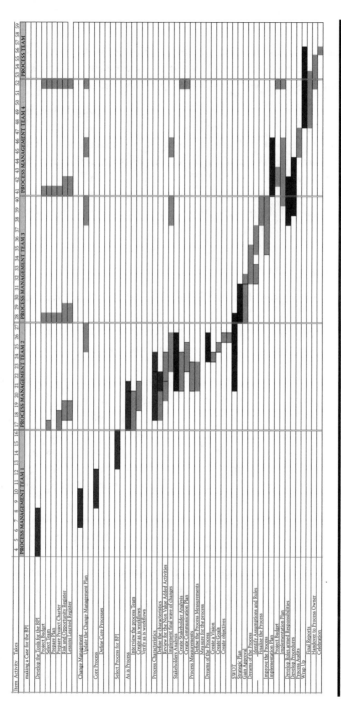

Figure 9.4 BPI project plan.

Risks

> The Chinese use two brush strokes to write the word "crisis." One brush stroke stands for danger; the other for opportunity. In a crisis, be aware of the danger—but recognize the opportunity.
>
> **—John F. Kennedy**

Each project has risks that if left unmanaged will endanger the project. The risk register determines the probability of the risks occurring and displays an assessment of the way that risks will affect the project. The team needs to identify mitigating actions that would eliminate or limit the effect of risk on the project. The impact of the mitigation, and its other effects on the project, is also assessed. The team continues to address risks as they develop.

Risk Register

Complete the risk register shown in Figure 9.5 with the columns as instructed:

1. Item—a sequential count of the risks identified. Risks are not to be deleted from the register. They are noted as being inconsequential by changing the status to closed.
2. Risk—describe the risk that has been identified; eg, late release of funds may impact timing and jeopardize the project schedule.
3. Risk owner—identify the team member responsible for leading the effort to eliminate the risk.
4. Impact—assess the impact of the risk on the project outcome using a scale of 1 (low impact) to 5 (stops the project). For example, answer the question "On a scale of 1 to 5, what will be the impact of not releasing funds on the project outcome?"
5. Probability—assess the probability of risk using a scale of 1 (unlikely) to 5 (highly probable) by answering the question "What is probability that the risk will occur?"
6. Total risk—equals impact times probability. This is calculated as the impact score multiplied by the probability score $(I \times P) =$ Total Risk.
7. Mitigation strategies—list the actions that may be taken to reduce the risk.
8. Effect—what is the effect of each mitigation? Scale whereby 0 eliminates the risk and 5 has no impact on risk.
9. Result—equals Total Risk × Effect. The product of Total Risk (from item 6 above) multiplied by the product of the Effect $(TR \times E) =$ Result

BPI RISK REGISTER – PROJECT ISSUES

Doc

Last Updated:

Item	Risk	Risk Owner	Risk Impact			Mitigation Plans	Mitigated Risk		Effect	Status
			Imp	Prob	Total		Prob	Total		
	BPI PROJECT									Open/Close
1	Timely release of the project funds.	MA	5	3	15	Prepare the project timetable identifying the impact of this on the budget. Meet with the executive to impress the need for timely resales of funds.	0	0	Executive guaranteed release of funds by the 3rd week in the project. Project team to press on with activities.	Closed
2	Vacation schedules of the project team members classed with the project plan.	GB	4	4	16	Revisit the project plan to make allowances for the Vacation schedule. Meet with staff to determine if any changes can be met to the holiday schedules e.g., payment in lieu of.	1	4	Meetings held with the staff. In principle 75% agreed to accept the monies. Need to work out the details with HR.	Open

Figure 9.5 Project risk register.

10. Action—the actions taken to mitigate the risk and the consequences or results are fully documented.
11. Status—open: the risk still exists; closed: the risk no longer exists.

Opportunity Register

> A pessimist sees the difficulty in every opportunity; an optimist sees the opportunity in every difficulty.
>
> **—Sir Winston Churchill**

Not all is gloomy for the project. As the project evolves, a number of opportunities will present themselves—new ways to save money, time, or create a business opportunity. The opportunities need to be documented as they will boost the team's confidence and are evidence of real and tangible benefits of the team's work.

Complete the opportunity register shown in Figure 9.6 with the following:

1. Items—a sequential count of the opportunities identified. Opportunities are not to be deleted from the register. They are shown as less consequential by changing the status to closed.
2. Identify the opportunity that exists; eg, some process team members have been trained in business process improvement.
3. Opportunity owner—identify the team member who will ensure that the team fully evaluates the opportunity.
4. Benefit to project—determine how the project benefits from the opportunity; eg, the project schedule can be accelerated.
5. Comment—how the opportunity has been used; eg, co-opt new employee for the PMT team.
6. Status—open: the opportunity still exists; closed: the opportunity has been exploited.

Lessons Learned

This project is going to generate new discoveries, findings, and intelligence for your organization. It is necessary to capture learning from the project so that the full benefits of the project are documented for the organization. Lessons learned can jump-start other projects as future teams will learn from both the positive and negative experiences of your team.

Determine how often the register will be updated and assign the responsibility to one person for maintenance and accuracy.

Document No:

Last Updated:

	Opportunity Description	Opp'y Owner	Benefit to Project	Date / Status	Status
▶	BPI PROJECT	▶	▶		▶ Open/Closed ▶
1	Some process team members have been trained in BPI.	JW	Saves the project money and schedules.	Ongoing	Open
2	Free one day training courses being offered in BPI at local university.	TO	Send rest of the team for training so that we are all on the same page with the BPI.	Three team members attended the training. Five more to go.	Open
3	The organization has a well established document control system. The project can piggy back off of these resources.		Cost savings. The project does not need a document controller.	One of the company's document controllers agreed to work for the project.	Closed
4					
5					
6					
7					

Figure 9.6   BPI opportunity register.

Use the four-step method to generate the lessons learned:

1. Identify the issues for the project that worked or did not work.
2. Examine the causes for the issues that developed.
3. Extract the lessons learned from the supporting causes and mitigation taken (or not).
4. Identify the action step recommended from the lessons learned.

Step 1: Identify the issues for the project that worked or did not work.

The issues, challenges, problems, and successes for the project provide elements of the lessons learned. Help your team to unearth the issues for the project by having each team member complete the statements below:

- I did not like …
- I think that … could have been done better.
- … did not work well for the project.
- Sometimes …
- I feel that …
- If I had to do this again I would never …
- Our team never should …
- I think that … worked very well.
- I think that … was a major achievement.
- I felt proud that our team …
- Our team did well to …
- If I had to do this again, I would repeat …

The statements for the team can be aggregated since it is likely that the members have similar thoughts and opinions about what took place during the project.

Step 2: Examine the causes for the issues that developed.

The issues may have occurred because of something that the team did or did not do. The analysis is necessary for the unearthing the causes behind the issues. To understand causes, we can use the Five Whys tool. This question-and-answer method encourages deeper understanding about true root cause. It works as follows:

Issue

The process management team was formed late, so we are off to a slow start.

Q: Why?

A: Because the managers did not release the team members sooner.

Q: Why?

A: Because the executive sponsor did not demand that team members be released sooner.

Q: Why?

A: Because he was waiting on the board of directors to approve the BPI team charter.

Q: Why?

A: Because the board of directors had many questions about the BPI document.

Q: Why?

A: Because the board of directors did not receive a thorough explanation of the need for the project.

Step 3: Extract the lessons learned from the supporting causes and mitigation taken (or not).

The lessons learned can be a combination of the following:

- What can remedy the situation
- What we know (experience)
- What we accept as true (rule, assumption, standard)
- What we think should be adopted—create something new

From the example, our lessons learned may be …

- Present a thorough document when presenting to the board of directors (ie, remedy).
- Get a preapproved format from the board of directors on how reports should be provided them (ie, adopt a new practice).
- Walk through future presentations with senior managers who may be familiar with how the board of directors "thinks" to get their insight (ie, new practice).

Step 4: Identify the action step recommended from the lessons learned.

The lessons learned may provide an immediate corrective action for the current project or organizational learning. This may not be applicable for all lessons learned.

In our example, the team may take the actions around—

- Develop a format for board of director presentations
- Get senior management to commit to preapproval from the board of directors for all BPI projects

Table 9.5 BPI Lessons Learned

Item	Situation	Action	Lesson Learned	Type of Lesson
1	Objectives were not set for each goal. Some goals seemed to have no objectives.	Team revisited the goals and used the gap analysis to identify what was needed to identify the goals.	Use the gap analysis to determine objectives.	Vision
2	Team members were released late in the project. Managers were unaware of what the team's plans were for the staff.	Team met with managers and revealed plans with managers. Regular meetings were planned to update managers.	Owners of resources need to be engaged and updated throughout the project to ensure compliance.	Communication

The lessons learned can be presented in tabular form, providing easy reference and future use as shown in Table 9.5.

At the start of the project, the team is inclined to place a host of lessons on the register. As the business process improvement continues, the team becomes more discerning and will combine lessons and learnings for greater impact.

Documentation Plan

Documentation is frequently underinvested in projects. Documents are tangible evidence of the whys of the decisions made. They provide an audit trail for the project, settle disputes, jog memories, and provide learning for the organization.

The documentation plan should include items as follows:

- Custodian—identify custodian for the entirety of the project documents. This role is typically one individual who becomes the recipient and distributor of project documentation that is received and submitted by the team.
- Distribution—the protocol for distributing documents; to whom and when.

- Document numbering—number the documents and determine the file-naming convention. An example of a numbering system:
  - E-Date – XXX – Number – Email document numbering system
  - L-Date – XXX – Sequence – Letters
  - M-Date – XXX – Sequence – Memo
  - F-Date – XXX – Sequence – Scan
- Rights—the rights of each team member to view, edit, save, update, and perform other actions among the archived documents need to be agreed upon and reflected in the SharePoint or file server security setup.
- Roles—the roles of each team member in receiving, updating, and so forth are identified.
- Storage—how and where the documents are stored, soft and hard copies, who can access the documents, and confirmation of any security challenges.
- Updates—when revisions are completed, how team members are notified of revisions.

At the end of the project, all the files should be approved by the process owner.

The project plan, risk and opportunity registers, and lessons-learned register will assist the project assess the opportunities and predict where pitfalls may threaten success. These tools help document the team's findings and add to the organization's aggregate intelligence while accelerating the learning curve for other project teams.

Chapter 10

Process Selection

> You see things; and you say, "Why?" But I dream things that never were and I say, "Why not?"
>
> **—George Bernard Shaw**

At the end of this chapter the process management team will select the process(es) for improvement. The team needs to select a process that will easily attract an executive champion.

Think of the first time you went on a date with your significant other. Much thought and mental preparation were invested in deciding the place, timing, and other factors of the event. Why? You knew that the first date would largely determine if you received a second chance.

The eyes of the organization will be focused on the business process improvement (BPI) project and the process management team. The success of the project will largely determine the future enthusiasm that the organization has for BPI. Just as a suitor, the process management team needs to build the organization's confidence in its competency and credibility to have a successful project. The approach must be seen as critical in terms of the amount of money consumed or the amount of resources generated and its contribution to the achievement of organizational goals, customer satisfaction, and employee commitment. The team may select more than one process for improvement, as the available resources will allow.

Introduction

A selection methodology that is both transparent and an auditable process will increase the project's credibility as the process management team will face challenges by stakeholders or other parties about *why* and *how* the choice was made. Be warned that executive management reserves the right to ultimately approve the process for improvement.

The methodology for process selection involves three steps as shown in Figure 10.1:

Step 1: Establish *what* is important to the organization
Step 2: Match each *what* to one or more processes
Step 3: Select from the competing *what*s

Step 1: Establish *What* Is Important to the Organization

The organization's strategic plan, vision, mission, objectives, and goals identify *what* the organizations considers important over the next two years and beyond. The process management team needs to reacquaint itself with organizational intentions and identify *what* is important to the organization. The purpose of the organization as developed earlier should also be considered. URHere's real estate division had three main goals.

■ To increase the inventory of company-owned properties—income generation
■ To limit maintenance on properties—expense reduction
■ To increase the income of the division—value-add

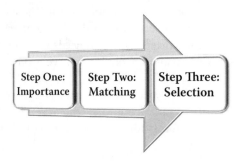

Figure 10.1 Process selection.

Table 10.1   Matching Goals and Processes

Goal/ Process	Asset Disposition	Contracting	Maintenance
Increase the inventory by 20 percent	⊗		
Limit maintenance by 10 percent		⊗	⊗
Increase overall market share 20 percent		⊗	

Source: Adapted from *Process Redesign: The Implementation Guide for Managers,* by Arthur D. Tenner and Irving J. De Torro. Published in 2000 by Prentice Hall. Table 6.1, page 61, Chapter 6, "Identifying Core Processes."

Note: ⊗ indicates high match of goal with process.

Step 2: Match Each *What* to One or More Processes

Each goal or *what* is matched to the core processes to show the correlation between the processes and the organization's goals.

The real estate division's core processes were mapped to its goals. Table 10.1 shows that contracting contributes to the achievement of two of the company's stated goals, while asset disposition and maintenance relate to only one goal each. Based on the Table 10.1 analysis, the team may select the contracting process for improvement since it potentially generates the most impact.

Step 3: Select from the Competing *Whats*

When more than one process seems viable, a more sophisticated analysis that builds on Step 2 might be used.

1. Determine the core criteria of the goals—the real estate company identified income generation, market share, and expense reduction (see Table 10.2). Be aware that the executive team may have additional and undocumented goals and objectives.
2. Attribute a weighting to each criterion—on a scale of 1 (lowest) to 5 (highest), determine the importance of each criterion for the organization's business plans. Discuss the weightings with the executive team, and get agreement before moving on.

Table 10.2 Weighting Processes to Goals

Weight 1 to 5	Criteria	Asset Disposition	Maintenance	Contracting
4	Increase Generation	3	2	5
3	Reducing Expenses	3	5	4
5	Increase Market Share	5	3	3
	Total Rate	11	10	12
	Weighted Rate	46	38	47

Source: Adapted from *Process Redesign: The Implementation Guide for Managers,* by Arthur D. Tenner and Irving J. De Torro. Published in 2000 by Prentice Hall. Table 6.1, page 61, Chapter 6, "Identifying Core Processes."

3. Compare each criterion to each process—identify on a scale of 1 (lowest) to 5 (highest) the contribution that each core process makes toward achievement of the criteria. Discuss among the team and with executive management to arrive at a consensual rating.
4. Calculate the total score for each process—add the total scores assigned to each of the criterion.
5. Calculate the weighted total for each process—multiply the assigned marks by the weight applied to the criteria, and then sum.

The division's weightings were agreed upon as shown in Table 10.2. Each core process was compared to each criterion and calculated a value to represent the level of contribution. Contracting was selected as the primary process upon which to focus, as it received the highest score of 47:

$$(5 \times 4) + (4 \times 3) + (3 \times 5) = 20 + 12 + 15 = 47$$

As long as the reasons behind the weighting of the criteria or goals and the scoring can be clearly explained and justified, the weighted calculation can stand up to scrutiny.

Core process selection is critical to the success of the business process improvement. Each team member must be able to explain exactly why the process was selected and the methodology for selection. Senior management needs to approve the choice before the team can progress further. A phase gate approval now helps to ensure that any undocumented goals or criteria are brought to the foreground.

Chapter 11

Process Characteristics

> There is nothing like a dream to create the future. Utopia today, flesh and blood tomorrow.
>
> **—Victor Hugo**

This chapter identifies the characteristics of the selected process. Process characteristics are the activities, tasks, and resources of the process that also help the process management team to anticipate pockets of resistance as the existing power base potentially shifts.

We are all familiar with sweet and delicious cakes. Activities such as creaming the butter and sugar, preparing the pans, mixing the ingredients, baking, and decorating the cake are involved in making cakes. In a commercial environment, production occurs in different areas—the baking furnace will be in a safety area and the cake decorating will likely occur in a climate-controlled room.

The creaming of the butter and sugar involves separate tasks such as weighing the butter and sugar and blending or whipping them together. Raw ingredients are transformed into a creamy substance that will be used in the next activity or process.

Flour is added to thicken the consistency of a batter. The pan is greased and powdered with flour. The oven is heated and the batter is poured into a pan. The baking in the oven continues until—voila—a perfect cake! These characteristics are not unique to cake making.

In a process, a set of linked activities transform inputs into outputs, for use by another process or activity, up to and including the end customer. Ideally, the activities transform the input to create a useful and effective output for the next step and its intended recipients.

Introduction

URHere's centralized accounts payable process comprises the following characteristics:

- Activities—processes reflect a series or sequence of ordered activities that imply underlying assumptions:
  - Adds value—each activity adds value as inputs are converted to outputs.
  - Cross-functional—activities occur over a period of time and potentially across departments.
  - Tasks—activities are a function of ordered tasks, or the *how-to* steps that aggregate into a sequence we call an activity.
- Customers—people, systems, and organizations that benefit from or use the output. Customers also provide feedback about the process.
- Inputs—things provided by suppliers at the start of the activity, typically in raw or less refined form. Inputs are converted by activities and tasks into outputs. Suppliers provide the invoices (input) required for paying bills (activity) that are completed through specific tasks (write checks) that result in new outputs (payments).
- Outputs—justify the reason for the activity; to produce a service or good for a client. Inputs are converted to outputs through a series of activities. Invoices are converted to checks at the end of the accounts payable process.
- Process owners—each process has an owner who is ultimately responsible and has a vested interest in the outputs. The finance manager may own the accounts payable process.
- Sources—people, systems, and organizations that provide inputs. Suppliers are sources that provide the invoices. Each process needs to find a way to monitor or control the quality of inputs to the process.

Definitions

Before process improvement can occur, the process characteristics must be well defined.

- Activities—what do people do in the process? What activities and tasks are performed within the process?
- Customers—who (people, systems, and organizations) benefits from or uses the process output?
- Inputs—what are the tangible/ intangible things that go into the process? What is converted during the process by activities and tasks into outputs?

- Outputs—what does the customer receive at the end of the process? What are the inputs converted or transformed into during the process?
- Process owners—who in the organization has the most to lose if the process fails? Who has the most to gain when the process succeeds? Who should be in charge of the process?
- Sources—who (people, systems, and organizations) brings or sends things through the process?

Process Characteristics Illustrated

Table 11.1 and Figure 11.1 show two different ways to illustrate the process defined for improvement. The SIPOC (supplier, input, process, output, customer) diagram shown in Figure 11.1 provides a graphical representation of process characteristics. The SIPOC diagram enables a one-page glance at the characteristics of the process.

Table 11.1   Process Characteristics

Items	Accounts Payables	Comments
Activities	Match purchase order with invoices received Match invoices with good received notes Approve invoice for payment Generate check for payment	These actions will convert an invoice to a payment.
Customers	All departments of URHere Bank (ie, financial institution)	This includes both internal and external customers.
Inputs	Invoices, delivery notes, purchase orders	These start the accounts payable process.
Outputs	Checks, updated reports	These are tangible and intangible.
Process owner	Finance manager	The buck stops at the finance manager, though a role such as the accounts payable supervisor may have some ownership of the process. This is the person with the ultimate responsibility for the process.
Sources	Suppliers, inventory department, purchasing department	These are both internal and external to the company.

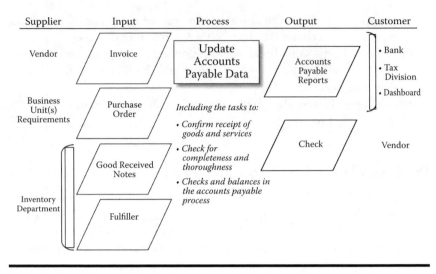

Figure 11.1   Illustrative process characteristics.

Chapter 12

Workflow Diagrams

Overview

At the end of this chapter, the process management team will understand how the current process works and will be able to produce a process workflow diagram of the process.

Ever purchased a new printer? Ever tried to install it yourself? Today it is easy to install and print on a new printer, rather quickly. Printers include a DVD, manual, and a large quick-start diagram that shows step-by-step how to install the product. Without reading the entire manual, one can set up and use the printer in less than 10 minutes by following the process workflow diagram.

Workflow diagrams are similar to a printer's quick-start diagram: they take us from start to end of the process, show us what do in sequence, identify where we are in the current process, and illustrate the next steps to be taken to get to completion. Our first workflow diagram represents the as-is state of the process. The team needs to understand what exists before it decides what to improve.

URHere's credit union operated offices in multiple locations and managed assets of more than $100 million. In the credit union environment, members are voted into positions of executive management during their annual meeting. For years, the credit union was run by managers who had little understanding of financial matters, and the organization's finances suffered accordingly. As the credit union's members became more professional, they clamored for an executive with a greater fiduciary duty. Leadership responded by calling for an immediate review and overhaul of the systems and procedures.

The review of the accounts payable process started with interviews of the customers, suppliers, process members, and other stakeholders. Samples of the process inputs and outputs were also collected. Workflow diagrams that showed the activities, documents, decisions, people, and departments were drafted from interviews with staff.

The interviews revealed that staff and managers did not share the same opinion of how the process actually worked. Managers were not intimate with the activities, nor did they know how staff met daily challenges. Staff members took advantage of loopholes in the process and manipulated the technology to circumvent procedures. They were not always aware of why actions were taken or other supporting rationales for the process. Staff also had many ideas about how to improve the process.

Workflow diagrams verified the process characteristics and confirmed the relationships between the people, systems, and processes. The diagrams helped establish where and when the process crossed departments and helped to identify areas of potential conflict.

Introduction

Just as a printer manual shows the parts of the printer and how they work together, workflow diagrams create an illustration of *how* the people, things, and technology interact to convert inputs to outputs. When creating diagrams, it may be best to conduct a workshop. If you interview each person involved in the process, each will reveal different opinions and methods.

However, the interviewing advantage is attributable to our personal desired to be heard and give perspective about the process. The interview is an opportunity to gauge staff's feelings and to give the project some credibility and visibility. Document the interview, but consider asking permission to take notes, since the interviews ought be considered *confidential*.

Questionnaire

Modify standard questionnaires that are agreed upon by the process management team. Build on the questionnaire below and tweak it to suit your needs. Ask for clarification, documents, reports, and the screen shots that are used in the process and created by the process.

SAMPLE QUESTIONNAIRE

- What do you do?
- Who gives you the information you need to do your job?
- How do you receive the information?
- What do you do with the information? Walk me through it, step by step.
- How long does it take if everything is going well?
- What delays the action?
- How do you know if the information is correct?
- What happens if the information is incorrect?
- What happens if your result or output is incorrect?
- What happens if the work is not done on time?
- Whom do you depend on to complete your work?
- What is the result or output of your work?
- Who uses the result or output of your job?
- What does this person do with the output of your job?
- What reports are generated from the work that you do?
- Under what circumstances is work returned to you?
- What reports are generated from the person after you in the process?
- What is the role of your supervisor or manager?
- Who audits your work?
- What audits do you do on your work?
- If you could change three things, what would they be?

Creating Workflow Diagrams

Workflow diagrams can be created using pen and paper, spreadsheet, word processing tools, or some specific software for drawing models. General tips that will assist with the creation of workflow diagrams include the following:

- Use the standard symbols—examples are presented in Figure 12.1.
- Start at the top left of the page and move the workflows to the right.
- Start with the activity, document, or event that begins (ie, triggers) the process.
- Place each activity in a separate activity box.

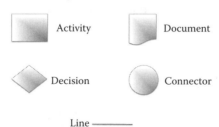

Figure 12.1   Standard workflow symbols.

- Describe the activities using the naming convention *action–noun*; for example, an accounts payable clerk will *pay bills*.
- Use the roles in the diagram, not the person's name; for example, use *supervisor* instead of *Mrs. Rose*.
- Attach a document symbol to each activity box that generates a document or report.
- Use a decision diamond where a decision needs to be made.
- Each decision diamond asks a logic question—with two likely answers (ie, yes or no) that lead to different paths.
- Although not illustrated, there may be a third conditional answer of 'maybe.' If so, conditions are noted under which it would or would not apply.
- Link activities with lines and arrows.
- Use connector symbols when the process goes to another page.
- Stop when the process ends.
- Use the same terminology and maintain the order and sequencing of activities as the interview suggests.

Test the Workflow

Facilitate groups of people or conduct additional interviews with staff to verify the completeness and accuracy of the diagrams. Archive the diagram electronically or post in a public space to solicit feedback and get the diagram right, as defined by consensual agreement and understanding.

Walkthrough

A walkthrough provides an independent verification of the process. The project team can physically walk or remotely track an input through the process, noting when and where it goes, the actions that are taken and by whom, and the duration required by each processor. The sample in Table 12.1 was tracked through URHere's accounts payable system.

Departmental Flows

Workflow diagrams can effectively illustrate when the process crosses departments. The department lines of site may be called *swim lane* diagrams.

Table 12.1   Business Process Improvement Walkthrough

Name	Action	Date	Time Taken
Maxine	Write up voucher Attach to check	12/09/20xx	2 minutes
Louisa	Confirm accuracy of data Initial voucher as checked	13/09/20xx	1 minute
Sandra	Sign check voucher	15/09/20xx	10 seconds

Conclusion

Workflow diagrams help us understand the process and the sequencing of activities within the process. Now that we understand what happens in the process, we can begin to think about improvements.

Chapter 13

Workflow Characteristics

By the end of this chapter, the process management team will be able to identify the non-value-added activities in the process and make some adjustments to immediately improve the effectiveness and efficiency of the process.

Consultants love low-hanging fruit. These small, immediate changes can be made to boost client confidence and to prove that the consultant is working assiduously to improve the process. The easy-to-grab fruit are usually found as an existing opportunity or an indisputable weakness. These changes are usually obvious to staff, but not management, and can be easily implemented. However, when the process has not been thoroughly analyzed and the root causes clearly identified, quick-win recommendations may prove subversive, in the end.

Analysis of the process workflows may give the process management team some accolades. Immediate recommendations that will positively affect process results can be made. The flowcharts can be used to develop improvements and discover the root causes of problems within the process. The team should present the changes to executive management and share the glory with other stakeholders. The business process improvement (BPI) project has already made a positive impact and provided returns on the investment.

Introduction

Standard workflow characteristics represent low-hanging fruit because they can readily be improved or eliminated without hindering long-term solutions for the improvements.

Value-Added Activities

Value-added activities transform and directly contribute to the conversion of inputs into desired outputs. For value-added activities, focus on reducing the time taken to complete. Examples include the following:

- Approving the invoices for payment
- Preparation of the checks
- Approval of the disbursements

Non-Value-Added Activities

Non-value-added activities do not directly contribute to the conversion of inputs to outputs. Examples include handovers, delays, rework, duplications, inspections, and redundant activities. Non-value-added activities in the process are identified and defined as follows:

- Bottlenecks—points in the process that slow down the rest of the process, like the neck of a ketchup bottle that narrows to control the flow. URHere bottlenecks are found at the receptionist as she has other mail to log, at the accounts payable supervisor, the accountant, check signatories, and the contract owners who have other responsibilities to pursue. Identify where the process slows or where there is an excessive buildup of work. Is there any point in the process after which the work flows faster? What part of the process is longest? Reduce any pressure points by diverting work around the bottleneck.
- Delays—sitting ... present in all of the aforementioned processes. Where in the process does work stop or wait? Whom or what is waited on across the process? The reasons for the delay need to be investigated.
- Duplications—same actions are repeated at different points in the process with the same results. Internal duplications can be eliminated. Those that occur externally to the process or department are dealt with during process.
- Handovers—whenever a document is handed over to another agent (or role), electronically or manually. Count the handovers and try to eliminate or reduce as many as possible. Most problems and inefficiencies are introduced when transferring outputs from one activity to another, typically in a different role. Our illustrated accounts payable process, in Figure 12.2 in the chapter on Workflow Diagrams, has four potential handovers.

- Inspection—all approvals, checks, and balances that occur as separate activities are identified. Set aside inspection points until the process is thoroughly understood. The accounts payable process as illustrated has four inspection points.
- Redundant activities—repetition of activities to reduce the probability of errors; for example, recalculating invoice values.
- Rework—work that was returned to an earlier point in the process is considered rework. Rework in our example is reflected in content that is incomplete or inaccurate or that is returned to the vendor, the accounts payable processor, or supervisor. Where in the process does rework occur and why? Eliminate internal causes for rework; the external factors should be set aside until later. *Internal* is defined as something you can control. *External* is defined as something beyond your span of control.

In our illustration, there are no value-added activities; 100% of the activities do not add value.

Inspection points, handovers, duplications, and bottlenecks are the most common low-hanging fruit. Simple changes can make your process more efficient almost immediately.

The process management team can spend time analyzing the reasons behind the non-value-added activities using fishbone analysis, also known as root cause analysis (optional and not always necessary). Our methodology does not focus on the *whys* because we are focused on creating a new process. Extra effort should ensure that the non-value-added activities are not repeated and that value-added activities are performed as efficiently and effectively as possible.

The non-value-added activities (see Figure 12.2 in the prior chapter) allowed some immediate and significant changes to be made (Table 13.1).

These recommendations have the immediate effect of reducing the number of handovers in the accounts payables process from three to one. They also empower the accounts payable clerk to make decisions and improve the relationships between the accounts payable process and its customers, both internal and external.

An organization may be satisfied with simple recommendations, but given the importance and potential of a BPI project, we are not satisfied at all. The BPI project must obtain the highest possible return on investment for the organization. We want to push beyond what we know and can fix quickly. We want to build an optimal process that can support change by substantially improving the current situation.

Table 13.1   Optimization

Action	Immediate Change	Removes Non-Value-Added/Adds	Effected
Receptionist sends invoices to finance. Does not log these.	*Invoice reaches the finance area as soon as it is delivered.*	**Removes:** Rework Redundant activities	*Immediately*
Explain the accounts payable (AP) input requirements to vendors.	*Vendors will include purchase order numbers on invoices. Vendors will include copies of goods received notes signed by URHere's personnel with the invoice.*	**Removes:** Delays Handover Rework	*Vendor workshop to be hosted in one month's time*
Explain the AP input requirements to URHere personnel.	*Goods received notes will be sent to the finance department as soon as goods are received. Contract owners to indicate the percentage of services/contracts received on a monthly basis.*	**Removes:** Handover Rework Delays **Adds:** Value Accuracy	*Operator workshop to be hosted in one month's time*
Use the goods received notes and the percentage of service contracts received to establish the amounts owed to vendors.	*The receipt of the goods or service triggers the AP process. At present, the receipt of the invoice triggers the AP process. URHere will now be fully aware of its liability at any point in time.*	**Removes:** Delays **Adds:** Flexibility to process Accuracy Completeness Control	*Implement one week after operator workshop*

Table 13.1 (continued)   Optimization

Action	Immediate Change	Removes Non-Value-Added/Adds	Effected
Change the rules for accepting an invoice for payment.	The invoice value is the maximum amount that has to be paid. Accept that an invoice can be partly paid.	**Removes:** Rework Delays **Adds:** Flexibility Control	Immediately
Electronic payments to be initiated.	Removes the need for manual checks. Vendors do not have to collect checks. No stale dated checks. More control over the banking function.	**Removes:** Rework **Adds:** Control Flexibility Increased efficiency	Implemented in three months time
AP clerk can determine payments to be made.	Frees up supervisor to be strategic and deal with exceptions.	**Removes:** Inspection Bottlenecks **Adds:** Empowerment	Considered for design of process

Conclusion

A process workflow workshop generates excitement about the BPI project, as staff often becomes fully engaged with defining, identifying, and generating solutions for non-value-added activities. The workshops connect staff to the project and give them a firsthand view of the process improvement promise and potential. Quick wins now provide an excellent opportunity for the BPI team to build its credibility, as shown in the before and after figures (Figure 13.1 and Figure 13.2).

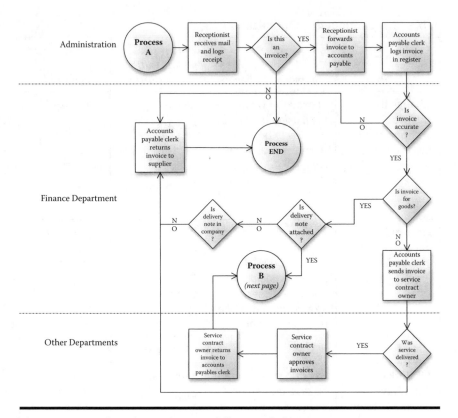

Figure 13.1 Before the process workflow workshop.

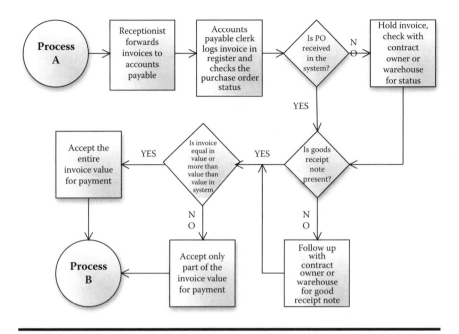

Figure 13.2   After the process workflow workshop.

Chapter 14

Phase Gate One

The process management team is handing over to the process examination team.

Accomplishments of the Process Management Team

The process management team has (see Table 14.1)—

1. Convinced the senior management team that there is a compelling need for business process improvement (BPI)
2. Successfully obtained resources to further prove that the problem exists
3. Made a promise to deliver a solution that would reduce the impact of the defined problem
4. Aligned the BPI project to organizational goals, objectives, and vision
5. Selected the process for improvement

Role of the Process Examination Team

The process examination team will (see Table 14.2)—

1. Examine the current process
2. Develop the vision, goals, and objectives of the process
3. Develop a strategic plan for the business process improvement

Table 14.1   Process Management Team (PMT) Deliverables

Deliverable	Completed
Project team charter signed by all PMT members	✓
Project budget	✓
Project timetable	✓
Risk register	✓
Lessons-learned register	✓
Documentation discipline	✓
Change management plan	✓
Communication plan	✓
Stakeholder analysis—process stakeholders	✓
Stakeholder strategy plan	✓
Stakeholder communication plan	✓
Selected process for improvement	✓
Process examination team members (names and responsibilities)	✓

Table 14.2 Process Examination Team (PET) Deliverables

Deliverable	Completed
Workflow diagrams of the current process	✓
Process characteristics defined	✓
Improvements on as-is process (removal of some non-value-added activities)	✓
Revised flowcharts (removal of some non-value-added activities)	✓
Process vision	
Process goals	
Process objectives	
Process action plans	
Process measurements	
Process SWOT (strengths, weaknesses, opportunities, threats) analysis	
BPI strategic plan	
Dream team members (names and responsibilities)	
Updated project team charter signed by all PMT members	
Final project budget	
Final project timetable	
Updated risk register	
Updated lessons learned register	
Updated change management plan	
Updated communication plan	
Updated stakeholder strategy plan	
Updated stakeholder communication plan	

Chapter 15

Dreams of the Process

It's really hard to design products by focus groups. A lot of times, people don't know what they want until you show it to them.

—Steve Jobs

By the end of this chapter, the process examination team will have set a vision and developed goals and objectives for the selected process. The goals and objectives will be used for evaluation by the process examination team and serve as a benchmark for process outcomes.

Clients usually want to increase sales, reduce expenses, or bring about some change in the way that operations are being handled. They know of some of the reasons why the process needs to be improved and some of the solutions to the problem. However, it is often difficult for the client to state the objectives of the business process improvement (BPI) project. In Figure 15.1 we define *vision* as the general outcome, *goals* as where we are headed with the improved project, and *objectives* as measurable or SMART (specific, measurable, adjustable and achievable, relevant and realistic, and time-based).

Test Driving the Vision

It is impossible to design a system so perfect that no one needs to be good.

—T. S. Eliot

Figure 15.1 Dreams of the process.

The selected process needs to have its own vision, a shared understanding about why it exists and where it is headed. As part of the exercise, consider creativity questions like: If our process was a motorized vehicle, what kind would it be? Why did you choose that type of vehicle? What are the characteristics of the vehicle that you want to have within your process? What does our vehicle look like in the future? Who drives it and how does it serve its community?

The process vision provides direction for the process examination team and identifies how the people, activities, and technology interact with each other. The vision becomes the team's reference for settling disputes about the design and how to deal with stakeholders. The vision may be modified as further assessments are made, but the results are seldom far from the team's original vision.

Setting Goals

The goals are the *what*s that help guide direction toward the vision. The process goals identify what we want the process to accomplish. They may represent improvements on existing process characteristics or set new criteria for them. The process characteristics are the *foci* around which we build the process goals. The goals can focus on improving the existing characteristics, removing a deficiency, or placing a new requirement on the characteristics. Table 15.1 was completed to identify the goals for URHere's accounts payable process.

Goals identify what we want from the process and its general characteristics. Set a goal for each process characteristic to ensure completeness, and use the overall outcome to set encompassing goals for the process. Use Table 15.1 to assist in the identification of what the team wants. What are the goals for the people, their activities, and the use of technology in the process?

Table 15.1   Process Characteristics and Goals

	What We Want (Goal)	Process, People/ Technology (Classify Impact)	Internal/ External
Input	Accuracy, zero defects	Process	External
	Supplier invoice to be accurate		
Supplier	Flexibility, updated systems, compliance	Process	External
	Supplier to comply with the needs of the accounts payable (AP) system		
Output	Timely, accurate, zero defects, satisfaction	Process	Internal
	Payments must be accurate and timely		
Customer	Satisfied, trust in the process	Process	Internal and external
	Vendors to be sure that contractual arrangements are met		
Activities	Value-added, no non-value-added	Process	Internal
	All activities contribute to the payment		
Process owner	Overview, troubleshoot	Technology process	Internal
	The AP owner must know at a glance where the process is at any time		

The vision for the accounts payable system was stated as, To provide an accurate, complete, and efficient payment system that realizes the needs of all our stakeholders.

At the end of the exercise we can ask, What are the goals that we have for the technology, people, and the processes? Goals frequently relate to a quality input, a quality output, and stakeholder satisfaction. From Table 15.1, the goals can be identified as follows:

1. To have ready-for-processing invoices
2. To process invoices accurately and within contractual terms
3. To make all payments as per contracts
4. To ensure that all activities add value in the process
5. To ensure that the process owner knows what is happening with each invoice

Align Goals to Vision

To ensure alignment, goals are mapped or related directly to supporting the vision. Where the goals do not map clearly to the vision, they may need to be modified or the vision restated. The goals can be mapped to the vision like in the example in Table 15.2.

Perform Gap Analysis

Make a list of the skills and resources that are needed to achieve the goals. Compare the list with the process characteristics, people, and technology.

Table 15.2 Align Goals to Vision

Goal	Part of Vision	Comment
To have ready-for-processing invoices	Efficient payment system	A quality input allows for efficiency
To process invoices accurately and within contractual terms	Accurate and complete Stakeholders needs	Vendors and contractors want to be paid on a timely basis
To make all payments as per contracts	Stakeholders needs Completeness and accuracy	Ensures that URHere makes all payments as contractually obligated
All activities must add value in the process	Stakeholders needs Efficient payment process	Elimination of non-value-added activities results in a more efficient process
Process owner must know what is happening with each invoice	Completeness Stakeholder	Process owner is stakeholder as well

■ What is needed to achieve the goals?
■ Which skills and resources are not present or void within the existing process?
■ Is it possible to obtain these skills and resources?
■ How will this be done?

Set SMART Objectives

From the gap analysis, the SMART objectives can be more easily determined. The objectives provide a way of measuring progress toward the goals of the vision.

The columns in Table 15.3 titled How to Achieve Goals and Skills/Resources Needed provide the level of detail required to set SMART objectives. We provide a more detailed definition below for the term SMART.

For each goal, at least three SMART objectives will be set to measure achievement toward the goals. Some of the objectives may be shaped by the gap analysis to ensure that the process focuses on getting the right skills and resources to achieve its goals, and ultimately its vision.

Table 15.3   Resource Gap Analysis

Goals	How to Achieve Goals	Skills/Resources Needed
Ready-for-processing invoices	Define the characteristics of a "ready-to-process" invoice for supplier Meet with suppliers Assist suppliers where necessary	Communications Vendor workshop
Accurate, timely payments and within contractual terms Payments as per contracts All activities must add value in the process	AP staff to understand contracts Remove bottlenecks and non value-added activities from process Invent a new process	Process examination team (PET) BPI facilitator Contracts training
Process owner must know what is happening with each invoice	Implement a technological solution	Technology Technologist Money

S—set significant and *specific* objectives. Objectives must not be fuzzy or argumentative when competing for resources. Objectives should be logical and methodical in the statement of what and how they provide results that support the organization's vision.

M—objectives should be *measurable*, and stated as a value. Use the results from the measurement exercises to get the reference. For example, in Table 15.3, the term *money* should stipulate how much money and in what unit of currency.

A—all parties must agree that the objective is *adjustable*. Think of the fuel or power gauge in your motorized vehicle. It can go up or down and you can set limits for alarms when it gets too low.

R—objectives must be relevant and *realistic* with a focus on results.

T—objectives are set to be achieved within a particular *time period*. The outcome must be timely to maintain the momentum and belief in the organization's goals and vision. For example, in Table 15.3, the value of that *money* might fluctuate because its value against other denominations will change on an hourly basis. While not important for a small project, currency fluctuations have been known to kill projects in excess of $100 million.

Objectives

An Illustration

1. To host a vendors workshop by March 31, 20xx.
2. To visit main contractors or vendors offices to ensure compliance by December 30, 20xx.
3. To host a contract management workshop for the accounts payable staff by January 31, 20xx.
4. To secure management approval for the project implementation team to design the accounts payable system by June 30, 20xx.
5. To implement the new accounts payable design by September 30, 20xx.
6. To ensure that the new system has the following design elements:
   - Vendor compliance to be tracked
   - Contractual terms to be readily available to processors
   - No non-value-added activities
   - Zero errors
   - Process overview for the process owner
   - Feedback on processing time and non-value-added activities to all process members
   - Empowerment of data processors

Note that objectives 1 and 3 are short-term measures that aim to correct obvious shortcomings of the accounts payables process. These objectives (1 and 3) represent low-lying fruit and are very valuable to both the process examination and implementation team members. The successful completion of the objectives provides immediate relief to the process stakeholders, gives the teams credibility, and provides tangible results for process. Early successes add momentum to the project.

Develop Action Plans

Each objective can now be broken down into small tasks that provide the road map for reaching the goals (see Table 15.4). Each task will be assigned a time line and will have an owner. Where there are monetary concerns, state them as well. The action plan for objectives 1, 2, and 3 are much simpler that those stated for objectives 4, 5, and 6. However, the most complex objectives need the most levels of details.

Table 15.4 Accounts Payable (AP) Objectives Action Plan

Objective	Tasks	Responsibility	Time Frame	Cost
Host vendor workshop	Set date	Process owner	Day 1	
	Invite vendors	AP team	End on Day 8	600
	Book conference room	AP supervisor	Day 1	
	Order food/drinks	Receptionist	Day 12	
	Develop presentation	Process owner	Day 14	
	Dry run of presentation	Process owner	Day 16	
	Host workshop	AP team	Day 24	

Check for Alignment

> See first that the design is wise and just: that ascertained, pursue it resolutely; do not for one repulse forego the purpose that you resolved to effect.
>
> **—William Shakespeare**

The selected process exists to support the strategic objectives of the organization. For this important purpose to be served, the process vision, goals, and objectives must match and be aligned with the organization's vision, goals, and objectives. Any decisions that the process management team makes about the purpose of the process must be confirmed by senior executives, as not all of their intentions are overt or openly known.

Since the selected process may consume sizable resources during the BPI project, it is important to confirm that the selected process is contributing to the overall organizational aspirations.

The trade union's improved collection process called for a 50 percent reduction in staff members. The trade union opted to retain the services of all the staff members. The leadership stated that as a trade union, they could not retrench staff members because of a change in process, because process changes were indicative of the types of issues regularly challenged with employers. The objective of increasing the process efficiency clashed with the union's undocumented objective of maintaining employment at the current levels and maintaining their bargaining power.

Conclusion

The selected process vision, goals, and objectives are critical to guiding the BPI project and to helping communicate the process examination team's remit to stakeholders. As the BPI project evolves, information will be gleaned about the selected process, and some of the information will be calibrated. Get the approval of the project sponsor and executives around the BPI project's vision, goals, and objectives to ensure alignment with stated and unstated organizational goals.

Chapter 16

Process Measurements

The measure of a country's greatness is its ability to retain compassion in times of crisis.

—Thurgood Marshall

Success is to be measured not so much by the position that one has reached in life as by the obstacles which he has overcome.

—Booker T. Washington

We use products and services every day, and every day we evaluate what we use: The staff was friendly, or the service was excellent, or I am not spending my money there again. We perform a valuable service for our inner circle and ourselves by measuring the performance of the services and products that we experience. First-hand information is highly useful and would greatly assist the organization to determine if its goods or services are satisfying its targeted customers.

Client satisfaction is the ultimate measurement of the product or service offered. Feedback from clients makes an impact if it is used to adjust the organization's offerings. Feedback frequently comes in the form of reactive or corrective measures. Ideally, the organization can access internal measurements that offer proactive and timely indication and can be used to adjust offerings and maximize customer satisfaction.

This chapter reviews the measurements around the selected process.

Why Measure?

Imagine that you are an executive of URHere and most of your clients are frequent travelers. You are interested in ensuring that your customers positively influence more sales, enjoy your global positioning system (GPS) services, and tell their friends and acquaintances about your products and services. You will need to walk in your customers' shoes, understand their experience, and think about what they consider important:

- What features of your selected process do your customers measure?
- How will you know if your product or service is successful?
- What features or aspects of your product or service can clients live without?
- What features or aspects of your product or service can clients not live without?
- How well does your product or service serve your client needs on a daily basis and under different conditions—recession, inclement weather, traffic congestion?

The questions above focus on what the customer views as important. The URHere executive will also be correlating answers from these questions with considerations of technology, employee activities, and costs to locate opportunities where customer satisfaction can be increased.

Measurement System

It is important to develop a measurement system that generates continuous feedback about the performance of the selected process. Measurement systems answer questions such as the following:

- *Why* is it important to measure?
- *What* will we measure and why?
- *How* will we measure the what?
- How will we collect the data?
- What data will we collect?
- How do we process the data collected?
- What will we do with the results from the measurements?
- What are the corrective or other actions that will be taken from the measurement result?
- How will we know if results of the measurements are true and that conclusions drawn are accurate?

The *why*, *what*, and *how* of the measurements must be established and explained to the people involved with the process. Measurement focuses on both internal and external methodologies of capturing, sorting, processing, and reporting the data and using the results to draw conclusions and take actions where necessary. To maintain confidence in the improvement, the results of the measurement system must be published regularly and be open to scrutiny. The method should be simple, so that a wide cross-section of the process stakeholders understands the measurements.

As conditions of the environment (internal and external) change, the appropriateness of the measurements should be challenged and changed as required. Customer preferences change with increased market options, knowledge, and expectations. The organization that is insensitive to market changes may suffer a loss in customer base and will need to invest heavily to bring customers back. The measurement system allows the organization to develop awareness about changing needs and work proactively to keep customers delighted.

Figure 16.1 illustrates the relationship between customer needs and the level of service provided. Customer needs are not static; they change over time, stabilize, and then change again. Depending on the industry, the period of stabilization will vary. Think of the dynamic market of mobile telephones and compare to the more stable market of automobiles.

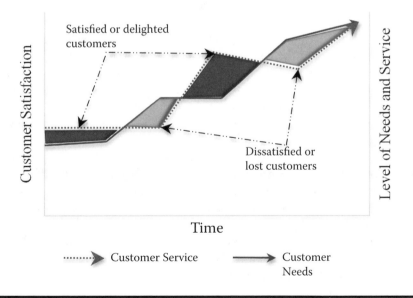

Figure 16.1   Customer loyalty.

Policies and procedures within an organization should support and encourage the behaviors and decisions that support the desired measurements. For example, reward systems need to reflect the desired process outcomes, to both reward and incentivize staff for excellent performance.

Measurement Types

The true measure of a man is how he treats someone who can do him absolutely no good.

—Samuel Johnson

There is a measure in everything. There are fixed limits beyond which and short of which right cannot find a resting place.

—Horace

When URHere began operations, performance was measured by collecting data on actual performance—quantities produced, resources consumed—and matching actual records to the budgets and standards. In the past, variances were acceptable within 10 percent of budget; variances greater than 10 percent required explanation.

Performance measures were quantitative; they focused on the consumption of resources and the conversion of inputs to outputs. Data analysis was completed at least six weeks after events occurred, since variances were part of the financial monthly reports. The emphasis on quantitative measurements increased the efficiency of the processes. Vast improvements were made on the conversion ratios of inputs to outputs and activity duration rates, with substantial reductions to the cost of manufacturing.

Not much emphasis was placed on the qualities of the GPS receivers. As a result, customers became dissatisfied with the performance of it GPS receivers. The radio frequency filters (RF devices that filter unwanted signals and amplify the desired noise) were calibrated too low or too high to provide high-quality signals.

Quality was considered a by-product of reduced sales. Customer needs and opinions became important only to boost sales.

Twenty years later, URHere no longer operates in that fashion. Qualitative measurements are now made in real time throughout the process, not only at the end of the financial monthly reporting period.

Process Measurements

Three sets of measures are used to gauge the process:

1. Process/efficiency—measures the time that activities take to convert inputs to outputs
2. Output/effectiveness—measures how well the output meets the design requirements
3. Outcome effectiveness and customer satisfaction—measures how well output meets customers' needs

Process/Efficiency Measures

Ideally, one measure identifies the minimum possible level of resources to be consumed during the process. Actual resource consumption is quantified and assessed against set standards as a variance, variation, or deviation. The results lead to the control of people, materials, methods, machines, environment, and the way each factor interacts with the others. Resource consumption is an easy measure since it is tangible. Standards are set based on the experience or target of an ideal; for example, for a printer, five pages will be printed in 10 seconds. Standards should have a stretch factor that can be realistically achieved with special effort. If you are new to standard setting, the best practices of other organizations in the world—within or external to your industry, country, and so forth—provide an ideal place to begin. Best practices may have to be modified to reflect your situation, but there is value in knowing how your process ranks with the best in your comparative world.

In the accounts payable process, the efficiency measures focused on the following:

- Inputs—the number of invoices received for the month. Invoice quantity was independently verified with suppliers.
- Time—the time taken for an invoice to be processed and for the vendor to receive payment. Rework factors, the availability of the technology, and human factors affect time components.
- People—a review of the payroll costs, indicated where and when, over time, value-added was created, how people were used in the process, and the level of training or skilled labor used in the process.
- Equipment—the availability of the technology and its ability to adapt to real-time data.
- Output—the number of accurate payments generated per month and reasons for delays.

Selected Process Measurements

For the accounts payable process, efficiency measurements were calculated using equations that are shown below.

Measuring Inputs

The accounts payable process owner determined that 360 invoices should be processed each week. At the end of the week, the efficiency ratio is calculated as follows:

- Actual number of invoices processed divided by the standard number of invoices to be processed times 100 percent.

$$\left[\frac{Actual\ Quantity\ of\ Invoices}{Standard\ Quantity\ of\ Invoices} \right] \times 100$$

- In the week that 320 invoices were processed, the efficiency ratio for the process was (320 divided by 360) times 100 percent, which equals 89.9 percent.

$$\left[\frac{300}{360} \right] \times 100 = 89.90\%$$

- The calculation above means that the process is not working as it should, because 100 percent minus 89.9 percent equals 10.1 percent.

$$100\% - 89.9\% = 10.1\%$$

- Note that if fewer than 360 invoices are received for the week, then the number of invoices received becomes the standard for that week. For example, if only 320 invoices are received and all entered, then there is 100 percent efficiency. If 300 of the 320 received were entered, then the ratio is calculated as (300 divided by 320) times 100 percent equals 93.75 percent.

$$\left[\frac{300}{320} \right] \times 100 = 93.75\%$$

Measuring Time

The standard processing time for an invoice is five minutes. The average time for processing invoices in the month was recorded as six minutes. The efficiency time ratio is calculated as follows:

■ Efficiency time ratio equals 100 percent minus [(standard time less actual time) divided by standard time multiplied by 100].

$$100\% - \left[\frac{Standard\ time - Actual\ time}{Standard\ time} \times 100 \right]$$

■ Efficiency ratio for the accounts payable process equals 100 minus [(5 minus 6 divided by 5) times 100].

$$100\% - \left[\left(\frac{5-6}{5} \right) \times 100 \right]$$

■ Efficiency ratio equals 100 percent minus [(–1 divided by 5) times 100].

$$100\% - \left[\left(\frac{-1}{5} \right) \times 100 \right]$$

■ Efficiency ratio = 100 percent minus (–20 percent) is the same as 100 percent plus 20 percent equals 120 percent.

$$100\% - (-20\%) |$$

$$100\% + 20\% = 120\%$$

(Remember that in math two minus signs coming together make a plus.)

The calculation above means that the process takes 20 percent more time than it should to be complete.

Measuring People

The labor costs for the process can be determined from the monthly payroll. Costs for people who are fully employed by the process can be easily identified. Costs for people who support the process—people external to the finance department or have other duties (accountant)—are allocated to the process based on an average time worked on the process. The accuracy of allocated times can be verified as input for the measurement, if the costing exercise is not too expensive.

■ Total staff costs (accounts payable process) equals payroll costs of direct staff plus indirect staff.

Staff costs = Direct staff cost + Indirect staff cost

■ The cost of the accounts payable direct staff equals $1,000 and the cost of the indirect employees equals $200.
■ Total staff costs equal $1,000 plus $200, which is $1,200.

The staff costs can provide the standard, and on a monthly basis, any increases or decreases from standard costs might be investigated.

Output Cost

The total costs for the process can be used to identify the costs per output, that is, the payment. The total costs can include an allocated cost for expenses associated with the department and overhead. We keep our illustrative calculation simple and use the staff costs to identify the cost of the output.

Output cost is calculated as follows:

■ Output cost equals total staff cost divided by the number of outputs.

$$Output\ cost = \left[\frac{Total\ staff\ costs}{Quantity\ of\ inputs} \right]$$

■ Cost per payment = total staff costs divided by the actual quantity of payments generated, which is $1,200 divided by 320 equals $3.75.

Purpose of Efficiency Measures

Efficiency measurements are used to drive decision making around improving the process. Each measurement tells the story about the process. The process may be operating within or outside of the set limits, and the process owner needs to understand the causes before changes can be made to improve the process.

Decisions about Inputs

To assist with decisions around inputs, teams can ask the following types of questions:

■ What quality checks can be built into the process?
■ What can be done to ensure that the process inputs include the required quality?

- What interface can we have with suppliers to ensure input quality?
- Will new standards be set for failing suppliers or will others suppliers be sought?
- Can we get more output from the same level of inputs (eg, in manufacturing, change formulas, change technology)?

Decisions about Time

The timing ratios may indicate parts of the process that need to be improved.

- Which activities could be sped up with improved technology?
- How can we make the process quicker?
- What can we do to reduce the total process time?

Decisions about People

Almost anything that interrupts or stops the process flow will increase the payroll costs; for example, emergency payments, absenteeism, technological malfunction, and downtime enable waste. Teams need to acknowledge that productivity may be subjective since a person's output can also be affected by personal situations and other job scenarios. Some of the relevant questions to ask are as follows:

- Are people sufficiently trained to do the job?
- What special circumstances—personal, departmental, or otherwise—increase or decrease performance?
- How is the output (eg, for the day) comparable to other days?
- How can we limit exceptions to the process?
- How can we reduce the number of hours (or minutes) invested with each activity?
- What triggers the need for overtime personnel?

Output/Effectiveness Measures

Here measures are concerned with how effective the process is at converting inputs to outputs, the amount of activity required within the process, the amount of product produced, and the number of customers served.

Output measures help to evaluate the ability of the process to deliver products or services according to internal or external specifications. Each specific feature, value, and attribute of the output as expected by the customer is scrutinized.

Internally between processes, information is easily obtained since the output of one process becomes the input for another. When the output serves an external customer, the information needs to be obtained through customer surveys and ratings or other appropriate feedback mechanisms.

Whereas the efficiency measures deal with a predetermined or set standard for process output, effectiveness measures are set by evaluating the trend of output performance over time. If quantitative numbers are obtained, the results become logical and auditable. For the accounts payable process the output/effectiveness measures were identified as follows:

- Output measures—the number of payments generated for the year. Total output for the year 20xx was 34,800 payments (comprised of checks, wire transfers, etc). When trended with results over the past two years of 45,000 and 42,000 payments, there seems to be a reduction of output for the department. The reasons why the output was reduced can be myriad. The causes may reflect purchasing or contractual decisions to use fewer vendors or the type of work performed. As conditions change, standards may become irrelevant and need to be modified.

- Features of the payments—percentage of the payments that were accurate, timely, and met the vendor's requirements. The number of returned payments or the amount of payments that required rework provides a measure of the noncompliance features of the payments. The standards for errors may be zero tolerance—no late payments.

- Conversion—inherent in the measurement of the output is the conversion of the inputs to outputs. How many invoices or payment requests were processed to generate 34,800 payments for the year?

- Other processes—the contribution of other processes or departments to generate output can be identified. The role that the warehouse has in accurately receiving and recording stock will affect the ability to make accurate payments.

- Customer satisfaction—how well the customers are satisfied with the process. Are the financial institutions satisfied with payments? Are suppliers satisfied with the accuracy, timeliness, and completeness of payments?

- Customer preferences—how will different types of customers prefer to be paid: one payment per invoice, one payment per purchase order, one payment for all outstanding invoices regardless of purchase order? What mechanism do they choose for payments: PayPal*, electronic banking, wire transfers, or other?

The measures above will change over time to reflect the process and the changes in the customer preferences. The standards that are set at zero tolerance may not change over time.

Purpose of Effectiveness Measures

The output measures assist us to make decisions about the output and by extension how the process operates so that customers are satisfied.

Decisions about Output Measures

In the accounts payable process, the one-on-one relationship between payment and invoice was changed to a one-to-many relationship, one payment to many invoices. Vendor invoices were paired across purchase orders and contracts. The pairing allowed maximization of the resources and the minimization of rework.

Decisions about Features

We focus on aspects of the process that are undesirable. A zero tolerance for defective outputs captures a primary measurement, any defects imply a process failure. Any incorrect or late payments suggest that the process has failed. The team needs to give reasons for each failure and eliminate factors that contribute to the cause. Some of the defects were caused by calculation errors, incorrect inputs, and human error. Where the defects were caused by external factors, we worked with the external parties to limit the occurrence.

Decisions about Conversion

The conversion factors for the process are not standardized. A payment could be generated for one or multiple invoices or other request. Two of the standards developed as guidelines for the checking of the system were:

- No payments of less than $1 million for vendors with multiple contracts or purchase orders in the system
- No one-on-one relationships between invoices and payments

All exceptions need to be justified. The justification process discovered that exceptions were mainly for immediate mobilization of contractors, catering for a meeting, purchase of year-end gifts, and advertising. The process owner and staff should have an awareness of the acceptable deviations from the set standards.

Other Processes

The terms and conditions set out in the vendor contracts and purchase orders were changed to reflect the payment policies of the accounts payable process and the standards for quality of inputs (accurate, timely, and complete processing).

Decisions about Customer Satisfaction

Internal customers were satisfied as the vendor or contractor did not complain about late or inaccurate payments or threaten to stop work because of nonpayments. Banks were satisfied when they were paid within the credit arrangements. Customers were satisfied if payments were on time and accurate.

From understanding what the customer considered valuable, we were able to measure each instance of not living up to the customer's needs and examine the underlying causes. We used questionnaires to cement ideas. Table 16.1, a questionnaire, provides an example.

Decisions about Customer Preferences

Our process outcome is simple to measure. A payment is either on time or late, accurate or inaccurate, complete or incomplete. We need to stay current about new payment methods and new ways to receive inputs. Processes with more sophisticated outcomes need to continuously poll customers to establish trends or to set new trends for their customers according to the organization's overall strategy. A sample questionnaire is shown in Table 16.1.

Outcome Effectiveness and Customer Satisfaction

Outcome effectiveness is a measure of the ability of the process to satisfy customer requirements. It is often difficult to differentiate between the output and the outcome measurements. The outcome measure is about the success of the process, but the output is a measure of the activity. The outcome measure is subjective.

The purpose of the organization is to satisfy customers' needs. Customer satisfaction derives from product or service delivery, so there is an inherent delay to problem solving that occurs after receiving negative feedback from customers.

Feedback from customers comes as a mixture of facts, opinions, and emotions that may change with the clients' physical and emotional state at the time the product is being used. Customer variability makes customer satisfaction challenging and reinforces the need to survey larger populations over time to normalize the effects of personal exceptions and emotions.

For your selected process, both internal and external clients need to be surveyed to gauge how well the process serves customers.

Table 16.1 Measurement Questionnaire

Output/Effectiveness		

Type of client: ☐ Internal   ☐ External

Service provided: Maintenance

How often do you receive payments?   Monthly

Average number of payments received for the year   24

Average value of payments received for the year   3MM

Rate the following statements about the payment process from 1 to 5:

    1 means that the statement is never true.

    2 means that the statement is true some of the time.

    3 means that the statement has no impact.

    4 means that the statement is true most of the time.

    5 means that the statement is always true.

Statement	Rank	Comments
Payments are accurate	4	
Payments are made on time	3	Payment are never early
Payments are complete—for all outstanding invoices that are due	4	Most times
The payments process can handle exceptions	5	
The payment process is flexible	2	
Payments are made speedily	3	
When things go wrong I am contacted immediately	5	
When things go wrong I am given the chance to fix it	5	
When things go wrong I can work with the people to fix it	3	
When things go wrong they are quickly resolved	5	

Continued

Table 16.1 (continued)   Measurement Questionnaire

Statement	Rank	Comments
Customer service is excellent	3	
The banking process works	5	
The banking process is timely	4	
I get information from the payables process with ease	5	
URHere's bankers are willing to help if I have a problem	2	
Staff in the payment process are always ready to help	5	
My invoices are never lost	5	
I can easily check on the status of my invoices and payments	2	
I know exactly what is needed to get a timely and accurate payment every time	5	
There is no problem with the invoices that I submit	3	

Purpose of the Output Effectiveness Measure

Output effectiveness can be used to identify how well the process serves clients' needs. Feedback identifies where and how the process can be improved as envisioned by customers. From survey to survey, the hope is that the gap between what clients and what the organization provides will be narrowed.

Feedback from the financial institutions helped us make decisions about how and when we made payroll payments to temporary staff. Feedback from our clients assisted in streamlining the input requirements for the accounts payable process.

Sample questionnaires as shown in Table 16.2 are used to gather information from clients.

The previous questionnaire is more open-ended than the one used of the output/effectiveness measures, because we are trying to get a feel for customers' perceptions about the process. Table 16.2, Customer Expectations, can be used to collate data from different stakeholders to get a comprehensive view of what customers want and how they perceive the delivery of the service.

Table 16.2 Customer Expectations

Outcome Effectiveness and Customer Satisfaction *URHere Payment Process Questionnaire*		
Type of client: ☐ Internal ☐ External		
Service provided:		
How often do you receive payments?		
Complete the table below as per the following instructions:		
• List your expectations of the payments process in the column labeled Expectations.		
• Rank your expectations from 1 (lowest) to 5 (highest) in terms of importance to you in the column labeled Rank.		
• Rate how the process meets your expectations using 1 (it does not meet your expectations) to 5 (it exceeds your expectations) in the column labeled Rate.		

Expectations	*Rank*	*Rate*
1. To hear about invoice problems before the payment due date	4	2
2. To receive more than one payment a month if invoices are in the company	4	2
3. To receive a coherent answer when I ask about the status of the payment	4	3
4. To get paid when the payment is made—that URHere has cash to make payment	5	5*

5. Which one of your expectations can you live without? Place an asterisk next to it.
6. List three things that we can do to better meet your expectations. • Call clients as soon as a problem is noted • Make exceptions to the process based on the client history, situation, and so forth • Not transfer calls to different people before giving feedback on the status of a payment
7. List two things in the payment process that you would change • The rigidity or inflexibility of the payment schedules • The number of people I have to talk to to get the correct answer

Continued

Table 16.2 (continued)   Customer Expectations

8. Complete this sentence: If I were the manager in charge of the payment process …
I would ensure that everyone knows the status of payments or can find the information. I would make sure that all complaints are listened to and that feedback is sought on a regular basis. It would make the employees work better.
9. List three things that work for you in the payment process • Money is always available. • The monthly check is on time and for all outstanding invoices at that time. • Some staff members have the information and are willing to help.
10. Complete this sentence: The payment process … • works. URHere needs to be more flexible in its arrangements with contractors; we should be paid as soon as invoices are due, not wait for the monthly cycle for our checks. I wonder if there is a cash flow problem.
Thanks for completing the questionnaire. Your feedback will help us to make improvements in our level of customer service.

Goals, Objectives, and Measurements

Process measurements provide the details to further define goals and make objectives SMART—specific, measurable, adjustable, realistic, and timely. Setting measurements for the process characteristics allows the team to state in clear and tangible terms how the process should perform on a sustained basis. When supported by measurements that are consistently and accurately used, the process can be continuously improved to meet changing customer requirements.

Teams should ensure that across a process, all measurements are directed at the same expectation. A goal of zero defects for the accounts payable system translates into 100 percent on-time transactions and 100 percent accuracy. No tolerance is shown for late payments.

Conclusion

Measurements are especially valuable when they are consistently recorded and the sampling is applied to all the results. A measurement system ensures that results are consistently interpreted and seen as valid. Each measurement tells the tale of some aspect of the process. Together they tell about the health of the entire process. The team needs to understand the importance of measurements before they take decisions or actions to improve the process.

Chapter 17

Strengths and Weaknesses

The preparation of a five-year strategic plan for URHere's micro credit agency began by comparing the agency's services to that of its competitors. Results highlighted activities that its credit union performed better or worse than its competitors. Table 17.1 compiles input from the analysis.

The team identified internal factors that caused the credit union to excel (strengths) and the factors that caused their ratings to be lower than competitors (weaknesses). The external environment that provides opportunities and threats was also reviewed to provide input for the SWOT (strengths, weaknesses, opportunities, threats) matrix shown in Table 17.2.

Process SWOT

A SWOT analysis for the selected process serves to validate the feasibility of the goals and objectives set for the process. With SWOT, the process and its results are compared with those of other organizations. The lack of information does not limit the validity or cheapen the veracity of the SWOT.

The SWOT analysis shown in Table 17.3 for the accounts payable process was completed by following the five steps that are discussed below:

1. Identify the internal strengths and weaknesses
2. Scan the external environment
3. Prepare the SWOT matrix
4. Develop strategies
5. Validate goals and objectives

Table 17.1   Analysis of Competitors

Issue	Competitor A	Competitor B	Competitor C	Credit Union
Years in existence	Less than 5	12	15	20
Number of members	100,000	75,000 (estimated)	75,000 to 100,000	>100,000
Management experience	5* Former bank executives run the company.	3 Mix of professional and nonprofessionals run the company.	1 Nonprofessionals are the executives.	3 Many years in the business. Few executives are professionals.
Delinquency ratio	1 Uses bank ratings to issue loans and banking collection methods.	3 Gives unsecured loans.	1 More on a savings drive and for purchase of tangible items for repossession.	5 Invests in the members' businesses. During start-up of business, the delinquency ratio is high. Because of family relations, there was leniency with members.

Client care	5	The customer care models from the banking system are used.	3 to 5	Seen as customer-friendly.	3	Unsecured loans are discouraged without explanations.	5	Members feel like family (and often are). Long-standing relationships with members for generations.
Risk taking	1	Not perceived as an option. Seen as cold and too businesslike.	3	Will give secured loans.	1	Not risk takers.	5	Will give unsecured loans for start-ups.
Branding	5	Logo, branded products, Web presence.	3	No logo or branding. Low name recognition. Web presence.	1	Logo. Now branding. Now getting Web presence.	3	Logo established. Low name recognition. Web presence.

* Ratings are on a scale of 1 (low) to 5 (high), as follows: 5 (high) means, "Pay any price"; 1 (low) means, "Want it for free; not willing to pay extra for it"; 3 (moderate) is all the stuff in between, meaning we are "willing to pay a reasonable price" without being forced to define "reasonable."

Table 17.2　SWOT Matrix for Credit Union

Strengths	Weaknesses	Opportunities	Threats
High customer satisfaction Committed management and staff Ready access to funding from URHere's main office	Limited managerial experience Customers and staff are related— conflicts of interest Not all process and systems work well High delinquency rates on loan portfolios	Government initiative to increase the number of micro businesses Government training programs for entrepreneurs and small-business owners Links to external markets for customers	Increased regulatory framework for operations Global credit crunch—may affect URHere's overall business Social conditions in the villages within which the micro credit operates

Table 17.3　SWOT Matrix for Accounts Payable Process

Strengths	Weaknesses	Opportunities	Threats
Long-term relationships with vendors Committed staff and management	Internal controls are weak Invoices received do not comply with the process requirements Increasing vendor complaints Internal customers do not always comply with our needs	Higher levels of technology within the banking sector Increased security in using the Internet Vendors are willing to work with us for solutions	Hackers update the Internet with viruses on a regular basis Vendors hold up services or want payment up front New government regulations that may result in litigation for late payments

Step 1: Identify Internal Strengths and Weaknesses

The credit union worked the questionnaire below to identify its strengths and weaknesses.

- Identify three things in your process that you cannot live without.
  - The staff's willingness to work
  - The long-term relationships with vendors, especially when things go wrong

- – The commitment of the accounts payable manager
- ■ Identify three things in the process that you do not care for.
  - – Late payments to vendors
  - – The constant loop of returned invoices to vendors for noncompliance
  - – Constant vendor queries for late payments, returned invoices, and the like
- ■ What advantages does your process have?
  - – The people who work in it
  - – We get the job done—it may be late but we do it.
- ■ What does your process do better than any other similar process?
  - – We have ongoing dialogue with our customers—internal and external.
  - – We work with customers to solve problems.
  - – Our customers are interested in our success.
- ■ What you think that customers will say about the process?
  - – That it fails them
  - – That we try
  - – That they want a better process
- ■ What do you think customers want to change about the process?
  - – No returned invoices
  - – No late payments
  - – Fewer queries
- ■ What could improve the process?
  - – Late payments
  - – Fewer queries
  - – Returned invoices

Step 2: Scan the External Environment

The external environment may offer opportunities and present limitations that can influence the process design.

Government

- ■ Will a change of government affect the process?
  - – No
- ■ What are the impending legislative changes and how will they affect your organization?
  - – There is pending legislation for the protection of small business owners from delinquent debtors. We often pay late, so we may face litigation under the new law.
- ■ What threats or opportunities may political situations present?
  - – Not applicable

Economic

- How does the economic situation affect suppliers and customers?
  - Suppliers do not want any further delays. They are demanding money before services are rendered.
- How do inflation rates and trends affect your industry or organization?
  - Goods and services are more expensive. Vendor relations are essential to getting good prices. Accounts payable now becomes critical.
- How easy is it to implement changes in the environment as described?
  - There is a great incentive to change as things tighten.
- How easy is it for competitors to surpass the organization?
  - Easy
- What are the opportunities or threats that new conditions present?
  - We have to please vendors to ensure that we maintain good relations and can get competitive prices.

Technological

- What are the new and emerging technologies in your industry?
  - Internet banking
- How are other companies using technology?
  - To make secure payments
- What opportunities or threats may evolve from the technology?
  - Hacking

Step 3: Prepare the SWOT Matrix

Identify answers from Step 1 as strengths and weaknesses and Step 2 as opportunities and threats. For each SWOT element identified, look for ways to exploit the strengths and opportunities and eliminate or reduce the impact of the weaknesses and threats as shown in the example below.

Refer to Table 17.3 for a sample SWOT matrix.

Step 4: Compile Strategies

Answer the following questions:

Weaknesses

- What do we do to transform weaknesses into strengths?
  - Improve the accounts payable systems.

- What do we do to eliminate the negative impact of weaknesses?
  - Make timely and accurate payments.
  - Get vendors to comply.

Threats

- What do we do to reduce the effects of external threats?
  - Work with government to understand the implications of the new legislations, so that we can anticipate how it will affect us and influence the outcome if we can.
- What can be done with the strengths to counteract the threats?
  - Continue to work closely with vendors to solve problems.
- How do we prepare ourselves for future threats?
  - Develop close working relationships with government officials and vendor personnel.
- What do we do to eliminate or mitigate the threats?
  - No control over new legislation
  - We can limit vendors' reactions by changing our systems to comply with their needs.
- Which, if any, weaknesses limit our ability to counteract threats?
  - Until we fix the internal process, we are vulnerable to both vendor demands and new legislation.

Opportunities

- What should we do to position ourselves to take advantage of future opportunities?
  - Get our technology up to date.
- What internal strengths can be leveraged to take advantage of the opportunities?
  - Resources at URHere—external to the accounts payable process
- What internal weaknesses limit our ability to take advantage of opportunities?
  - None—staff is willing to learn.
- What threats can be converted to opportunities?
  - The government can see us as willing to comply and be part of a new initiative. Our compliance may auger well for future leniency.
- What opportunities can we put to use now?
  - Vendors' willingness to work with us

Strategies

- Strategies that results from consensual agreement about the analysis could be ...
    - Improve the accounts payable system
    - Explore the technological opportunities with Internet banking
    - Protect our systems from hackers
    - Have accurate and timely processing of invoices
    - Help vendors get their invoices right the first time
    - Understand the new regulations

Step 5: Validate Goals and Objectives

The goals that were set for the accounts payable process were as follows:

- All activities must add value to the process.
- Be ready for processing invoices.
- Make all payments as per contracts.
- Process invoices accurately and within contractual terms.
- Process owner must know what is happening with each invoice.

These goals are all compliant with the outcome of the SWOT analysis. The team added the following goals:

- To explore using the Internet for payments
- To understand the pending regulations
- To update firewalls and maintain security more thoroughly

For the new goals, new objectives were also set:

- To determine the new firewall system and the maintenance of it by December 31, 20xx
- To set up a committee to meet and attend stakeholder meetings with the government by March 30, 20xx (ie, during the next three months)

Conclusion

The SWOT analysis provides the team with a mechanism to check that they have set realistic and effective goals and objectives for the process. SWOT analysis recognizes that dreams of the process may not be locked into the existing environment. The SWOT analysis provides a "reality check" against the way things could be.

Chapter 18

Business Process Improvement Planning

Companies and organizations make large investments in the development of strategic plans. For example, the market rate for professional support services to help develop strategic plans may cap off at 4 percent of the investment sums sought to support the plan, and sometimes more. Planning consultancies can provide a lucrative business, especially for the service provider with a tried and tested methodology.

Over the years, we too have developed templates that we use repeatedly to bring about consistent results. We use facilitated workshops to extract information and build consensus from senior management about their articulated hopes for the organization.

The strategic plan is a statement of what the client wants to do; why, how, and when the client wants to do it; how much it will cost; and the estimated return-on-monies invested. The strategic planning document is a clear statement of the organization's intent and should be used to benchmark performance.

The business process improvement (BPI) strategic plan crystallizes executive sanction before the BPI project can move ahead and transition from the process examination team to the dream team.

The process examination team's process improvement plan provides clear communication to senior management about the team's intention for the BPI project as a whole, and specifically as to how it supports the organization's strategic initiatives.

Your team has worked hard; now is the time to sell the project to the executive team, receive its approval, and release the resources needed for completing a successful project. You will develop a BPI strategic plan by the end of this chapter.

Purpose of Business Process Improvement Plan

The business process improvement provides a reference point against which the process examination team will be evaluated. The BPI plan also provides a synopsis of what all the BPI teams have been working on over previous months. The document legitimizes the critical nature of the proposed BPI project.

Now is a wonderful opportunity to sell the project. For success the team must—

- Be prepared to defend the tables, statements, and figures presented
- Document known assumptions
- Ensure that the methods and results used are auditable and transparent
- Establish the accuracy of the data
- Include charts and tables
- Plan carefully
- Prepare an oral presentation with visual supplements for management
- Sell the project—your organization's future may just depend on it
- Solicit support from the project sponsor

Business Process Improvement Plan Elements

The BPI plan is the process examination team's last action item before the project is handed over to the dream team and is a culmination of the team's findings and decisions over recent months. The BPI plan includes the following components:

- Executive Summary
  - The Problem
  - The Solution
  - Resources Needed
- The Process
- Vision, Goals, and Objectives
- SWOT (strengths, weaknesses, opportunities, threats) Analysis
- Project Team
- Risks and Opportunities

- Resources
- Next Steps
- Conclusion

Executive Summary

Create a snapshot of the project that will capture the imagination of the executives. Concisely state why the project is critical and the results that will be created by its completion. Include the project costs and expected return on the investment. Bear in mind that the executive summary may be all that an executive has time to read, so the summary may serve as the deciding factor of whether the project gets approved or not.

The Problem

Business process improvement is either in response to or in anticipation of a changing environment. The reader needs to identify with and believe that the problem is real and that the organization's ability to meet its goals and objectives will be compromised if the problem goes unresolved.

State the pain that the process causes to the stakeholders and why it needs to be stopped. Process measurements and workflows provide evidence of what is wrong with the existing process.

The Solution

Develop a lofty purpose for the BPI project. State *how* and *why* the BPI project will resolve the problems identified.

Resources Needed

The project budget shows the investment needed by type of expense. The Return On Investment made and the period for the returns should be clearly stated. Include the assumptions that went into the number-crunching.

The Process

Clarify the reasons why the particular process was selected for improvement. Demonstrate that an auditable and transparent methodology was used for the selection of the process to be improved, and include the results of the analysis.

Vision, Goals, and Objectives

Paint a picture of the future process, what it will look like, and how it will assist the organization achieve its strategic objectives. Include the vision, goals, and objectives of the BPI project and align them to the organization's vision.

SWOT Analysis

Strengthen the argument for the process vision, goals, and objectives by showing how strengths and opportunities accommodate the vision. Determine how the weaknesses and the impact of threats will be reduced, converted, or eliminated by the project.

Project Dream Team

Explain the remit of the dream team and how and why the members were selected. Explain the selection criteria and present the dream team charter.

Risks

From the risk register highlight the risks with the highest probabilities for impacting the project, and explain the mitigation or elimination strategies. Summarize the change management plan and the stakeholder analysis.

Opportunities

Highlight the opportunities that successful business process improvement presents. Identify any opportunities that have been taken advantage of thus far, such as the quick wins discussed earlier.

Resources

Include the updated project budget and highlight the critical costs. Show the basis of the project rate of return and the payback period.

Next Steps

Present an updated project plan and give an overall view of the next steps and the estimated dates. Highlight the key activities, such as BPI plan acceptance by management, dream team training, process design, project testing and implementation, and project completion.

Conclusion

In the conclusion, provide a review and wrap-up of all the above. No new information should be introduced in the conclusion. All members of the process examination and dream teams need to sign off on the document (literally obtain signatures) showing commitment and buy-in to its contents.

Chapter 19

Phase Gate Two

The process examination team is handing over to the process dream team.

Accomplishments of the Process Examination Team

The process examination team will have provided the deliverables shown in Table 19.1, including the following:

1. Documented the existing or as-is process
2. Developed the vision, goals, and objectives of the improved process
3. Tweaked the current process to gain credibility
4. Measured or developed measurements for the current process
5. Performed a SWOT (strengths, weaknesses, opportunities, threats) analysis to test feasibility of vision and goals
6. Generated a business process improvement (BPI) strategic plan for executive approval
7. Obtained executive approval of the BPI strategic plan

Role of the Process Dream Team

The process dream team will work on the deliverables in Table 19.2 including:

1. Design the new process
2. Document the new process
3. Test the new process

Table 19.1   Deliverables for Process Examination Team (PET)

Deliverable	Completed
Workflow diagrams of the current process	✓
Process characteristics defined	✓
Improvements on as-is process (removal of some non-value-added activities)	✓
Revised flowcharts (removal of some non-value-added activities)	✓
Process vision	✓
Process goals	✓
Process objectives	✓
Process action plans	✓
Process measurements	✓
Process SWOT analysis	✓
Approved BPI strategic plan	✓
Dream team members (names and responsibilities)	✓
Updated project team charter signed by all dream team members	✓
Approved project budget	✓
Approved project timetable	✓
Updated risk register	✓
Updated lessons learned register	✓
Updated change management plan	✓
Updated communication plan	✓
Updated stakeholder strategy plan	✓
Updated stakeholder communication plan	✓

Table 19.2   Deliverables for Dream Team

Deliverable	Completed
Workflow diagrams of the improved/designed process	
Process characteristics (improved/new) defined	
Assumptions and rules of improved/new process	
Statement on how design achieves the process vision, goals, and objectives	
Benchmarks for improved process	
Process measurements for new process	
Process implementation plan	
Implementation project team members (names and responsibilities)	
Updated project team charter signed by all dream members	
Updated project budget	
Final project timetable	
Updated risk register	
Updated lessons learned register	
Updated change management plan	
Updated communication plan	
Updated stakeholder strategy plan	
Updated stakeholder communication plan	

Chapter 20

Assumptions and Rules

Of all the preposterous assumptions of humanity over humanity, nothing exceeds most of the criticisms made on the habits of the poor by the well housed, well warmed, and well fed.

—Herman Melville

In this chapter, we review the underlying rules and assumptions that guide decision making about the business process improvement (BPI) process. The current assumptions and rules will prove to be either relevant or easily discarded to make way for new thinking.

Working with artists can be inspiring, and yet challenge us to think in new ways. An architect, an artist, and a writer get together and create a wonderful space for creative processes to occur. In the yard, dance, discussions, exhibitions, and mixed-media presentations by both seasoned and novice artists are given equal billing for expression. The architect, as patron, pumps loads of money into the project. No one knows just how much. There are opportunities to access funding from various international organizations that give annual grants for such creative endeavors. To access the funding, a proposal document needs to be completed. The proposal highlights past activities and monies spent and outlines the amount of funding the project needs to achieve its goals and objectives. Sounds like a business plan, but not to the artists.

Example

> I love that sometimes we need to go to the opposite side of the world to realize assumptions that we didn't even know we had and realize that the opposite may also be true.
>
> **—Derek Sivers**

We meet at the space and we say, "What's your vision for the space."

Silence. We hastily repeat the question. Bristles go up.

"We don't think like that. We don't think vision and goals and those things."

After a retracted apology, we try again. "What do you want this space to look like in 10 years? How do you want it to feel and what do you want the community to say about it?"

Bingo! Talk now comes easily, quickly, and smoothly. Information for the business plan—sorry, proposal—was gleaned.

Introduction

> The harder you fight to hold on to specific assumptions, the more likely there's gold in letting go of them.
>
> **—John Seely Brown**

> Hell, there are no rules here—we're trying to accomplish something.
>
> **—Thomas A. Edison**

The thing about communication is that we make an assumption about what other people mean. Our backgrounds help us see a vision as commonplace and nonthreatening. To the artist, it presents a rigid thought process, associated with unappealing "isms." Different language and terms can help evoke a positive response.

Processes communicate the multitude of activities within the organization in which they reside. Very often, what we believe about our organization, people, and technology is evident in the process design and the way the process works. In hierarchical structures, there is a strong tendency for control. Hence, processes tend to be laden with inspection points along with the corresponding delays and bottlenecks. Flatter organizations, with less hierarchy, tend to empower employees to make decisions about the way work is done—fewer inspection points, bottlenecks, and delays. Virtual organizations tend to have even less structures, since there may be no need for time frames, but rather deadlines as people are flexible to work when they will as long as they satisfy their deadlines.

The existing design of the process is linked to the culture of the organization. Process improvements may result in a cultural shift or resistance as the rules, procedures, and the way things are done on a regular basis may change.

To increase the success of cultural shift, the assumptions that underlie the processes need to be unearthed and tested for validity. This can be tricky, as assumptions may be insidious and supported by long-held beliefs. Challenges to the assumptions may be met with strong resistance from stakeholders who have vested interests in the status quo.

Before going further with analyzing assumptions, the dream team needs to review its stakeholder management and communication plan. Be warned that previous supporters of the business process improvement may now feel threatened and withdraw support for the team and project as a whole.

Assumptions

To unearth the process assumptions, each activity in the current process needs to be examined. The assumptions about *what* is done to support the process, *who* performs activities in the process, and *why* activities are completed need to be explained and tested for validity.

Testing

The four steps below are used to discover and validate the underlying assumptions of each activity:

1. Identify assumptions.
2. Validate assumptions.
3. For assumptions that are no longer valid, change the activities and generate ideas about how the modified activity can be performed.
4. For assumptions that are valid, think about ways to reduce the risks associated with the assumptions.

The credit union's accounts payable flowchart is revisited to work through its assumptions. We look at the check distribution process and examine the role of the receptionist: "Receptionist receives all the checks."

Table 20.1 Assumptions

A: Items	Assumption
Receptionist	Has downtime—therefore can open and distribute mail.
Postal service	Is inefficient and the mail is often lost.
Vendor	Has a resource for check collection.
Bank	Service charges to regularly transfer funds to vendors' accounts are more expensive than generating checks.
Evidence	Vendor signs for—collecting checks as evidence of payment.
Liability	Vendor signing for check removes liability from the company.

Step 1: Identify Assumptions

Q: Why does the receptionist hold the checks for collection by the vendor?

A: To ensure that the checks are signed for when collected; the signature indicates that the company has transferred responsibility for the checks to the collector.

Q: What are the assumptions underlying transferring responsibility?

Table 20.1 displays some of the primary assumptions that are further validated in Table 20.2.

Step 2: Validate Assumptions

Review each assumption and state whether or not it is valid in the current environment. Refer to Table 20.2, Validation.

Step 3: Change the Activities That Are Invalid. Replace with New Ideas or Discard.

Discard Assumptions

The following items and assumptions are discarded because they are invalid (Table 20.2):

- Postal service—Inefficient and mail is often lost
- Evidence—Vendor signs for collecting check as evidence of payment

As a result, the credit union no longer needs vendors to collect checks and sign for them as the assumptions of an inefficient postal service and evidence of check collection are no longer valid.

Table 20.2   Validation

A: Items	Assumption	Still Valid?	Comment
Receptionist	Has downtime— therefore can perform this function.	Yes	The role still has downtime.
Postal service	Is inefficient and the mail is often lost.	No	The postal service has dramatically improved both its efficiency and effectiveness.
Vendor	Has a resource for check collection.	Not sure	Vendors regularly send for checks. This may be because we ask them to collect.
Bank	Service charges to regularly transfer funds to vendors' accounts are more expensive than generating checks.	Yes	Wire transfers are more expensive than checks.
Evidence	Vendor signs for—collecting checks as evidence of payment.	No	Bank returns all cashed checks to the company on a monthly basis with the bank statements. Returned checks are equivalent to receipts and are evidence that the checks were collected.
Liability	Vendor signing for check removes liability from the company.	Yes	If check is lost, we have evidence that vendor's agent completed the collection.

Generate New Ideas

The postal service is now a viable option for check distribution. The updated process that does not require a vendor to sign for checks reinforces the acceptability of using postal service delivery. However, it does not remove the company's liability if in fact the check is lost.

Uncertain Assumptions

The team needs to glean more information about the uncertain assumptions. Vendors will have to be asked if they can regularly send for checks.

Step 4: For Assumptions That Hold True, What Can We Do to Change Them?

The following assumptions hold true:

- Receptionist has downtime.
- Bank transfer charges are more expensive than check generation.

For the two assumptions above, we may change the way that we operate.

- For the receptionist we can look at enriching the role. This may be outside the scope of our process improvement.
- What are the other service options that the bank has to offer? Online payment services provide an entirely new way of paying vendors. The cost per transaction is less than that of a check.

This change in assumptions about the bank's options will influence the way that the accounts payable system is improved.

Results

Vendor payments are now made via online transactions. Monies are transferred directly from bank to bank. As a result, the check preparation and check collection activities were entirely removed from the process.

Some assumptions may reflect negative experiences that the organization is trying to recover from, such as an information technology limitation, an avoidance of liability, or other litigious situations. When such assumptions are unearthed, the team should involve expert organizational members with the technical skills to assist with the process redesign—for example, human resources, legal, and the information technology departments.

Processes carry the tales of the organization and its history. The organization must understand and reconcile the origins of its processes before it tries to change or improve them.

Before the credit union could begin to electronically transfer monies to vendors' accounts, the information technology department played a major role in ensuring that the right security and authentication codes were in effect. This change in the process added more responsibility to the information technology department.

Unearthing the assumptions makes a powerful argument for the need for change. The team can meet and explain future challenges about decisions with the improved design.

Rules

If you obey all of the rules, you miss all of the fun.

—Katharine Hepburn

There are two rules for success: (1) Never tell everything you know.

—Roger H. Lincoln

The general manager at the real estate division was a real trooper, very enthusiastic about the BPI project and a firm believer in its benefits. She was an active participant in the workshops and used her influence to encourage stakeholders to buy in to the business process improvement.

The workflow diagrams of the existing process identified the manager's desk as a bottleneck and a delay point. The logic of passing all incoming mail through her office for subsequent redistribution to the staff was questioned.

The manager calmly explained that her control over distribution was essential for the smooth operation of the agency. She explained that all mail was passed through her office for distribution, delegation, decision making, and filing. This was the method that enabled her to control what took place at the agency on a daily basis.

Most of the staff members were strongly in favor of maintaining the workflow since the delay was never more than 48 hours.

Rules reflect a firm and proven belief about the environment and often determine who performs the activity and the sequencing of the tasks required to complete the activity.

Each rule is supported by one or more assumption(s) that need to be identified, checked for validity, and eliminated or changed. Organizations resist changing rules because rules often express the way activities are traditionally performed and are considered as must-haves, imperative, and critical. There is a strong belief that rules are good and they work.

Rules often belie redundant activities, inspections, delays, and other non-value-added activities in the process design. To unearth the rules, we work through eight steps with the group.

1. What is the problem area (as defined by the process characteristics identified earlier)?
2. Why is it a problem?
3. What is the rule?
4. Identify what happens when the rule is not applied.
5. What are the assumptions that support the rule?
6. Are these assumptions still valid?
7. For the assumptions that are no longer valid, change the activities and generate new ideas about how the activity can be performed.
8. For assumptions that are valid, think of ways to reduce the risks associated with the assumption.

The outcome of the discussions of rules regarding the bottleneck at the general manager's desk is demonstrated below:

Q: What is the problem area?
A: The manager's desk is a delay point and a bottleneck for work coming into the agency.
Q: Why is it a problem?
A: Because there is a backlog on the manager's desk. She has to sort all the mail but is often called away to meetings. Sorting is not done as quickly as she would like to do it.
Q: What are the rules?
A: All mail must pass through the general manager.
A: The general manager determines the allocation of work.
A: The general manager determines how things are to be filed.
A: The general manager only must sort all incoming mail.
Q: What happens if the rules are not applied?
A: In the past, the information went to the wrong department or was misfiled. She indicates how everything is to be filed and distributed for work.
Q: What are the underlying assumptions that support the rules?
A: No one else can control distribution.

A: If someone else performs the sorting task, things will go wrong.

A: The general manager is the only person who can do it correctly.

Q: Does the assumption still hold true?

A: Yes, in the past mistakes have been made. Things go wrong when the manager is not here and someone else did it. There are serious repercussions for misfiling.

Q: How can we make changes to the process?

A: We cannot make changes.

Q: Are there any types of mail that are obvious to anyone, as what to do with them?

A: Vendor invoices. This is for the account staff only.

Q: Are vendor invoices obvious in the mail?

A: Yes. They come in envelopes with the vendor's logo or are hand-delivered with goods and services.

Q: Can vendor invoices be removed from the batch that the supervisor has to look at?

A: Yes. These can be sent straight to the accounts department.

Q: What other types of mail come into the agency?

A: Technical reports, valuation reports, and other reports from other professionals who report on the structural soundness of a building and the rental prices.

Q: Are professional reports obvious in the mail?

A: Yes, they come in envelopes with the vendor's logo on it.

Q: Can professional reports be removed from the batch that the manager has to look at?

A: Yes, professional reports can be sent straight to the property processing or the real estate acquisitions department for approval.

Q: What other types of items come in the mail?

A: Client requests for properties to rent or purchase, and client offers of properties to rent or purchase.

Q: Are property offers obvious in the mail?

A: No.

Q: What does the manager do with property offers when she receives them?

A: She determines who should do what and distributes the work.

Q: What are the criteria for distributing the work?

A: Depends on the casework that each person has, the location of the property, and other factors.

Q: Can the employees distribute work themselves?

A: No.

Q: What are the assumptions that support as-is thinking?

A: That the work will not be evenly distributed within the department.

Q: Can we devise a method for the even distribution of the work?

A: We can try.

Q: Who will be involved in designing the method and when will it be brought for agreement?

A: The supervisors and the general manager can discuss and present something in two weeks' time.

Q: What other types of mail are received?

A: Mail for general filing. Information for auctioned items, where the property has already been rented or sold but the information is for general filing.

Q: Are general information items obvious in the mail?

A: No. The receptionist can open them but the mail *must* be sent to the general manager to be sorted for filing.

Q: How can we remove filing types of mail from the manager's desk?

A: We cannot.

Q: Can we train anyone else to sort the mail or distribute to the relevant person?

A: They will need to be trained on how to read and understand the incoming materials.

Q: Can we develop a standard filing system?

A: It is not so easy, because sometimes it is a lease, but the letter may say rental and might go to the wrong place.

Q: How do we make sure that everyone understands?

A: We could develop a glossary or dictionary so that anyone can read the letters. However, it will take time.

Q: Will it help?

A: It might but it will take a while to get it right.

Q: If we had a glossary, who could do the indication for the files that need updating with the incoming mail?

A: The receptionist. She receives the mail but she will need a lot of training.

Q: Who is going to train her?

A: The general manager.

Q: How will the general manger be informed about who has what or is doing what?

A: We can develop internal reports and scan documents. We can think about other options some more.

Impact

Rules can change only if the underlying assumptions are proven no longer valid or if the team can present alternatives. The general manager resisted the change in workflow at every step, and the staff supported her resistance. It is only by asking the questions about each assumption that underlies the rule that we begin to understand the inherent problems that the rule safeguards against.

Not all assumptions are incorrect either. For our example, we met many instances of where the assumptions held true. It is only by exercising the *whys* of the assumptions that we can determine its relevance.

This is a good time for the dream team to review and update the change management and communication plans. Hold on—the ride is about to get rocky.

Chapter 21

Improve the Process

Life coaches believe that all people are born creative. They believe that as kids grow older, experiences that cause pain and hurt cause people to lose their innate creativity. When kids take a box and create a rocket ship and the adult passes by and says, "Clean up that mess!" the child loses a little bit of the willingness and the freedom to be creative. When a child has an invisible friend and is encouraged to "Give them up!" the child loses a bit of creativity and imagination.

> Capital isn't so important in business. Experience isn't so important. You can get both these things. What is important is ideas. If you have ideas, you have the main asset you need, and there isn't any limit to what you can do with your business and your life.
>
> **—Harvey Firestone**

Many adults have difficulty with the notion of *being*. We are accustomed to *doing* and not being. Being creative describes an intangible attitude that is difficult to explain or measure.

When is the last time you did something creative? We are so caught up with the job, the kids, the aging parents, and success and achievements that we rarely take time to think about being creative. We get to work and there is a way to do things accurately. We have a daily routine that sees us do certain things at certain times. What need is there to be creative?

We often think about creativity as something big and huge, or something tangible—works of art, designer clothing, or the new Swiffer® mop. It may be simpler than that; cooking with leftovers, selecting an adorable gift for the person who has everything, and keeping kids entertained all require creativity. When did you last do something creative?

In our business process improvement project, we are asked to redesign a process, dream up very new ways of doing things, think of new ways to address issues, and come up with new solutions. Creativity may be revolutionary and make everyone *ooh*, or it could show itself as smaller, evolutionary efforts that provide incremental change. Either way, we can do it.

Alignment

Process design establishes how we will execute the vision we have of our improved process. The objectives and the goals for the process narrow the vision to identify the targets that we strive to hit with the design.

The dream team needs to review the vision, goals, and objectives that have been set for the process for alignment.

Begin to Design

> Too much of our work amounts to the drudgery of arranging means toward ends, mechanically placing the right foot in front of the left and the left in front of the right, moving down narrow corridors toward narrow goals. Play widens the halls. Work will always be with us, and many works are worthy. But the worthiest works of all often reflect an artful creativity that looks more like play than work.
>
> **—James Ogilvy**

Get a whiteboard or large sheets of paper so that the team can diagram the process on a flowchart as it is being designed. Visual feedback makes it easy to see what is happening in the new process, at a glance. The benefit of using paper is that we can quickly move around activities until we are satisfied with the sequencing.

The initial design should be completed as if there are no constraints. Develop consensual agreement around the following:

- All suppliers and customers are compliant with the process needs.
- The process has all the resources—technology, money, people—that are required.
- There are no barriers to what we could do.

To illustrate the process, start with the outputs that are desired from the process. We call the illustration "right-to-left thinking." The activities include:

- Determine the process name and process owner.
- Describe the process vision.
- Explain each activity that is required to generate the outputs, and detail the specifics of each.
- Identify the optimal activities and then sequence them.
- Confirm that you have identified the ending point of the process or the process output.
- Associate each output with its client(s) or customer(s).
- Identify the inputs required to generate the desired output.
- Identify the supplier(s) or source(s) of the inputs.
- Identify the starting point (what event, document, or other triggers the process).
- Minimize the time allowed for business valued-added activities.
- Minimize handoffs and inspection points.
- Remove bottlenecks.
- Remove all non-value-added activities.
- Use technology or automated sources wherever possible.

Questions

Some highly valuable questions that will assist in the design are as follows:

- Who and how many sources of inputs are there?
- Is it possible for the inputs to come from one source?
- Are the inputs clearly defined?
- How can we remove inspecting inputs and continue to receive the quality we need?
- How can we receive inputs so that they are immediately ready for processing?
- How are these inputs going to be processed to achieve outputs in a manner that will reduce the quantity of necessary inputs?
- What is the first activity that is performed with each input?
- Who performs that activity?
- How is the activity performed?
- What is the direct result of this activity?
- What is the next activity and what is its output?
- Can the two activities be joined or must there be a handover or transition?
- Can one person perform both activities sequentially?
- How can we ensure that the outputs from each activity provide the necessary inputs for the next activity?
- How can one person perform more than one activity?

- How do we ensure quality throughout the process?
- What decisions need to be made?
- What changes occur from these decisions?
- How do we know when the process is complete?
- How do we package the output and in what format?
- Will the output serve more than one purpose?
- How can we use technology to make the activities more efficient?

The dream team used the following guidelines to develop the new design.

- All manual steps need to be fully automated.
- Checks and controls can be reduced.
- Data forms serve multiple purposes.
- Each customer service representative should provide the same level of service.
- Each person is responsible and accountable for the tasks they perform.
- Every action must add value to the input.
- Every action performed must contribute to the process outcome.
- Inputs should be standardized.
- Outputs should be standardized.
- Processes have variable pathways but the quantity of pathways is finite.
- Process steps should be performed in a natural order.
- Reconciliation should be minimized.
- Targeted customers must be delighted.
- The customer should have a one-stop shop—should not be moved around to be served.
- The process is not designed for, but will allow for, exceptions.
- There is one standard way of performance for each occurrence.
- There may be more than one source for inputs.
- When a client leaves the customer center, all the related paperwork must be completed.
- Work is performed where it makes the most sense.

Non-Value-Added Activities

Review the flowchart in Figure 21.1 for non-value-added activities. Look for activities that occur more than once in the process or recur in various areas. Look for potential bottlenecks, delays, inspections, or checkpoints. Once identified, discuss ways to remove or reduce the bottlenecks. Count the number of handoffs in the process and bundle the activities to minimize handoffs. All non-value-added activities present opportunities for further redesign.

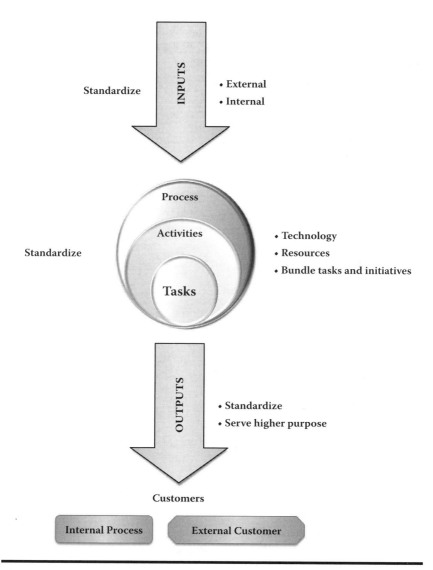

Figure 21.1 Diagram of the design process.

Value-Added Activities

The assumption is that every step in the design adds value to the input as it being converted to an output. To increase the efficiency of the process, it is important to determine the maximum amount of time that should be spent on each of the value-added activities. The design team should have a good idea on how long the entire process should take, and as a result, each activity and task should have a time limit. The time limit also helps to identify the exceptions and other scenarios that may require particular attention.

Rules and Assumptions

> All human development, no matter what form it takes, must be outside the rules; otherwise we would never have anything new.
>
> **—Charles Kettering**

The rules and assumptions underlying each activity need to be examined. For assumptions that are invalid, the team needs to find an alternative solution. Valid assumptions need to be served by the new design. The improved process should not accommodate any false assumptions.

Constraints

Are there any preexisting conditions that have been built into the design? Did we limit our design because of internal technology that exists, the amount of available resources, or the organization's response to the project?

> There is no doubt that creativity is the most important human resource of all. Without creativity, there would be no progress, and we would be forever repeating the same patterns.
>
> **—Edward de Bono**

Constraints and their impacts on the design need to be identified. It is challenging to design without being aware of the constraints, but discussing constraints will limit creativity. The team needs to take a flight of fancy and eliminate the effects of the constraints on the design. The team needs to dream and to go for it. The ideal may be closer than you think. We need to get the design as close to the vision as possible. Build the design as if all can happen. We design as we dream, with an open checkbook and limitless possibilities.

Technology

Technology may be used to accelerate the completion of activities and the speed of the overall process, or to break existing rules. The disruptive power of digital technology (eg, electronic funds transfer) can remove many of the limits that may exist in the current analog (eg, written check) design.

When technology is used to enhance, streamline, or improve activities already being performed, we may not be using its full potential. Technology can be used to identify and break long-standing rules. Think of paying bills by check. We need to get that check in the mail at least three days before the due date to ensure timely payment. With digital technology, we can pay bills online at 11:59 p.m. on the due date and avoid penalties.

The team can perform scenario analysis and ask, "What if?" to encourage the dreams of the process. When answers are not constrained, they help the team to take the process to another level. What if we could receive monies immediately when a customer pays? What if customers did not have to come in the door to pay bills? What if we had all the money to build an ideal process?

The "What if?" question provides another way of dreaming and ignoring constraints in the existing technology. To decide on the specific technology to be used is outside the scope of this manual, since the technology is ever-changing.

Design Again

Now that the process has been designed (drafted), do it again. Be bolder! We have identified the non-value-added activities, the constraints, and the rules and assumptions that are in our present design. We can now design the process again to further reflect the affect of the restrictions. Take a more fanciful flight! Assume the world is at your disposal! Now that you have done it for a second time, go for a third! Make it as fanciful as you wish.

Benchmarking

Your process is likely not unique. In the wider business world, processes are being repeated in other organizations, serving different stakeholders and purposes, and operating in different industries with similar outputs. Payroll will always be about ensuring that employees are paid on time and accurately every month. Differences across organizations include how they are paid, with what currency, and at what pay levels.

> The achievement of excellence can occur only if the organization promotes a culture of creative dissatisfaction.
>
> **—Lawrence Miller**

Benchmarking involves searching for the best practices and using them as a way to measure your process against the best in the world. Benchmarking might reflect another organization in the same field or in another industry or in any part of the world. The idea is to find the best with the process application and try to see how close your ideal design is to the best one. Every organization has its own culture and history, and therefore the benchmarking process may not be immediately applicable to your markets, customers, or resource levels—thus, the process cannot be adopted wholesale into your organization. The process may need to be adapted, or only relevant parts will be captured by your organization.

When URHere's credit union wanted to establish its acceptable delinquency rates, it surveyed its bankers to understand what was considered acceptable by the best in the market. The banks tolerated a 6 percent delinquency on their small loan portfolios. The micro credit union thought that 6 percent delinquency would be too stringent for the profile of its customer base, and it increased the rate to serve the needs of its customers.

Benchmarking is not solely about where your process ranks but understanding *what* the best process is, *why* and *how* it exists, and what parts of it to emulate. The micro credit union modified the bank's procedures to include more visits to the delinquent loan clients and involved a series of actions to help the clients get back on track. The banks did not include any social outreach as part of their delinquency procedures.

It is not necessary to benchmark the entire organizational enterprise, because it would be too costly and time-consuming. However, activities, processes, and transactions can be benchmarked.

How to Benchmark

It is possible to engage in online or other surveys to establish the best. This may include visits to other organizations, joining exchange forums, and exploring other networking options.

> It's easy to come up with new ideas; the hard part is letting go of what worked for you two years ago, but will soon be out of date.
>
> **—Roger von Oech**

Information can be gathered from research, surveys, and benchmarking visits. The team should be aware that participation in a survey is not benchmarking. Surveys provide an idea about the organization's process rankings against similar processes in other organizations, but they provide no further information about process improvement. The idea is to combine the best of the benchmarked designs with the idealized in-house or internal design.

Improvements at the Service Center

Once the service center is improved, customers will regard the new changes as miraculous. The service center may become a one-stop shop where they could finance purchases, make complaints, request services, and purchase new or additional products.

Each time contact is made with an input, value is added and a contribution is made to the output. There will be different situations that occur at the service center, but the updated process is well equipped to deal with varying situations.

The roles of the cashiers may include automatic updates of client accounts upon the generation of receipts and end-of-day balancing of cash with receipts. Activities might no longer be sequential. More than one cashier could perform simultaneous activities of collecting money, generating receipts, and updating clients' accounts to accelerate transactions within the process.

Activities can be bundled to empower workers to make decisions, while the role of the supervisor may be to escalate dealing with exceptional cases outside the remit of the frontline staff or would delay service.

Eventually, the supervisor would become involved when a client account could not be updated, at a customer's request, or when frontline staff could not resolve a new issue.

The process owner—the customer service manager—was also pleased with the changes; she received fewer complaints and did not have to work overtime to sort things out. Team members were in favor of the new process but became a little wary when three of their colleagues were sent home because of the changes.

> Creative activity could be described as a type of learning process where teacher and pupil are located in the same individual.
>
> **—Arthur Koestler**

Changes to the process generated new roles. The new design featured empowered workers with the information to make better decisions at their level. Inspection points were reduced and supervisory roles were empowered to spend time on anomalies, ongoing evaluation of the process, and its outcomes. Supervisors and managers began to play a strategic role and were freed from the minutiae of the process details. Wherever possible, manual processes were automated or earmarked for automation. Inputs were formalized, forms were unified to capture all pertinent information, and data capturing was simplified. The outputs from the process were forwarded in a format that the operators could immediately use and benefit from.

Design Details

Complete Table 21.1 to ensure that all the inputs and outputs have been considered.

What Next?

> Innovation is fostered by information gathered from new connections; from insights gained by journeys into other disciplines or places; from active, collegial networks and fluid, open boundaries. Innovation arises from ongoing circles of exchange, where information is not just accumulated or stored, but created. Knowledge is generated anew from connections that weren't there before.
>
> **—Margaret J. Wheatley**

When the team has completed the design, share the design with all the stakeholders of the process. The design may require a change in the way that suppliers interact with the organization. It is a good time to incorporate and involve suppliers into the design to understand if they have any problems with the new design. Most suppliers will comply if they want the business and if the changes do not require major technological investment. The supplier may have some ideas of how to generate the inputs in a manner that will assist in your objectives for streamlining the process.

Internally, there is need to liaise with other processes or departments as the proposed changes may affect them. Stakeholder meetings are critical in getting the new design approved, because frequently without the cooperation of the other departments, full benefits will not be realized.

At URHere, leaders in the production department were trained on how to approve invoices electronically. Feedback from the production team led to the creation of a data management system that included contracts, purchase orders, technical reports, and invoices by vendors that were shared across workgroups.

Table 21.1 Process Validation

Process Characteristics	Descriptions
Process vision	To have a one-stop service center for customers
Process goals	Timely and accurate information
	To have accurate data in databases
	To retain clients
Process objectives	To update client information within 10 minutes of client entering the service center
	To update loan information within 2 minutes of receiving payment
	To resolve customer problems within 30 minutes of entering the service center
Links to organizational goals	To be the leading micro credit financial institution
	To ensure client satisfaction and delight
Process owner	Customer service manager
Process start	When customer enters the service area
Process end	When the client information is updated in the database
Process inputs	Client requests, money
	Existing client records
	Supporting documents
Process outputs	Updated reports
	Loan statements
	Client balances
Process sources	Customers
	Internal reports
Process customers	Clients
	Loan department
	Accounting department

Return to the Vision, Goals, and Objectives

The design needs to be checked against the vision that was set for the process to ensure alignment. If the two are misaligned, then either accept the design and work on the vision, goals, and objectives, or modify the process.

Return to Stakeholders Analysis

The stakeholder analysis identified the stakeholders of the process and how they would gain or lose power in the present design. The dream team needs to return to the stakeholder forms and update each stakeholder analysis. Updates should be based on the new design and used to anticipate the stakeholder's response to the improved process. See Chapter 4, "Stakeholder Analysis."

Communications Plan

The communications plan needs to be updated for use during meetings with the stakeholders. The team needs to identify its approach for communicating with stakeholders and revisit the strategy for getting buy-in for the improved process. The team should have developed a series of meetings to discuss the new design with the stakeholders. The executive team and the project sponsors should be involved in the communications, as the team now needs to begin focusing on the implementation plan for the project. See Chapter 3, "Change Management."

Conclusion

The new design needs to be ratified by process stakeholders. The process improvement may need to compromise some of the design features for building consensus in the short-term. According to characteristics unique to the health of the organization, not all of the process may be immediately implementable. The team may have to implement the design in phases over a period of time.

Chapter 22

Phase Gate Three

The process dream team is handing over to the process implementation team.

Accomplishments of the Dream Team

At the start of phase, the dream team will have completed assignments in Table 22.1.

1. Improved or designed a new process
2. Prepared workflow diagrams for the new or improved process

Role of the Process Implementation Team

The process implementation team is now responsible for the assignments in Table 22.2.

1. Implementing the new/improved process
2. Documenting procedures for the new/improved process
3. Hand over to the process owner

Table 22.1 Deliverables for Dream Team

Deliverable	Completed
Workflow diagrams of the improved/designed process	✓
Process characteristics (improved/new) defined	✓
Assumptions and rule of improved/new process	✓
Statement on how design achieves the process vision, goals, and objectives	✓
Benchmarks for improved process	✓
Process measurements for new process	✓
Process implementation plan	✓
Implementation project team members (names and responsibilities)	✓
Updated project team charter signed by all dream team members	✓
Actual costs for the gate	✓
Updated project timetable	✓
Updated risk register	✓
Updated lessons learned register	✓
Updated change management plan	✓
Updated communication plan	✓
Updated stakeholder strategy plan	✓
Updated stakeholder communication plan	✓

Table 22.2 Deliverables for Process Implementation Team (PIT)

Deliverable	Completed
Revised workflow diagrams of the improved/designed process	
Identification of constraints to full implementation	
Implementation plan for process	
Action plan for removal of constraints	
Action plan for full implementation of improved/new process	
Process procedures	
Process measurements for new process	
Hand over schedule	
Updated risk register	
Updated lessons learned register	
Updated change management plan	
Updated communication plan	
Updated stakeholder strategy plan	
Updated stakeholder communication plan	

Chapter 23

Implementation Plan

Background

When you were 10 years old, what did you want to be? Some of us made elaborate plans for our future and had a clear idea of what our life would look like. We had a vision. How many of us today are living out childhood dreams in our daily lives? We consider ourselves good at making plans, setting visions, and generally saying what we want. Yet, for most of us, our personal plans often do not come to fruition. Why? Because most of us fail at execution.

Planning is safe, we can logically plan the three steps needed to get what we want, but we often stop at step two or three during implementation. Procrastination, lack of knowing how to complete the tasks, inadequate resources, fear to achieve, and past habits are some of the reasons that we fail to execute.

We have stated how we want the process to look and how we want it to work. All our previous work will come to naught if the improved process is not used or embraced by the process team, or the process owner is dissatisfied with the results. Implementation is the most visible phase of the project and represents what the team will be remembered for, especially if the improvements fail.

Illustration: New Payroll System

Wonderful plans were devised for the implementation of the new URHere payroll system. A data team consisting of four staff—two from human resources and two from accounting—was set up to transfer 250 payroll records over a 20-day period.

A payroll record comprises three sets of data:

1. Employee data—basic information about the employee; name, address, birth date, beneficiaries
2. Benefits and allowances—for example, car and travel allowances, insurance deductions, academic reimbursement, savings
3. Payroll data—basic salary, overtime rates, taxation assumptions, rates, and calculations

To complete a payroll record, employee data needs to be created first, then the benefits and allowances data can be accounted for, and finally the payroll data can be entered. The sequencing of the data entry was recognized as critical in the project plan.

The team relocated to a separate room and reported to a project manager. They worked from 8:00 a.m. to 6:00 p.m. on a daily basis and made significant progress in the first two weeks. After the third week, things started to go haywire.

Building the payroll data was not straightforward, and some of the data needed to be verified with the employees. Some of the obstacles were as follows:

- Employee data—multiple addresses, beneficiaries, banking data, and even multiple records existed for some employees
- Benefits and allowances—for example, a travel allowance is given to employees who need to travel beyond certain distances, regardless of their payroll grade
- Payroll data—verification of past data and reworking of calculations to ensure that taxation is accurate

The team began to suffer from cabin fever, as the room was not designed to host four people with computers and printers for multiple weeks. The team was tired and felt underappreciated. The accounting staff was annoyed, as they had to continue switching attentions and energies between the project and their departmental tasks. The other team members felt that they were doing the work of the accounting members and resented that, without the full commitment of the accounting staff, the quota was becoming unattainable. The project, which was formerly seen as recognition of individual ability, could now be a liability on the members' performance. The project went badly off track and the project manager met with the team to build some solutions (see Table 23.1).

The project manager set individual and team incentives, and an offsite fun day was planned to encourage performance. The payroll project plan was completed in the sterile conditions of the manager's room. No contingencies were

Table 23.1 Problem/Solution Matrix

Problem	Solution
The accounting team members were often recalled to their department to complete tasks.	Two temporary staff were hired to work in the accounting department until the project was complete.
Room is cramped for work.	Team would have more work breaks. The room could not be changed.
The project could not be completed as per the timetable.	The team reset the target to accommodate for delays.
Feedback was needed from the employees to verify the existing payroll records.	A questionnaire was sent to each employee. Line managers were responsible for the return of the questionnaire.

made for the departmental responsibilities or deadlines or for missing information. The project plan assumed that all data would be available, all records accurate, and human resources 100 percent committed to the project.

Implementation never occurs in a vacuum. The organization continues to operate and achieve its goals and other activities as other parts of the organization compete for resources that will result in unforeseen circumstances.

To mitigate against imbalance, we need to concentrate on the areas that we can control: the *who*, *what*, and *when* of the implementation

Who: Implementation Team

The process implementation team provides the transitional personnel between the earlier teams and the process members. Responsibilities include testing and tweaking of the design, rolling out the design to the process team, training, and finalization of procedures. The process owner may lead or work closely with the implementation team as its champion and provide and allocate resources, troubleshoot, and problem-solve. The team will comprise process members and co-opt the services of information technology, human resources, and other relevant professionals.

Implementation may be seen as the mundane part of the project. The creative people who were excited about the project and came up with wonderful suggestions may not be suitable for implementation and detailed duties. Assign people with the right temperament for the job. Some dream team members should be part of the implementation team if only to ensure complete understanding of earlier decisions made.

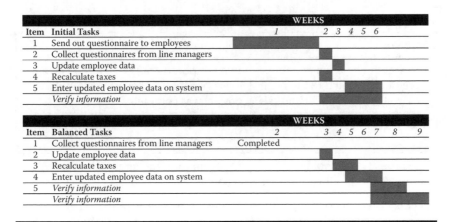

Figure 23.1   Action (implementation) plan.

What and *When*: Implementation Plan

The implementation plan (part of the overall project plan) can now be developed in detail as more information becomes available and decisions have been made. We want a timely implementation, with little rework and a schedule that will maintain interest in the project. The implementation plan is critical toward achieving urgency and quality.

According to the anticipated duration of the implementation, a 30/60/90-day rolling plan can be used. The plan highlights the activities that will be done for the next 30 days, by whom, and when. At the end of each week the plan is reviewed and progress is monitored. The plan is then updated to show what will happen during the next 30 days of work.

This method keeps everyone focused on the project, and allows constancy of adjusting steps, adding steps, and deleting activities on a regular basis. Constant review ensures adherence to the schedule, early problem detection, and timely interventions so that the schedule can be restored if it falters.

The plan needs to account for public holidays, team members' vacation schedules, departmental deadlines, and organizational events as social calendars will affect the established time frames as shown in Figure 23.1.

Implementation Budget

The implementation budget (part of the initial project budget) is now reviewed and updated for price changes and any other additional details that the process implementation team determines will ensure successful results.

Figure 23.2   The ASQ's Plan, Do, Check, and Act.

Testing

During testing, the process implementation team can gauge the feasibility of the improved process and identify any constraints to full implementation. The iterative process of the ASQ—Plan, Do, Check, and Act—is followed until the desired results are attained and accepted (Figure 23.2).

Some of the constraints to full implementation, like technological changes, may be beyond the scope of the process implementation team. In out-of-scope situations, the process implementation team needs to document the potential for future process changes and communicate potential updates to the relevant people. Some members of the process implementation and dream teams should be brought back into the project when future changes are made.

The new payroll system went live as scheduled, but two members of the data team stayed on the project to complete updating the allowances, benefits, and the effects on taxation.

Determine What to Do

How do we determine what to do first in the implementation? The procedures and the flowcharts are sequential and should be followed as presented. Start at the beginning of the action plan and perform the steps in the charted sequence.

Make decisions that result in both the yes and no answers and perform the suggested actions to ensure that the process can deal with each. Create scenarios that are anomalous to the process to see how exceptions are handled. Estimate the time for the entire process and identify the measurements for process activities and resources.

The risks and opportunities and lessons-learned registers may identify other actions for consideration during the implementation. The process implementation team needs to decide what additional issues will be dealt with during the implementation, as they have limited resources.

The critical success factors for the data team were accuracy, timeliness, and completeness, with a secondary interest in cost.

Opportunities for the data entry project system included the following:

- Building the payroll payments alongside the accounts payable process
- Incorporating the calculations of vacation, sick, and other leaves of absence as part of the financial system
- Entering all historical payroll data
- Merging the human resources performance management system with the payroll data (However, given technology constraints, the team could not seize this opportunity.)

Opportunities were ranked according to the impact each had on the critical success factors as shown in Table 23.2. Based on the matrix results, the order for implementation is shown in Table 23.3.

"Entering all historical payroll data" meets three out of four of the critical success factors and therefore is selected for implementation. "Build the payroll system into the accounts payable system" meets only one of the four critical success factors and therefore is not an immediate priority. The level of the existing technology in the organization did not allow for immediate merging of the two systems.

Preimplementation

The process owner and the team members need to be fully trained in the new process before it is implemented. Each operator (ie, process worker) must understand how the entire process works, what each role contributes, and why each activity is important. The emphasis is on the logic of the process, the measurements involved, and other process characteristics.

The roles and responsibilities and the key performance measurements for each role will be determined. Different levels of training will be needed for the process owner, team members, suppliers, clients, and other stakeholders who may be affected with the process. Training may also focus on the creation of experts within the process to whom the process implementation team can transfer responsibility for the monitoring and continuous improvement of the process. Individuals may be selected to be "super operators" so that they can serve as internal troubleshooters for the process team and its owner.

Table 23.2 Opportunity Ranking

Opportunity	Accuracy	Timeliness	Completeness	Cost
Build the payroll payments into the accounts payable system	No impact on accuracy	Delay delivery by six weeks	No impact on completeness	Additional costs for the interface between systems
Use calculations of vacation, sick, and other leave	No impact on accuracy	Delay delivery by four weeks	No impact on completeness	No additional costs—this is an internal fix
Enter all historical payroll data	Improves accuracy	Needs three weeks	Makes the system complete	No additional costs
Merge the human resources performance management system with the payroll data	No impact on accuracy	Delay delivery time by three weeks	Makes the system complete	Additional costs for interface between the two systems

Table 23.3 Implementation Ordering

Opportunity	By Whom	When
Enter all historical payroll data	Data entry	Next three weeks
Incorporate the calculations of vacation, sick, and other leave	Accounting	Next three months
Merge the human resources performance management system with the payroll data	Human resources and information technology	Next six months
Build the payroll payments into the accounts payable system	Accounting and information technology	Next nine months

Change Management

The change management plan identifies potential pitfalls and recommendations for the process implementation team. These should be reviewed at the onset of the implementation.

How to Implement

There are standard methods of implementing a new process from which the team may select.

In *direct implementation*, the new process immediately replaces the existing approach. There is no lingering use of the old process as operators instantly discard the old and use the new approach. There is nothing else to rely on if data are lost or to confirm that results are accurate. Staff must be adequately trained in the new process and all technological interfaces completely updated with files and data to ensure that the new process works.

With a *phased implementation*, the process is broken into phases and each phase is implemented and fully evaluated before another phase is put into practice. This is a structured, low-risk, and time-consuming approach as each phase is fully evaluated before another phase is implemented. Staff members are trained in stages and learn the skills during the relevant phase. When the final phase is implemented, the new process has been fully implemented.

If the organization structure allows, the improved process can be piloted at a branch, satellite, or subsidiary organization. When the pilot is successful, a full-scale implementation follows. This approach is slow and controllable, as the pilot can be stopped at any point in time.

With parallel implementation, old and the new systems are operated concurrently and independently. Failure of the new system will not result in data loss, and personnel are safe to make mistakes as they learn. This implementation uses a lot of resources. There is a large amount of rework and duplication of the efforts of staff and hardware. There may be confusion as the two different systems are run side by side.

An implementation can last indefinitely as the process implementation team strives for perfect results with the new approach. The business process improvement should have a finite end date that must be strongly signaled to the process owner and team members. The business process improvement project must end so that resources can be redeployed to other areas of the organization and the work of the team hailed as complete and, hopefully, successful.

Post Implementation

After implementation, the process implementation team needs to be disassembled and team members return to their respective teams or functional areas. A few members of the process implementation team will maintain relations with the process owner and members, monitor the process, and be the guardians or gatekeepers for the process.

The process guardians and owner must be consulted before any proposed changes are made to the implemented process. The organization cannot lose the vision of the improved process and how its design ensures alignment with the organization's vision, goals, and objectives. This ensures that all changes are consensually ratified and documented as part of the process.

Implementation Report

The process implementation team team is responsible for generating written reports during and at the end of the implementation.

During the implementation, a concise report is generated on a weekly basis. It keeps the process owner up to date on the status of the implementation. Problems, challenges, successes, achievements, and resources needed are highlighted. An updated rolling implementation plan needs to be included. Consider using a "30 by 30" report format—a report that does not take longer than 30 minutes to write nor longer than 30 seconds to read, as illustrated in Figure 23.3.

At the end of the implementation, the process implementation team generates a report that summarizes the weekly reports. This report also compares actuals with budgets, such as actual costs with budgeted spend, completion dates with forecast dates, and gives the reasons for the variances. Unresolved issues are also highlighted as illustrated in Figure 23.4.

After implementation, the report will add to the organizational intelligence.

Conclusion

The process is considered fully implemented when the process owner and members are satisfied with the results. The improved process will need to be monitored and the outputs evaluated to ensure that the process is working according to specifications. Success is not an event; rather, change management for the process needs to be ongoing and feedback sought from the process owners and members to keep it efficient and effective.

Date: _____   Report Number: XXX-xxxx

Week *X of Y*

To: _____

Achievements—Highlight team accomplishments and completed actions during the period.

Issues—Identify any threats or opportunities that the team may be faced with and state the mitigation strategies. Include potential impacts on the budget and schedule.

Need help solving—Identify issues that may need the sponsor's intervention to resolve.

Look ahead—For the next three weeks/months (according to the duration of the implementation) and identify:
- Anticipated achievements
- Upcoming activities
- Anticipated conflicts

Attachments—Include the updated rolling implementation schedule.

Figure 23.3   Implementation report "30 by 30."

Fast-Based Summary
State the total cost, duration, and the achievements of the implementation.
Outstanding implementation issues need to be identified.

Challenges Faced and Resolved
The risks and opportunities that were closed out for the implementation can
be included.

Outstanding Issues
State the implementation issues that are unresolved. Include the
implementation activities that are delayed because of existing constraints.
Make recommendations for future implementation and include an action plan
for these.

Team Performance
Give an overview of the team's performance. Identify people for special
rewards.

Budget Report
Rate of return and payback period are calculated. An analysis of money
budgeted and spent can be stated.

Schedule
An updated schedule that shows the dates of the implementation is included.
Focus on the steps after implementation.

Qualitative Perspective Summary
Concluding observations, conclusions, and
recommendations from the project.

Figure 23.4   Summary implementation report.

Chapter 24

Phase Gate Four

The process implementation team has implemented the process and will now hand over to the process (business) owner the items stipulated in Table 24.1.

The process implementation team has—

1. Tested the improved/new process
2. Implemented the process
3. Developed workflow diagrams for the new process
4. Prepared procedures for the new process

The process (business) owner will now assume responsibility for the items in Table 24.2.

1. Take ownership of the process
2. Disband the project team
3. Work with members from the management, examination, dream, and implementation teams to close out the project and generate project close-out reports
4. Evaluate and monitor the process on an ongoing basis
5. Continue to improve the process
6. Work with members from the various project teams to close out the process

Table 24.1   Deliverables for Process Implementation Team (PIT)

Deliverable	Completed
Revised workflow diagrams of the improved/designed process	✓
Identification of constraints to full implementation	✓
Implementation plan for process	✓
Action plan for removal of constraints	✓
Action plan for full implementation of improved/new process	✓
Process procedures	✓
Process measurements for new process	✓
Hand over schedule	✓
Actual implementation costs	
Actual implementation dates	
Updated risk register	✓
Updated lessons learned register	✓
Updated change management plan	✓
Updated communication plan	✓
Updated stakeholder strategy plan	✓
Updated stakeholder communication plan	✓

Table 24.2   Deliverables for Process Owner

Deliverable	Completed
Project report includes ■ actual versus budget ■ actual versus schedule plans ■ teams evaluations ■ process evaluations versus what was planned ■ final risk register ■ final lessons learned ■ final communication plan ■ final stakeholder analysis ■ final stakeholder strategic and communication plans	✓
Process audits	Ongoing
Process evaluations	Ongoing
Updated procedures	Ongoing
Removal of constraints to full implementation	Ongoing
Full implementation of improved/new design	✓

Chapter 25

Procedures

Bent Cookies

When we were kids, we loved to make "bent cookies." These are soft dough cookies sprinkled with almonds, baked soft, and then placed to cool on a rolling pin. The result—Pringles®-shaped cookies that melted in your mouth from pure sugar and almonds—yummy. We were able to make bent cookies perfectly as long as we properly followed the recipe and each of the steps.

A robust approach to process improvement may be likened to the bent cookie recipe. It provides systematic tasks that take the operator from the beginning to the end of the process to achieve the desired results. The operator should be responsible for following the procedure and ensuring that they understand the recommended tasks.

Recipe for Procedure

The bent cookie recipe provides a reasonable analogy for developing procedures:

- A pretty picture (ie, visual illustration) of bent cookies provides an example of what the delivered output should like upon completion.
- A list of the ingredients is provided at the beginning so that the operator has a checklist for success.
- The target audience is clearly identified. For example, all the bakers in our analogy are kids donned in oven mitts and aprons with a parent in the background.

- Step-by-step instruction from beginning to end complete with standard times, amounts, and temperatures for all the various stages of the process.
- The instructions are precise, easy to understand, and issued in universal language. A glossary provided further definitions for special ingredients.
- Conversions are provided to account for cultural differences—accommodating the various backgrounds of the audience. Tables are included to allow easy conversion from Fahrenheit to Celsius, kilograms to pounds, and so forth.
- Preparation and completion times provide estimation for how long the entire process will take.

Purpose of Procedures

A procedure provides the written and documented version of process. Documentation of the systematic activities that take the user from the beginning to the end of a process, revealing the *what, when,* and *who* of the process. Procedures help clarify and standardize specific ways that work is performed. They ensure that the predetermined results are achieved consistently, every time.

Procedures explain to team members exactly why they perform their role and what happens to the immediate output of each activity during the process. When more than one person is responsible for the process, the documentation ensures consistency throughout the approach. All staff can identify the role they play in the process, whom or what they affect, and how they interact during the process. When staff churns though growth, promotion, or attrition, the procedures ensure that the process remains consistent.

Procedures promote knowledge transfer and add to the organizational intelligence. The learning curve for new and existing employees is flattened as written procedures keep knowledge retained in the organization and allow for ongoing knowledge transfer. The rate of errors in the process is also diminished when the procedures are easily and readily understood.

Developing Procedures

There are three basic considerations that will affect the level of detail in the procedures.

The Target Audience

The team needs to carefully define the target audience. Is the procedure for a novice, an occasional operator, or a frequent operator? The maturity of the

Table 25.1 Audience Targeting

Type of Operator	Novice	Occasional	Frequent
Level of experience	Low	Medium	High
Priority	Learning the procedure	Explanation and navigation	Navigation
Type of procedure	Step by step, detailed	Explanation	Checklist
Needs instructions on …	Detailed work procedures	How and why things are done	Critical points, exceptions

audience determines the level of detail that the procedure provides, as shown in Table 25.1.

The more familiar the audience is with the process, the less detailed the procedures need to be. New operators need to be prepared to follow the procedure as quickly as possible. All need to be trained to complete the process in the shortest time possible. Operators need detailed instructions. The activity steps need to be outlined so that there will be no doubt about what to do, when to do it, and how.

Persons who are more familiar with the process need checklists, and the control/critical points to be highlighted. Such operators need to know exactly where to find the procedures so that they can reduce any other uncertainty they may have or that might develop.

Application of the Procedures

Procedures may be used for training new staff, for updating existing staff of changes in the process, or as part of an audit package. Each purpose brings different requirements. An audit procedure will emphasize control points, possible risk areas, and the separation of duties. For training, the relationships and interactions between the people, and how to perform the tasks, are emphasized. For existing staff, a comparison of the old and new procedures will normally suffice.

Life Cycle of the Process

Detailed procedures are required for both new processes and those that have been improved. Procedures are used to introduce the process and ensure that the operators get it right the first time.

Procedures Document

Each procedure should include the following:

- Purpose—each procedure should serve the target audience and its purpose for each discrete audience. Is the document for training or reminding persons about the procedure? (*Hint:* consider using the "Purpose is to ..." tool discussed in the appendices).
- Scope—the scope defines the extent of the process, what it covers, and where the process starts and ends. It also defines other systems or processes that the procedure affects and describes to whom or to what the procedure applies. The procedure can be specific so that it includes only a subset of the employee population or process, or it can be general and include the entire organization, location, or process.
- Definitions—all jargon and abbreviations are defined and clarified to ensure that general readers can understand the document. A dictionary or glossary of terms should be created and verified for each procedure.
- Background—the origin or the reason why the procedure is being developed is mentioned here. This includes any statutory or regulatory reasons, or associations that demand the need for the procedure.
- Responsibilities—the responsibilities for the direct and indirect execution of the process are defined. Provide responsibilities by job function and not by name—since the individual may change, but not the role.
  - The roles of the process owner and the other people directly involved in the process are also defined. Use the roles section to guide auditors (internal and external) and to train employees.
- Procedure—the step-by-step actions are defined here. Each activity is mapped within the procedure. Flowcharts can be used to illustrate the sequence of the activities. Instructions for the completion of forms and other related documents in the process can be included.
- Attachments—policy documents and pertinent reports should be included.
- Revision history—a record of the changes made to the procedure needs to be maintained. Archiving helps avoid duplication of mistakes and supports creating other processes, which saves money and time and reduces employee frustration. The revision history also allows the organization to review the development of the procedure to ensure that risks are mitigated and important opportunities are not lost.

Writing Procedures

The procedure deals with the *why*, *what*, and *how* of the process. The *why* explains the reason for the actions, the *what*s are the activities performed during the process, and the *how* provides step-by-step tasks that are described. Sometimes the *when* is included to set the time limits for each activity in the process. Follow these steps to develop procedures:

1. Present the *why* of the procedure. This allows the operators to understand the reasons for their various actions.
2. Start with the detailed flowchart of the improved process. These show all the inputs and outputs, documents, and decisions involved in the conversion of the outputs from inputs.
3. Provide a short statement of each *what* (ie, activity that at a minimum includes a verb–noun pairing) that occurs for each action box.
4. Follow the operator through a logical train of thought from one action to the next. This confirms the operators' *what* associated with each action.
5. Include the *how* of each activity so that the operator is clear on how each task should be completed.
6. People in the process should be referred to by their job titles and not by name.
7. Complete sentences should be made for each step. Use the convention object (noun) verb (action) subject (noun); for example, the accounts supervisor [noun] approves [verb] the time sheets [noun].
8. For each step, display one action performed by one person.
9. For decision trees, state the outcomes, typically arrayed as yes, no, or conditional (ie, maybe).
10. When you have reached the end, continue with the next procedure until all have been completed within the process.

Procedure Deployment

Written procedures need to be confirmed with the operators and matched to the process flowcharts. The process owner must sign procedures as accepted and approved. The procedures are rolled out to staff, placed in an easily accessible location, and made available to stakeholders—intranet, general files, and so forth.

All process members should be trained in the new procedures to ensure compliance. The process owner should host meetings with the team to ensure that each team member understands the procedure.

Processes need to be audited on an ongoing basis to confirm compliance with the procedures. Audits check for deviations from the procedures and highlight areas where the procedure may be compromised. The audit may also recommend improvements for a procedure within the process.

The process team should always be on the lookout for ways to improve the process and to reduce the time and effort needed to achieve a quality outcome. Any changes to the process must be accompanied by changes in the documented procedures. The reasons for all changes should be justified, and then documented.

Changing Procedures

A "management of change" is a good way to track changes to procedures in dynamic environments, and it removes any confusion about which revised procedure is relevant at discrete moments during the process.

Procedures should be updated to reflect what is actually happening throughout the process. All changes should flow through a formal process that includes the following:

- Automation of manual steps—what tasks are now automated
- Changes in roles—how each role is changed and affected by the new process
- Explanation of the change—why the change is needed and exactly what the change entails
- Impact of the change—the impact on time, efficiency, effectiveness, and resources that are consumed and generated by the process
- Impact on other departments or processes—any changes of input or output and how the changes support other activities within the process
- Improvements of the process—detail of the actual benefits of the process characteristics (input, activity, output) that are changed
- Rationale—the reasons that have brought about the need for the change

The process owner can make changes to the process only after discussions with the team and acceptance. These changes need to be captured in the process procedures and the accompanying flowcharts. The updated procedures should be archived, dated, and approved as a revision by the process owner.

Updated and modified procedures need to be formally rolled out to staff with appropriate training sessions. The training should be illustrated with highlighted exceptions, showing what has changed and why. After implementation, an audit should be conducted to ensure that the new procedure is fully implemented with the intended results.

Example: Procedure Management

In our URHere illustration, the document controller on the accounts payable team was the custodian of all the procedures and monitored the changes, ensuring that the most recent document was accessible by all operators. She also ensured that all the procedures were in a place (intranet) and accessible to appropriate personnel, ensuring the right security limits were assigned according to the sensitivity of the information. She monitored that the following rules were adhered to during ongoing process changes or modification, as further illustrated in Figure 25.1.

Revision History—This procedure was revised December 15 20xx.

Purpose
The purpose of the accounts payables process is to state the procedures, activities, tasks, roles, and responsibilities of the team members involved in the process so that the accounts payable process is efficiently, accurately, and completely performed each time.

Scope
The process deals with the receipt of an invoice for goods or services within the company and ends with the confirmation of receipt of payment by the vendor. The procedure deals with the accounts payables team and the stakeholders with whom they interface to complete their tasks.

Definitions
AP—accounts payable
FM—finance manager
BPI—business process improvement
GAAP—generally accepted accounting principles

Backgrounds
This procedure supersedes all existing procedures dated before December 15th 20xx, called the AP Process. This procedure reflects the changes made after the implementation of the BPI project and is in line with GAAP.

Responsibilities
The FM has overall responsibility for the implementation of the procedure. The AP manager has direct responsibility for the application of the procedure on a daily basis. The internal auditor is responsible for detection of significant deviations from the procedure.

Procedure
1. Invoices are received by mail, electronically, or delivered with the goods or services.
2. The receptionist logs all invoices on the data system within 24 hours of receipt.
3. The receptionist sends the invoices to the AP department within 24 hours of receipt.
4. The AP team members collect invoices according to the agreed assignment rules.
5. Each AP member confirms that the invoice is logged.
6. If the invoice is not logged, the AP member logs the invoice and flags it as an exception.
7. If the invoice is logged, the AP member confirms the accuracy of the invoice.

Attachments
A—Flow chart of the AP process
B—Sample of exception reports

Figure 25.1   Sample procedure.

- All changes must be fully approved—the team members should all review the procedures and ensure that the changes truly reflect the improved process.
- Review and approval of procedures—a planned review of the procedures should take place, followed by an update of the explanatory documents. An audit may affect desired results.
- Sign-off on procedures—all the documented procedures need to be approved and perhaps even signed. The team can choose to have each member, the process owner, or the executive sponsor add a signature as an endorsement of the contents and to show support for the use of the procedures.
- Standard set of procedures—at any point in time only one standard set of procedures should be used by everyone in the organization. This should be the most updated version of what is actually happening.

Chapter 26

Audit

Background

The audit department of URHere's global positioning system (GPS) group was charged with two responsibilities:

1. To ensure that processes and procedures were properly performed
2. To ensure that questionable practices were detected

The audit department has complete authority over where and when an audit will be conducted, and it reported directly to the CEO of the conglomerate—the department was considered her eyes and ears.

The audit manager defined the objectives, scope, and the time frame for audits and prepared the final reports. The senior auditors determined the scheduling of each audit and prepared draft reports, while the junior auditors conducted the audit.

To prepare for the audit, the relevant audit manual and process procedures were given to the junior auditors for briefing. The audit manager notified the relevant organizational group of the forthcoming audit dates.

Procedural audits require a process walkthrough to verify if activities are being completed as per the specific policy that governs the actions. The audit team noted exceptions, took evidence of the exceptions, and then met with the respective managers to discuss their findings. The onus was on the managers to explain the reasons for procedural deviations. At the end of the audit, an audit report was generated. The report included the procedure that was audited, the tests that were completed, and the findings listed. Recommendations to limit procedural deviations were made; and where deviations were deemed acceptable, the exceptions were mentioned in the report. All reports were supported by detailed audit papers that provided evidence or examples.

Other types of audits in the organization were more exciting and led to potentially disastrous results for the people in the audited organization, such as a written reprimand and, in some cases, dismissal. The audits were usually conducted systematically or in response to suspicions of a financial result, complaints, or unfiled reports. Two factors frequently instilled suspicion—materiality and impact.

Why Audit

Audits are conducted to ensure the *effectiveness* and *efficiency* of the processes. *Effectiveness* refers to the ability of the process to achieve the desired output, how consistently an internal control is applied, and by whom. *Efficiency* reflects how the process achieves the desired outcome.

Audits may be used for the following purposes:

- To ascertain compliance with internal procedures and policies and external statutory regulations and laws that govern the industry or country
- To confirm the reliability of the process as witnessed by external stakeholders
- To ensure the consistency of the process so that the same outcome can be achieved in more or less the same time frames over a period
- To verify the reliability of process reports—that the results are accurate and reflect what is going on within the process

The audit may determine an anomaly of the process reports or a consistent trend that needs to be examined. The process owner's assertions about the completeness of the process—all steps and documents to complete the procedure will have been accurately completed—can then be verified.

Materiality and Impact

Materiality varies from organization to organization. An external stakeholder with monies to invest may not consider a calculation error of $25 on a $1 million bottom line to be significant, but may have a different reaction to an error of $25,000.

If 99.9 percent of the process outcomes are as expected, then 0.1 percent deviations may not be considered material. If the percentage of deviations escalates to 2 percent or more, then anything above 2 percent may be considered a material impact that demands investigation.

A cashier preparing daily deposits may have timely and accurately deposited 1,000 checks for the month. However, she neglected to deposit one check for $1 million. The neglected deposit is a deviation of less than 1 percent of process output; however, its impact on the organization's cash flow or its ability to meet financial obligations in the short term may be material. Regardless of the amount, the stakeholder may consider it significant that an error has gone undetected for a period and may lose confidence in the organization.

Core processes will be audited more frequently because they have the ability to greatly affect the business.

Sampling

Chefs sample all the time. They dip a spoon into the sauce, take a sip, and make decisions about what the sauce needs—salt, basil, or nothing at all. A sample is taken to make an estimation of the actual characteristics of the contents of the saucepan and the spoonful is assumed representative of the whole.

What to Sample

The choice of what to sample is determined by the type of audit being done and the purpose of the audit. The sample should reflect the population that is being audited. It would be irrational to audit the payroll process and take samples from the inventory ordering process.

Audit samples can be taken from anywhere within the process boundaries or from the previous or next process in the value chain.

Materiality sets the floor for the sampling of transactions. All transactions over a set limit may be scrutinized for accuracy, completeness, and procedural integrity. Sometimes the limit may be a percentage (eg, 2 percent of gross sales) or an absolute figure (all transactions of $25,000 or more). Materiality may not be limited to one transaction; it may be an accumulation of transactions that calls for scrutiny of all the transactions conducted, regardless of the size.

How to Sample

Just as the chef dips his spoon, the sample is taken from within the population. Some guidelines for sampling include the following:

- Decide what part of the process you want to audit.
- Identify the population or range of items to audit.
- Determine what questions need to be answered by the audit.
- Determine how many samples will be drawn from the population, to be considered representative of the whole.
- Take samples that represent the whole.

Random sampling is based on the belief that each item in the population has the same probability of being selected as a sample. Types of random sampling methods include the following:

- Computer-generated algorithm
- Selection of transactions on a predetermined basis:
  - The last five transactions for any day
  - The first 10 names on the reports

For the sales audit, the list of commissions paid to the sales agents was scrutinized. The sample of sales for the audit comprised the portfolio of the three top-earning sales agents. This approach intended to capture a varied portfolio of customers and transactions over varying periods.

Even with the most sophisticated of sampling, the primary rule is to select enough samples to have a good representation of the entire population.

Sampling Results

Sampling can be used to test a particular attribute or characteristic of the population. The condition will either exist or not exist in the samples taken; for example, all paid invoices are stamped *paid*.

It can also be used to confirm the acceptable tolerance deviation range. Samples are examined in a *stop-and-go* manner; that is, the sample is checked to see if it supports a particular conclusion, and the sampling ceases as soon as that conclusion is supported.

Sampling Risk

A sampling risk is inherent unless the auditor examines 100 percent of the population. It is possible for a sample to mislead the auditor to make incorrect assumptions about the population, or that conclusions drawn from the sample may not represent correct conclusions for the entire population. (If the chef has added salt to the soup, but the salt has not yet dissolved in the soup, then the sample may not be representative of the whole pot.)

Other risks involve observing a difference when in fact there is none, akin to the soup not tasting salty when in reality it is. The other error is the reverse and reflects the auditor's excessive credulity where the difference is not observed when in fact there is one—the soup tastes salty when in reality it is not.

These risks are mitigated by using a larger sampling size; the greater the sample size, the less chance of sampling error as well as by the auditor's neutrality and independence.

When to Audit

An audit should be conducted to ensure that the process is compliant especially when the following conditions exist:

- A new process is implemented
- An existing process is changed
- Continuous improvement is valued
- New members join the process
- New statutory, regulatory, or other requirements are required because of industrial, governmental, or other requirements
- There is a new process owner

Audits can be conducted in response to nonconforming outcomes to establish why there was a deviation. Spot checks are conducted to ensure that the process is performing and that procedures are being followed. Regular and planned audits can also be part of the continuous improvement and maintenance of existing processes.

Audit Team

The audit team comprises members that are internal or external to the process. An internal audit team will be in charge of the audit and co-opt additional members where necessary. The process owner can request an audit at any time, or the audit department may independently schedule an audit of the process. Where an internal audit department does not exist, the process owner can subscribe the operators' team members or prior business process improvement team members to conduct the audit.

Ideally, an audit team should be independent of the process. When the team members are involved, they need to adopt an independent attitude and strive to be objective and impartial to the results. Audit team members should be proficient in and have the competence to conduct an audit, through either formal or informal education and training.

Audit Preparation

The audit manager may send a letter of engagement to the process owner outlining the nature and extent of the audit, start date, and other relevant information. An audit plan outlines the overall strategy for the conduct and scope of the audit that will be developed. The audit objectives, when established, will determine the type of evidence that is collected.

The audit team develops an understanding of the process—its objectives, measurements, and key transaction types—by examining all the process documents, flowcharts, systems, and interfaces.

Materiality limits, sampling methods, the number of samples, and the audit tests will be determined. An audit schedule that shows the duration and task assignment is also prepared.

Audit Method

The audit of a cleared check for $25,000 involved tracing the transaction from the decision to spend the amount to the approval of the purchase order to the receipt of the goods and services.

Some of the investigation points were as follows:

- Is there a purchase order that matches the goods or services ordered?
- Is the vendor registered?
- What type of bidding process was engaged to award the contract to a vendor?
- Was the decision within budget?
- Were the accounting procedures for the processing and payment of the invoice followed?
- Were the goods delivered in an acceptable manner?

An audit once led to the discovery that some outstanding artworks were being boldly displayed at the home of one of the executives. After the audit report, valuable paintings, sans executive, were visibly present in the office.

For our process audit, we want to make several determinations:

- Are the process time frames being maintained?
- Are there any bottleneck delays or other non-value-added activities in the process?

- Are there any exceptions to the process?
- Are there any improvements that are being made or recommendations for procedure change?
- Are there any loopholes in the process?
- Have the procedural changes been documented?
- Is there any challenge in using the documented process?
- Is the outcome as expected?
- Is the procedure being followed?
- Is the procedure representative of what is happening in the process?

We want to ensure that the process is being conducted in the prescribed manner at all times.

Audits may fail because of a nonsampling audit risk (ie, the deviation was not part of the sample). The procedure applied to the transactions or balances may fail to detect a material misstatement. The auditor may also select an audit procedure that is not appropriate to achieve a specific objective. For example, confirming recorded receivables cannot reveal unrecorded receivables. Nonsampling risk can be reduced to a negligible level through adequate planning and supervision.

Conducting the Audit

Each sample will be walked through the process from beginning to end to ensure completeness—that all steps are followed, that all compliance controls are operating as intended, and that the accuracy of transactions is vouched and verified. The audit can focus on quantitative aspects of the process, such as number of checks processed, or on the qualitative aspects of the measurement.

Some of the tests that the auditor will employ in conducting the audit are as follows:

- Analyze—identify and classify items for further study
- Ascertain—determine or discover with certainty; for example, to ascertain the date when a transaction occurred
- Assess—to determine the value, significance, or extent of a transaction
- Confirm—communicate with external stakeholders parties to authenticate internal evidence
- Corroborate—strengthen with other evidence to make a conclusion
- Count—enumerate some characteristic, such as the number of items in inventory
- Examine—look at the transactions critically
- Inquire—ask questions of client personnel

- Inspect—scrutinize or critically examine a document
- Recalculate—perform procedures again and compare with original results
- Reconcile—agree between separate sources of information, such as accounting records reconciled with the financial statements
- Reperformance—repeat of a computation to check its accuracy
- Review—to examine again
- Test count—count done by auditors, qualitative
- Verify—prove accuracy of numbers or existence of assets
- Vouch—prove accuracy by tracing to supporting documents

Audit Findings

Test results provide the audit findings. Working papers (written audit documentation), procedures applied, tests performed, and information obtained must be able to withstand scrutiny to ensure that the claims in the report are accurate.

The process owner has an opportunity to explain the deviations that exist before the final audit report is generated. The discussion focuses on the problems identified, recommendations, and action plans to address the problems.

Recommendations

The auditor must perform a rudimentary cost–benefit analysis to ensure that the cost of implementing recommendations (time and money) is met with the expected returns. The process owner may challenge the recommendations and give reasons why certain actions are taken during the procedure. Negotiations can end with a scheduled implementation plan for the accepted recommendations or with the acceptance of the reasons for the deviations by formally including the deviations in the procedure. The auditor must bear in mind that procedures alone, no matter how well designed and operated, cannot guarantee that an organization's objectives will be met.

Audit Reports

The audit report reflects audit findings and explains how the findings were determined. The process audit report needs to establish if the process is conforming to the standards. The audit reflects the process characteristics and highlights whether measurements are in line with the stated objectives. The auditor may provide an opinion on the process in the areas of effectiveness, operational effectiveness, and efficiency. The auditor can include observations and comparisons of the results from one year's (or one period's) audit to the next.

The audit report is formatted to include the following:

- Introduction—identifies the audited process and the responsibility of process owner and the auditor.
- Scope—details the scope of the audit, sample size, and the tests conducted. Any assumptions that have been made about the process need to be stated herein.
- Findings and recommendations—findings and the associated recommendations are listed in the document with or without explanations. Findings may be listed as an appendix.
- Opinion paragraph—the auditor's conclusions are stated in an opinion paragraph. The process can be compliant with the procedures or noncompliant, efficient or inefficient, effective or ineffective, or any other conclusion that the auditor determines.

Audit Meeting

After the final report is issued, a final meeting is held with the process owner to discuss an action plan to rectify the anomalies and other findings of the audit.

Audit Check

The audit team may want to follow up on the reported findings at appropriate intervals. Audit checks will determine the progress of the process team in implementing recommendations and allow an assessment of whether or not the recommendations are working.

Issue Closure

The process owner has responsibility for closing the issues raised during the audit. The auditors can perform spot checks to confirm that the implementation has been completed.

Date _____   Requested By: _____

Process: Audit of the accounts payables process

Objective: To identify that the process works as documented

Conducted by: _____   Approved By: _____

Sample, invoices – 3001, 45001

No	Audit Item	Tick	Comment	Reference
1	Invoice logged within 24 hours of receipt	√		Log report
2	Invoice was accurate	√		Invoice 4001
3	Invoice was matched to purchase order	√		Purchase order #44-556
4	Invoice matched to goods received note	√		GRN#65
5	Invoice was paid on time	√		
6	Invoice was fully paid	√		
7	Invoice was part of multiple payment	√		

Figure 26.1   Sample audit working papers.

Audit Evaluation and Findings

At the end of the audit, an evaluation can be made on the auditors' performance and the appropriateness of their recommendations, illustrated in Figure 26.1.

Conclusion

The audit process is dynamic. In the mode of process improvement, process team members may devise new ways of achieving process objectives. The audit confirms through a series of tests that the process objectives are being met in a manner that conforms to agreed-upon procedures. The audit is an independent review of the process and ensures that valid changes are formally accepted and documented within the process procedure.

Chapter 27

Phase Gate Five

The process owner now has responsibility for maintenance of the process on an ongoing basis, further improvements, and where the implementation is incomplete, a plan to complete the same.

The process owner will have ongoing responsibility to—

- Ensure that the process is working as designed
- Develop audit programs for the process
- Test on a regular basis that the process is continuously effective
- Work on implementing the fully designed process where necessary
- Update the procedures when changes are made

Deliverables are—

- Audit program
- Implementation plan (for outstanding issues)
- Training program
- Updated procedures
- Updated workflow diagrams
- Maintenance of change program for the process

Chapter 28

Wrap-Up

"It's a wrap," the producer says, to signal the end of the movie. A cast party follows, as well as dismantling of the sets and everyone adapting to their new life as influenced by the film.

As the URHere payroll project neared completion, a number of closing activities were to be completed. Final checks were made to ensure that the data entry was accurate and that the system was ready for adoption by the human resources department. The project manager prepared a final report to document challenges that were overcome and opportunities created. Outstanding implementation issues were included, with a brief outline of how open tasks would be completed. The impact of the project and the expected outcome of the new payroll process were confirmed.

Final Report

At the start of the business process improvement (BPI) project, the project management team communicated its intentions and projected outcomes to the senior executives to gain sanction for the project. Now, at the end of the project, the team is obliged to update the executive on the outcome of the project, including a focus on outstanding issues and a comparison of projected-against-real outcomes. An objective comparison of the plan to the actual outcomes needs to be made.

Executive Summary

Create a synopsis of the project results. The focus should include cost savings that resulted from the project and the return on the monies spent for the project. Any project team members who need to be specially mentioned for outstanding service or performance might be included here. The executive summary should give management a quick snapshot about successes that were realized during the project.

Problem and Solution—the Report

Remind executives of the reasons for launching the project—in response to or in anticipation of a changing business environment. No need to go into the analysis of the decision-making process because the analysis was justified at the start of the project to gain sanction. This report focuses on specific outputs and the overall outcome. The vision, goals, and objectives for the selected process should be stipulated for clarity.

Project Teams

Identify the teams that worked on the project at the various phases. Be certain to mention individual contributors to each team's success. The team may have set targets for its performance before the process, so use the targets to measure members' performance at the end of the project. The team can develop its own criteria or use others established with human resources, or the project management office for other such projects, using consensual guidelines along with measures that team members contribute to the project.

New Process

Flowcharts of the improved or new process with an explanation of the type of changes that were made are included in the report. The measurements for the process and the roles and responsibilities for members are outlined.

The results of the new versus the previous process should be highlighted. The time to completion, the number of delays, the non-value-added activities that were removed, and the empowerment of the operators all need to be emphasized.

The overall savings for the new process should be calculated. The procedures, organization charts, and swim lane diagrams that show the interface with other departments are included as appendixes.

Table 28.1   Stakeholder Shift

Stakeholder	Power Before	Power After
Collections supervisor	Limited recognition by shop stewards (difficult to provide the information that they needed)	Recognition as a performer by the shop stewards (as information was readily available)
	Controlled the assignment of work and roles Inspector of the process Prepared all the reports for the various users	No control over the work flows as inspections were removed No control over the reports or contents–happens without her intervention
Accounting staff—junior	Less powerful than senior members	Empowered to perform work from beginning to end, with limited interruptions or supervision Equal power in the process with senior staff
Accounting staff—senior	More powerful in the process than junior staff	Equal power in the process as all junior staff

Stakeholders

Changes in the stakeholders' power and interest in the process must be included. If the process has gained any new stakeholders or omitted the presence of others, these changes also need to be documented. A return to the United Front trade union's improved collections process allows us to complete Table 28.1.

Risks and Opportunities

None or very few risks should be remaining in our project risk register. The project team should have found ways of mitigating the risks and ways to build the mitigations into the new process design. The opportunities should have also been woven into the design. The project risk register should be included as an appendix to highlight challenges that the team faced and how they were overcome.

Lessons Learned

The lessons learned register is completed to display all new findings the team unearthed during the project. This provides learning residue for the organization's intelligence and is a good starting point for future BPI teams.

Budget Comparisons

The project team would have kept track of the project expenses. The expenses should be compared with the budget, with variances explained. The return on the investment needs to be calculated on the actual expenses and included in the project, as shown in Table 28.2.

Timetable

The timetable needs to be updated to show the actual dates when milestones were achieved. The variance in days for the milestones are also noted and explained (Table 28.3).

Return-on-Investments (ROI)

Return on resources consumed by the project—money and time—must be calculated. The calculation permits the team to quantify the benefits and positive outcomes of the program and correlate benefits to the investments made. If the team cannot calculate the ROI, the lack of a calculation reflects that the team did not pay attention or keep track of expenses and time and perhaps remains uncertain of the outcome of the program.

Outstanding Issues

Some issues may remain incomplete during the implementation. For example, there may be technological issues that are beyond the technical competency of the process implementation team. A list of outstanding issues should be presented as an action plan along with the responsibilities and time frames projected.

Conclusion

Provide a quick wrap-up of all the above. No new information should be included here. Members from all of the BPI teams ought to sign off on the final report showing commitment and buy-in to its contents.

Table 28.2 Budget Comparisons

Item	Description	Budget ($)	Actual ($)	Variance (+/– $)	Comment
1	BPI launch	1,800	500	–1,300	Used the organization's rooftop to launch—no rental cost. The project champion gave a speech—no speaker hired.
2	BPI team cost	11,000	7,000	–4,000	Team members did not want to be paid for their holidays.
3	Conduct of BPI	7,000	10,000	+3,000	Three team members were trained in facilitation to lead the workshops. No external facilitators used.
4	Team costs	1,100	4,500	+3,400	Team hired a technical writer and a document controller for the project.
	Subtotal	20,900			
5	Contingency 10%	2,090	0	–2,090	Used in other areas
	Grand Total	**22,990**	**22,000**	**–990**	**Savings of $990**

Handover

The project team must send a strong signal that the project is over and return ownership of the entire process to the process owner. A handover meeting should be set with a clear objective: at the end of the meeting, the process will be handed over to the process owner.

Table 28.3 Timetable

Milestone	Budget Date	Actual Date	Variance	Comment
Design completion	Feb 15	Feb 28	+13 days	Needed to get stakeholder buy-in.
Design acceptance	March 15	March 14	−1 day	Workshops were held with small groups.
Process implementation team formation	Feb 28	Feb 15	−13 days	Needed to get department managers to release staff.
Pilot acceptance	June 12	July 14	+32 days	Process owner challenges were resolved.
Implementation date	Sept 30	Nov 15	+15 days	Delay in staff training.

Even though the process owner may have been involved in the implementation issues and aware of what has transpired, there is need for a formal handover of the project documentation related to the project and the improved process. This is also an opportunity for any outstanding issues to be cleared up.

Dismantling the Project Team

Project team members need to return full-time to their primary functions. Team members are part of the intelligence of the organization and can be leveraged as reference points for future projects. They may provide training and troubleshooting resources for the process and future BPI initiatives. Individual and team evaluations should be completed.

Documentation

The project's entire documentation must be stored and archived to form part of the organizational knowledge. The documents can reside with the project owner and a named document controller in the organization.

Other Processes

Success of the business process improvement may encourage the organization to expand the concept to other areas of the organization based on a selection process or perceived needs. The lessons learned and risk and opportunity registers are important documents that will accelerate the learning curve of new project teams. The members of the previous project teams may provide a source of facilitators for new teams.

Conclusion

It has been a rocky, exciting ride in which we learned new things about the organization where we spend large portions of our lives. Assumptions were revealed and challenged; rules were broken. We understand the fears and concerns of our colleagues and have come to appreciate the strength and knowledge of our stakeholders. During the process, we studied, worked together, and changed together until we found a way that would work for everyone. Constrained by resources, limited by our own thinking, we saw a new way emerge. We got excited, soaring beyond our expectations, tried and failed, and eventually succeeded. We created a new process, one that works by providing a strong return on investment and a source of pride. Now on to the next, new challenge.

Appendix A: Structuring Your Workshop

Well Codified

Just as the life cycle of a workshop (or meeting, or session) has three steps (Get Ready, Do It, and Review), we find that within each meeting, three pieces need to be systematically managed to ensure success. All agendas should include a beginning, a middle, and an end. Many meetings fail because they fail to include all three pieces. Even a lousy book or movie includes a beginning, a middle, and an end.

The Beginning

Manage (and rehearse) your introductions carefully. Make sure your participants understand your meeting's purpose and importance. Remember to use the integrative and plural first-person term *we* or *us* and avoid the singular *I* or *me* so that you can begin to transfer responsibility and ownership to the participants, since they must frequently own the results.

Have your room set up to visually display the meeting's purpose, scope, and deliverables. If you cannot convert these into 50 words or fewer (for each), then you are not ready yet to launch your workshop. Let us repeat, if you do not know what the deliverables are, then you do not know what success looks like, nor are you prepared to lead a group of people.

Consider displaying the purpose, scope, and deliverables on large Post-it® paper, along with a set of ground rules appropriate to your politics and situation. The following sequence is typically optimal for a robust introduction:

1. Introduce yourself and explain the importance of the workshop; that is, how much money or time is at risk if the workshop fails. Try to avoid using the first-person singular pronoun *I* after this moment. It is hard to stop saying *I* but at least be conscious of whenever you do use this pronoun.
2. Present the purpose, scope, and deliverables and seek assent. Make sure that all the participants can live with them. If they cannot, you probably have the wrong agenda prepared since it is designed around your deliverables.
3. Cover any of the *administrivia* to clear participants' heads from thinking about themselves, especially their creature comforts. Explain how to locate the lavatories, fire extinguishers, emergency exits, and other necessities particular to your group and situation.
4. Cover the agenda and carefully explain the reason behind the sequence of the agenda steps, and how they relate to each other. Relate all of the agenda steps back to the deliverable so that participants can envision how completing an agenda step feeds content into the meeting deliverable, thus showing progress for their efforts as they get closer to ending the meeting.
5. Share some (not more than 8 to 12) ground rules. Consider supplementing your narrative posting of ground rules with some audiovisual support, including humorous clips, but keep them brief and appropriate.
6. For a kick-off, have the executive sponsor explain the importance of the participants' contributions and what management hopes to accomplish. For ongoing workshops, consider a project update but do not allow the update or executive sponsor to take more than five minutes. Your meeting is not a mini town hall meeting (unless it actually is).

Note: For multiple-day workshops, remember to cover the same items at the beginning of subsequent days (except executive sponsor or project team update). Additionally, review content that was built or agreed upon the day(s) before and how it relates to where you are located in the agenda.

The Middle Steps

The agenda steps between the Introduction and Review and Wrap-Up comprise the middle steps. The remainder of this manual is focused on *what* to do during the middle steps, based on where the team is in the project life cycle and what deliverable is required at the moment. For right now, we will skip over the middle steps. The sections after this all provide content on tools and activities for the middle of your meetings.

Review and Wrap-Up

For the ending, walk through the outputs or deliverable (decision, functions, data, priorities, reports, etc.) created during the meeting, ensuring that the pieces fit together and form one cohesive product.

Walk through the documentation from the workshop. Review it, but do not relive it. As the walkthrough captures process, insert some real-life examples to see how it performs.

Action Plan

Have the group list the action items that they have already agreed to or will undertake—starting with tomorrow. List the actions, clarify them, have someone take responsibility, and have the group assign a deadline (month, day, year) for each action to be completed. Consider applying the RASI tool (responsible, authorizes, supports, informed; see Appendix B) to manage the action items. Absence or silence is unacceptable during assignments, so do not permit assignments to go to someone who is not in the meeting, either live or virtually.

Open Issues (Parking Lot)

Conduct an open issues step after the review of completed items and agreed-upon action items. An open issue reflects a topic too important to discard, but not relevant at the moment, and frequently something that is key and the scope of the meeting or project. During your meeting, record open items as they arise. Review each open item. First, make sure it remains valid. Over the course of meetings, some open issues will no longer be open; therefore, these can be deleted or marked accordingly (eg, OBE = Overcome by Event, or taken care of). Append each open issue with the following:

- The item status—along with a complete, coherent statement
- Who is responsible for communicating back to the group on the status of the open item (frequently viewed as who "will do" or complete the open item)
- When completion is expected (month, day, year)
- How the resolution will be communicated to this group
- Consider e-mail, file naming, and file-server security restrictions

There are various ways of describing open issues that arise during meetings. Other terms used by organizations include issue bin, coffee pot, water cooler, elevator speech, limbo, chestnuts, popcorn, and our favorite, refrigerator (a term

Figure A.1

used in the Middle East because the items temporarily stored there can be pre-served and cooked up later). Regardless of the term you use or the phrase that is embraced by your existing culture, open issues need to be managed properly rather than left unattended without context or next steps.

Note: A simple method for managing open issues is called the "2 by 4." Meant to connote the piece of lumber as shown in Figure A.1, the method suggests a tripartite approach, namely:

- ■ To: Do what?
- ■ By: Who and when?
- ■ For: What purpose or benefit?

Evaluation

Obtain comments on the method used and the session leader's (facilitator's) performance. Use an evaluation form shown later or create two *plus* and *delta* columns to capture what went well and what should change. Others terms used to describe the Plus/Delta tool include OFI, or Opportunity for Improvement, Benefits and Concerns (also known as the B's & C's) and Star/Delta.

Appendix B:
Workshop Tools

Brainstorming

How We Think

We believe that human beings

- Are creative
- Are intelligent
- Have real power to do amazing things

We are challenged with how to express our creativity and intelligence and to take the risks associated with power. We accept what we know. Tim Hurson in his book *Think Better* shares that most times our brains are engaged in three activities: distraction, reaction or following well worn patterns.

In brainstorming sessions, be aware of these natural limitations to creativity. Humans will revert to animalistic behavior when uncomfortable or challenged. Once aware of how the brain works the group leader can push the group to true creative thinking that is needed for brainstorming.

Monkey Brain

This is an avoidance strategy. Participants will display:

- Chatterbox mind—participants talk and talk but don't say anything valuable.
- Stream of consciousness—participants relate events without any conclusions.
- Daydreaming—particpants zone out and are not present or aware in the workshop.

Gator Brain

This is another avoidance strategy. Alligators have few standard responses to conditions; ie, a new creature that ventures into its territory. Particpants in a workshop often react the same way.

- Fight—the gator will fight a same sex gator
- Flight—if the intruder is a larger creature the gator will flee
- Feed—if the intruder is a smaller creature the gator will try to eat it
- Mate—if the season is right and the intruder is of the opposite sex, the gator tries to mate
- Freeze—if the intruder is none of the above, the gator will freeze until the creature is gone or does something that triggers one of the above responses

Elephant Brain

This is an energy conservation strategy. Particpants will be comfortable with the familiar and it will be difficult to generate new thinking around a topic. Look out for:

- Patterning—the brain forms patterns by recognizing, restoring, and retrieving past experiences, and uses these to assess and deal with current situations. This survival technique serves us well in everyday life, but limits the generation of new and creative ideas.
- Making assumptions—we approach new situations with information from the past. Most of us when we hear "the secretary" think of a female.
- Resisting change—what we know is safe, we know how to respond, new situations generate fear and confusion.

In brainstorming sessions, we have to find ways to get participants beyond the avoidance and patterning ways of thinking, to reach true creativity.

Brainstorming

Lead groups through brainstorming session when:

- Many ideas are needed—the more ideas generated the greater the chance of getting the best idea
- Group wants a solution

How to Brainstorm

Explain to the group that they are going to generate ideas about the topic at hand. Read and explain the ground rules:

- Build on the ideas of others—if someone says red, it may generate the idea of colors or ripe tomatoes
- All ideas are accepted—all answers are good, no judgment
- No discussion of ideas presented—discussion leads to analysis and limits creativity
- Be creative—crazy, wild, silly ideas are okay
- Everyone participates—no one in the group has your idea
- Fast-paced thinking—keeps judgment and discussions at bay
- When in doubt, leave in—all ideas are good enough

As the group generates ideas, capture these—using the group's language—on Post-It notes and paste these on flip chart paper. When the group has finished generating ideas, read the ideas off the flip chart encouraging the group to add ideas as and when they think of them. When the group seems to have exhausted all ideas, ask them "What else can you think about the topic?" This will generate even more creative ideas as the group is encouraged to think.

Group Ideas

Invite the participants to group the similar ideas together. Name each group of similar ideas, eg, dog-horse-cat. The group name becomes pets or animals. Note that there will be some ideas that are dissimilar and stand alone. That is acceptable as well.

What Next?

The ideas generated can now be worked on by the group. They will need to further discuss, define (to ensure common understanding), and analyze the ideas to determine which they will continue to work with.

Brainstorming is not an end in itself, unless the group just wanted to generate ideas. It is usally one tool that can be used in a workshop.

Wrap Up

- We have better results when we get to the third area of creativity.
- In the third area, magic happens.
- We often get quiet, but the struggle is worth it.

Responsibility Matrix

Roles and responsibilities take on different names depending on your organization. All capture a sense of *who* will be doing *what* and *when* we can expect an update or completion. The intersection of *who* does *what* and *when* is called a Responsibility Matrix. Frequently it is called a RASI chart where R stands for who is responsible, A stands for who is accountable, S stands for who will support the person responsible, and I standards for needing to be informed by the person responsible.

Purpose

To define the roles and responsibilities for an action plan.

Rationale

The RASI method clearly defines "who does what different tomorrow" by producing a responsibility matrix.

Method

Import your action plan (ie, *what*) from a separate activity such as the gap analysis. The action plan includes the *what*, *who*, and *when* of the assignment. Define the roles and responsibilities using the RASI process noted below.

Note: The *who* dimension might include business units, departments, roles, or people; but be consistent across the board and match closely to the appropriate level of responsibility for the nature of *what* needs to be done.

■ Define each of the four areas of responsibility—note that each implies the ones that follow:
   – R = responsible—is held responsible for the success and completion of a given task
   – A = authorizes—approves or signs off on the method or results of a given task
   – S = supports—provides assistance, information, and so forth in the completion of a task—if requested
   – I = informed—is kept informed of the progress or results of a given task.
■ Portrait view: If you are using an easel or flip chart, write the people involved (units, job names, etc.) across the top (the *who*) and the tasks, jobs, projects, and so forth down the left side (the *what*).

- Landscape view: Build a matrix on a whiteboard or other large writing area with the tasks, jobs, projects, and so forth across the top (the *what*) and the people involved (units, job names, etc.) down the left-hand side (the *who*).
- Have the group fill in the intersections with the appropriate level of responsibility.

Rules to Follow

- One and only one R per row (ie, for each activity)
- At least one A who is not the R—may be more than one
- I if individual must only be informed
- S for people supporting the *what*

Note:

- R implies A, S, I
- A implies S, I
- S implies I

Build the matrix using a large sheet of paper. Use a bright-colored marker to document the R for each assignment. Go back to the empty cells and complete the relationships as appropriate, as illustrated in Figure B.1.

Consider also capturing the deadline and resource request (eg, the amount of man hours required or the amount of money or other resources being requested to complete the assignment) so that you can convert your RASI chart into a project planning tool or Gantt chart. (See Figure B.1 below.)

		WHO			
		Role 1	Role 2	Role 3	Role 4
WHAT	Task A	R	A	I	S
	Task B	A	R	S	
	Task C	R	A	S	I
	Task D	S		A	R

Figure B.1   Landscape view of a RASI chart.

The chart reads as follows:

- Role 1 is responsible for completion of Task A.
- Role 2 will approve the resources required to complete Task A.
- Role 3 is kept informed about progress with Task A.
- Role 4 provides assistance and support for task completion.

Note: Not all tasks need an I or an S. All tasks require one and only one R. Typically, the A may be true for all the tasks in a plan.

This step takes one to eight hours. The major difficulty for the session leader is the logistics. You must plan the logistics of capturing the matrix well in advance. Large sheets of white paper or numerous flip charts taped together are the best means to capture the information.

Guardian of Change (Communications Plan)

Purpose

Our guardian of change is more commonly known as a communications plan. Our experience shows that it is best to guard and protect the message rather than to shout out and be a champion or a cheerleader. Different audiences need different parts of the message and may react differently to descriptive terms used and the media used to communicate results.

The overall purpose is to get a group to agree on how it will communicate the results of its meeting and workshop efforts to others. Generally, students in study groups have a grade point average that is 0.50 points higher than students without groups. Why? Socialization.

Rationale

At a minimum, team members need an "elevator speech" that can deliver an effective synopsis of the meeting results. At the other extreme, if the meeting is strategic, there could be numerous audience types such as the investment community, suppliers, trade personnel, and others. If so, identify the key audience members before discussing the message, medium of communication, and frequency of communication for each audience.

When it is important that a message given to two or more different audiences sounds the same, consider agreeing on the rhetoric used to describe the meeting. Typically, the two major audiences are:

1. Our bosses or superiors
2. People dependent on our results

Method

After identifying each target audience, ask for each, "What are we going to tell _____?" List the messages as bullet points that homogenize (ie, create consistency) the meeting participants' descriptions in the hallway about what was accomplished.

If necessary, discuss *how to* communicate with the target audience such as face-to-face, e-mail, or otherwise. For complicated communications plans, further discuss frequency or how often to set up regular communications. It may be necessary to schedule the communications so that the superiors are informed before other stakeholders. When communications are not planned, meeting participants will use different methods and different rhetoric that will generate different understanding among stakeholders who may required shared or at least similar understanding.

Proactively consider a "30 by 30" report, a written summary of results that should take no longer than 30 minutes to write and no longer than 30 seconds to read. The 30 by 30 report may be ideal for executives and other team members who are interested but not fully invested.

Assessment

It remains important to assess your own performance, so frequently obtain feedback about how you did and what you could do to be better, as illustrated in Figure B.2.

Power Balls

Purpose

To help a group quickly and simply prioritize.

Rationale

Apply the Pareto Principle (or the 80–20 Rule) to help a group deselect and to eliminate as many options as possible so the group can stay focused on the most important or powerful options.

FACILITATION EVALUATION FORM

FACILITATION: LOCATION:

DATE: FACILITATOR:

ITEMS	Met participants Needs?				
	1	2	3	4	5
	NO		OK		YES
	Place an X in the appropriate column				
WORKSHOP OBJECTIVES					
Were you aware of the workshop deliverable before you attended today?					
Were you involved in defining the workshop deliverable?					
Was the workshop deliverable well defined?					
Was the deliverable achieved?					
WORKSHOP CONTENT					
Was the material appropriate?					
Simplicity of material (1 = not simple 5 = Perfect)					
Volume (1 = too much, not enough, 5 = Perfect)					
Did the handouts fit the training? Did they help?					
FACILITATOR METHODS					
Did the facilitator allow sufficient discussion?					
Did the facilitator encourage participation?					
Did the facilitator help to bring out new ideas?					
Did the facilitator help to close out discussions?					
Did the facilitator control the session?					
Did the facilitator consider my opinion?					
Did the facilitator listen to my inputs?					
Facility and Time					
Was the session well managed in terms of time?					
Were lunch and other breaks adequate?					
COMMENTS AND CONCERNS: This is your space to comment					

Figure B.2   Illustrative assessment form.

Caution

Be aware that the effective approach suggests that you prioritize the criteria, not the options directly.

Method

The following steps should be read with an understanding that some of the material and examples used to support prioritization and other tools are discussed elsewhere in this book.

- ▪ Establish the purpose of what the team is doing ("The purpose of … is to … so that … ").
- ▪ Build a list of options (brainstorm). Set the list of options aside.

- Build a list of criteria (be prepared to define *criteria*).
- Look at the criteria to see if any options are in violation. For example, if Sally is allergic to flowers, then "buying her flowers" is probably an option we should eliminate.
- Consider asking the participants if they can live with all the remaining options. If someone objects, eliminate that particular option.

Once they can live with the balance, you have consensus.

To improve the quality of the decision, lead the group through a method of weighting the criteria.

5: High, means "Pay any price."

1: Low, means "Want it free; not willing to pay extra for it."

3: Moderate, all the stuff between 1 and 5, meaning "willing to pay a reasonable price" without being forced to define "reasonable."

Separate the most and least important criteria. Code the remaining as moderate by default, without discussion. Attempt to force-fit the candidates into thirds as high, low, and moderate—but be flexible.

Appeal to the high criteria and isolate the option(s) that best satisfy them. To further optimize or guide discussion (if required), appeal to some of the fuzzy factors that may be hard to measure.

Appendix C: Workshop Agendas

Vision and Goals Workshop

Deliverable

At the end of the workshop, we will have defined the vision, goals, objectives, and action plan for our organization.

Simple Agenda

- Introduction
- Vision
- Goals
- Skills/Resources
- Objectives
- Action Plan
- Responsibility Assignments
- Guardian of Change

Introduction

Refer to Appendix A, "Structuring Your Workshop."

- Our purpose today is to …
- Our scope today is …
- Our deliverable today is …

- Administrivia
- Today's agenda is ...
- Ground Rules
- Ice Breaker

Vision

Follow one of three options:

1. Develop the vision before workshop—usually by the head of the organization—and review for consensus in the workshop.
2. Develop a draft vision before the workshop and modify in the workshop.
3. Use a creativity exercise—draw a picture of your business (a coat-of-arms picture is the most powerful) and extract a mission or purpose statement in the workshop.

Goals

Goals should be narrative; use one of three methods:

1. Define a goal statement and then have the group use a creativity exercise to draw their goals. Have each group describe their picture to the others and then capture the vision statement in narrative format on a flip chart using discussion.
2. Prepare a draft vision statement (usually gathered from the senior manager of the group) and write it on a flip chart. Define a vision statement; then review the statement with the group and have them modify it to meet their needs.
3. Have the group develop a newspaper or magazine headline that they would like to see in a major newspaper on the date of the vision—ask, "What would the newspaper headline read on January 15, 20xx?" Have them embellish the headline with the story behind the headline. This headline and story provide the foundation for the goals.

Skills and Resources

The gap analysis is a critical step that may provide an uncomfortable exposure of the organization's weaknesses. It also identifies the existing skills, competencies, and resources within the business process improvement that will lead to goal achievement. Teams that do not perform a gap analysis run the risk of not attaining goals in a satisfactory manner, as they may be unaware that they do not possess the skills or resources necessary to achieve the stated goals.

An honest assessment will align existing skill sets, resources, and competencies of the people, processes, and technologies with the goals. If the skills and resources are absent, the organization needs to determine how they will be attained—either externally through outsourcing or internally by developing existing resources.

To perform a gap analysis, a skills analysis is completed and then the gaps are identified.

Perform Skills Analysis

Ask the following questions of each goal:

- What skills are needed to achieve the goals (of the organization)?
- How will these skills assist in goal achievement?
- Which of these skills currently exist in the organization?
- What resources are needed to achieve the goals—time, people, and money?
- How can the organization get the skills and resources needed to achieve the goal?

The analysis may look like something like the following:

Q: What skills and resources does URHere need to increase membership usage and corporate revenue?

A: (1) Field officers to visit existing members and recruit new members (resources). (2) Proper accounting methods to maintain members' records (resources). (3) Accountant to maintain the records (skill).

Q: How will the skill assist in achieving the goals of increasing membership usage and corporate revenue?

A: The field members will meet with the members to increase visibility, early problem detection, and problem solving.

Q: What resources are needed to achieve the goal of increasing visits by field offices?

A: Accounting resources are needed. Field officers need to increase outreach to members.

Perform Gap Analysis

For each skill or resource that is identified as missing or absent from the organization, ask the following questions:

- What are the skills and resources that the organization does not have?
- How can the organization get the skills and resources needed to achieve the goal?
- How can we attain these skills?

Illustration

Q: What are the skills or resources that URHere does not have to achieve the goal of increasing membership usage?
A: Accounting skills, accountant.
Q: How can URHere get the accounting skills?
A: Outsource the function or develop it internally.
Q: How will the lack of accounting skills affect the organization?
A: The increase in membership will not be correctly or completely measured. Revenues may not be properly accounted for and members' accounts may be improperly maintained.

Table C.1 shows the results of the gap analysis. URHere's micro credit unit has identified the way that goals will be achieved and the skills and resources needed. More important, the unit knows exactly what skills are absent and can devise a plan to develop them.

Objectives

- Describe the rules of ideation in the brainstorming process.
- Define objectives using a visual prompt.
- When the group seems to have exhausted the list, review each candidate objective carefully. Roll up the list by looking for common themes. Objectives may embrace the following:
  - Financial criteria
  - Employees
  - Customers
  - Stockholders
  - Product and product quality
  - Environment
  - How they manage the organization
- When the group exhausts the list, review each candidate carefully—aim for no more than 6 to 12 objectives.

Table C.1   Skills/Resources Gap Analysis

Goals	*How to Achieve the Goals*	*Skills/Resources Needed*
To increase membership usage and corporate revenues	Visit members Promote for new members Maintain low delinquency rates for loans	Field officers *Proper accounting methods* *Outreach programs*
To retain funding capacity and partners	Meet regularly with partners	*Reports to funders*
To maintain a low delinquency rate	Visit clients regularly Develop relationships with clients Proper and regular reports	*Employee retention* *Membership database system*
Ensure timely and accurate reporting	Improve the accounting process Internally maintain and upgrade the system	*Accounting skills* *Accounting software* *Reporting system*

Note: Skills/resources in *italics* are lacked by URHere's micro credit business unit.

- ■ Review objectives and make them SMART. Do not show the SMART definition until after you have captured the raw input.
  - – Specific
  - – Measurable
  - – Adjustable and achievable (yet challenging)
  - – Relevant and realistic
  - – Time-based
- ■ Document the remaining objectives.

Action Plan

Complete the action plan described in Appendix A, "Structuring Your Workshop."

Responsibility Assignments

See Appendix A, "Structuring Your Workshop," for a discussion and illustration about how to make the assignments.

Guardian of Change

See Appendix A, "Structuring Your Workshop," for a discussion and illustration about how to build the communications plan.

Review and Wrap-Up

Follow the standard closure method (Review and Wrap-Up) discussed in Appendix A, "Structuring Your Workshop."

Stakeholder Analysis Workshop

Deliverable

The deliverable for this workshop is the identification and definitions of the process stakeholders.

Simple Agenda

- Introduction
- Purpose of the Process
- Inputs
- Contributors
- Outputs
- Beneficiaries
- Stakeholder Definitions
- Wrap-Up

Introduction

Refer to Appendix A, "Structuring Your Workshop."

- Our purpose today is to …
- Our scope today is …
- Our deliverable today is …
- Administrivia
- Today's agenda is …
- Ground Rules
- Ice Breaker

Purpose of the Process

You may develop the purpose outside the workshop and review it in the workshop for consensus. Preferably, develop a live view.

Purpose Written in Advance

- Sponsor or project manager drafts a statement of purpose.
- Mail the draft to all participants without identifying the author.
- In the workshop, review the draft (written on a flip chart) and solicit comments from the participants until all agree with the wording. Hang the final statement on the wall.

Purpose Developed in the Workshop

- Define the purpose of the process.
- Agree on a purpose of the process by asking the group to state the purpose in 25 or fewer words. Start with, "The purpose of … is to … so that … " and let the group finish the statement. This will be a run-on statement. Do not try to wordsmith the statement (get it perfect). Mount it on the wall.

Inputs

Identify the things—tangible or intangible—that come into the process and are converted into outputs. Ask the following questions to prompt the response:

- Are there any substitutes for the input?
- Can the input come in another form? If so, what does it look like?
- What does the input look like?
- What enters the process for conversion?
- What information is needed to begin the process?
- What is used at the start of the process?
- What raw materials are needed to begin the process?

Contributors

Each input comes from an internal or external organization, person, or other process. This step matches the inputs with the contributors. For each input identified, ask the following questions to prompt the answers:

- Is there any process or activity that needs to be completed before the input is generated?
- Where did the input come from?
- Who provides the input?
- Who provides the substitutes?

Outputs

Outputs are tangible or intangible outcomes generated by the process. Ask the following questions to prompt responses:

- Are there any substitutes for the output?
- Do all the outputs have the same use or get used the same way?
- Is there more than one output?
- What are inputs converted to by the end of the process?
- What comes out of the process?
- What does the output look like?
- What is the output used for?

Beneficiaries

Internal and external organizations, people, and processes that use the process outputs are the beneficiaries. Ask the following questions to prompt responses:

- Are the outputs ready for use?
- What are the outputs used for?
- Who benefits from the outputs?
- Who uses the outputs?

Stakeholder Definition

Check the prior four agenda steps for thoroughness and identify any omissions. Complete Table C.2 to match inputs and outputs with the stakeholders— sources or beneficiaries. Fully define each stakeholder group and be certain to illustrate with real-life examples from the organization.

Craft sentences that explain the relationship between the stakeholder and the process inputs and outputs. Make a complete sentence so that anyone can understand how the stakeholder interacts with the process and what they bring or use from the process. Carefully add and fully define any missing stakeholders, inputs, or outputs.

Table C.2   Stakeholder Involvement

Source	Input	Output	Beneficiary

Review and Wrap-Up

Follow the standard closure method (Review and Wrap-Up) provided in Appendix A, "Structuring Your Workshop."

Core Process Workshop

Deliverable

At the end of the workshop, we will have identified and defined the core processes in the organization.

Simple Agenda

- Introduction
- Purpose of the Organization
- Support of Each Purpose
- Core Processes
- Purpose of Each Core Process
- Activities of Each
- Process Life Cycle
- Review and Wrap-Up

Introduction

See Appendix A, "Structuring Your Workshop."

- I am …
- Our purpose today is to …

- Our scope today is …
- Our deliverable today is …
- Administrivia
- Today's agenda is …
- Ground Rules
- Ice Breaker

Purpose of the Organization

You may develop the purpose outside the workshop and review it in the workshop for consensus. Preferably, develop a live view.

Purpose Written in Advance

- Sponsor or project manager drafts a statement of purpose.
- Mail the draft to all participants without identifying the author.
- In the workshop, review the draft (written on a flip chart) and solicit comments from the participants until all agree with the wording. Hang the final statement on the wall.

Purpose Developed in the Workshop

- Define the purpose of the organization.
- Agree on a purpose of the organization by asking the group to state the purpose in 25 or fewer words. Start with, "The purpose of … is to … so that …" and let them finish the statement. This will be a run-on statement. Do not try to wordsmith the statement (get it perfect). Mount it on the wall.

Support of Each Purpose

Use the first step of brainstorming: list. Label the top of the flip chart with "Verb Noun" and ask the group to list *what* they do in support of the business purpose. Enforce the verb–noun pairing, as in, "Do this."

Following are some illustrative questions to modify:

- What do you do to support the purpose?
- You no longer have an organization and computers to do the work. You now have a warehouse with 100,000 clerks. What would they do?

Core Processes

A chunking exercise involves both art and science. There is more than one right answer. Review the list developed in the prior step and have the group reduce it to between 5 and 10 business processes. After you have reduced the list, place the processes on the front board, typically in the form of gerunds or verbals, and define the purpose of each process. Use the following guidelines:

- Look at the list for common nouns. Underline those referring to a common noun. Then, repeating the first activity, have the group define its purpose or goal—"*Why* do you do this?" Write the purpose next to the item. Continue with the next—if it has the same purpose, then it will roll up to a common process. When a number of items relate—due to a common purpose—have the group name the process. Put a visual box around the name for the process.
- Format process names as gerunds or verbals—a verb acting as a noun and usually ending with *-ing*, *-ment*, *-tion*, or *-ble*). Examples are accounts payable, budgeting, or resource generation.
- Avoid meaningless processes, such as management reporting, that have no specific goal. If the group includes a number of challenging processes, write the candidate titles as a side list of concerns and continue with additional activities. Revisit the problem areas or concerns later, after the group has developed some momentum.

Avoid letting the group simply define their organization. For example, insurance companies have a tendency to define their processes as underwriting, claims adjusting, and operations. What they do from a process perspective (regardless of how they are organized) is risk assessment, claims payment, portfolio management, and so forth.

Purpose of Each Process

Have the group define the purpose for each process—ensure that each purpose is distinct and a single purpose—not a process to "do this and to do that." Review all the goals with the group to ensure that the processes combine to support the business function.

- Define the purpose of each business process with the group.
  - Repeat the first step of this workshop: "The purpose of … is to …" for each of the process areas that have been identified.
- Consider using subteams to create the purpose statements and have them present and calibrate their work with the other subteams.

Activities of Each

This step duplicates the listing and analysis method described for the verb–noun (activities) step earlier. The main differences follow in the next step.

Process Life Cycle

- After gathering initial input as to what activities are performed to support the purpose, use *the plan, acquire, operate, and control* life cycle to help stimulate thinking about what activities may be missing.
- Identify in which category (plan, acquire, operate, control) each activity fits. Each activity fits into only one. Activities within a category roll up or stay separate depending on the goal of each process. Generally, you should find at least one to two planning, one to two acquiring, two or more operating, and one to two controlling activities for each process.
- Format activity names as "verb–noun" rather than gerunds or verbals. Examples of activities are open account or report discrepancies. If necessary, repeat the naming process, creating a separate purpose statement for any new processes discovered, and then push one level deeper toward the activity level.
- Each activity must occur only once—never the same process under multiple functions or the same activity under multiple processes.

Review and Wrap-Up

Follow the standard closure method (Review and Wrap-Up) discussed in Appendix A, "Structuring Your Workshop."

The Tools for Business Process Improvement: Budgets Workshop

Deliverable

At the end of the workshop, the participant will be able to develop a budget for any phase of the business process improvement project.

Simple Agenda

- Introduction
- Activities Supporting the Purpose of the Business Process Improvement
- Resources/*Whats*

- The *Costs* of Doing It
- *When* of the *What*s
- Impacts/Limits of Cost
- Wrap-Up

Introduction

See Appendix A, "Structuring Your Workshop."

- I am ...
- Our purpose today is to ...
- Our scope today is ...
- Our deliverable today is ...
- Administrivia
- Today's agenda is ...
- Ground Rules
- Ice Breaker

Activities Supporting the Purpose of the Business Process Improvement

The purpose of the business process improvement can be further broken down so that the participants have a clear understanding of what is required to support the purpose of the project. It may be useful to display the six phases of the Engage diagram (see Figure 3.1) and the responsibilities of the various teams to prompt the participants. A brainstorming approach can help generate answers. Some questions to create the supporting activities include the following:

- What do we need to do to get the business process improvement project off the ground?
- What do we need to do to complete the project?
- What do we need to do to host the workshops?
- What will we do when the business process improvement is completed?
- Do any of the teams have any special needs?
- Do we have the resources to complete each of the steps?

Resources/Whats

The budget comprises numeric projections. Each number represents the cost of resources required to support the business process improvement. The projections may be developed within the organization or derived from an external source. Use the activities and the purpose statement to focus the participants during the brainstorming sessions. For each activity identified in the previous step, ask the team, "*What* is needed to complete the activity regardless of how big or small?" The *what* may be a service or goods, tangible or intangible. Each activity may be associated with several *what*s. Use the questions below to prompt responses:

- What are some of the things we need to support the business process improvement activities identified above?
- What are some of the resources that we need to support the activities?
- Who needs to be involved with each business process improvement activity?
- Can these people (*who*) be involved full-time?
- Do we need to provide replacements for these people in their normal roles?
- Do we plan to work overtime?
- How many holidays occur during the project?
- Where do we need special help to complete each business process improvement activity?
- Do we need any external assistance?
- What events are we planning for the across each of the Engage phases? for the teams? for the staff? for the managers?
- Do we need any training? for the teams before, after, and during each Engage phase? for internal staff? for stakeholders?
- What are our specific needs for conference rooms, meeting rooms, stationery, Internet services, online tools, laptops, and other significant resource requests?

At the end of the responses, aggregate all the suggestions made. Remind the team that as the workshop continues they can keep adding to the list.

Costs

Each *what* is provided to the project at a cost. The cost may be already absorbed by the organization (eg, salary) or may be specific to the needs of the project (eg, hiring temporary staff to assist with the project). The team needs to understand the rules of cost allocation across the organization to confirm how they will be charged. For example, they may decide not to charge the project team the cost of staff team members since they were already budgeted for under the departments from which they came. Another organization may decide to charge the project for the use of the team members at a predetermined rate.

The team may not have all the information to generate the cost for each *what* and may need to research further. Table C.3 can be used to match each *what* with its costs.

Table C.3 Activity Costing

Activity	What/Resources Needed	Cost	Comment

Table C.4 Budget Phasing

BPI Phase	Total Cost	Start Date	End Date
1. Examine			
2. Negotiate			
3. Go For It			
4. Action			
5. Generate			
6. Engage			

When

The budget needs to be staged to match the phases of the project. Some costs may hold constant for each period (eg, salary costs). Other costs may be specific to particular phases of the project, such as the project launch, which only occurs once.

Since activities are already identified with the phases of the project, the phases of the project can be matched to costs. Work with the team to complete Table C.4 to match activities with the project phases. If the team has completed its project plan, then the phases can be matched with the plan so that the costs can be viewed on a periodic (eg, monthly) basis. The team can revisit the exercise to add time frames when the project plan is completed.

Impacts and Limits

Conduct a general discussion and overview of any constraints or limits.

Review and Wrap-Up

Follow the standard closure method (Review and Wrap-Up) discussed in Appendix A, "Structuring Your Workshop."

Process Selection Workshop

Deliverable

At the end of the workshop, we will have selected the core process for the business process improvement project.

Simple Agenda

- Introduction
- *What*s
- Matching to Goal
- Selection
- Review and Wrap-Up

Introduction

See Appendix A, "Structuring Your Workshop."

- I am ...
- Our purpose today is to ...
- Our scope today is ...
- Our deliverable today is ...
- Administrivia
- Today's agenda is ...
- Ground Rules
- Ice Breaker

Step 1: Importance—Establish What

The business/strategic plan, vision, mission, objectives, and goals identify *what* the organizations considers important over the next two years to life. The process management team needs to reacquaint itself with the planning documents to identify *what* is important. The purpose as developed earlier can also be used. URHere's real estate division had three main goals:

1. To increase the inventory of owned properties—income generation
2. To limit maintenance on properties—expense reduction
3. To increase the income of the division—value-add

Step 2: Matching—What to Process

Each goal or *what* is matched to the core processes to show the correlation between the process goals and the organization's goals.

The core processes of URHere's real estate division were mapped to its goals, as shown in Table C.5. This table shows that contracting contributes to the achievement of two of the stated goals, while asset disposition and maintenance relate to only one goal each. Based on the outcome, the team may select the contracting for improvement since it potentially generates the most impact.

Step 3: Selection—Competing Whats

When more than one process seems viable, a more sophisticated method that builds on Step 2 can be used.

1. Determine the core criteria of the goals—the real estate company identified income generation, market share, and expense reduction (see Table C.5). Be aware that the executive team may have additional and undocumented goals and objectives.
2. Attribute a weighting to each criteria. On a scale of 1 (lowest) to 5 (highest), determine the importance of each criterion to the organization's business plans. Discuss the weightings with the executive team, and get agreement before moving on.

Table C.5 Matching Goals and Processes

Goal/Process	Asset Disposition	Contracting	Maintenance
Increase the inventory by 20 percent	⊗		
Limit maintenance by 10 percent		⊗	⊗
Increase overall market share 20 percent		⊗	

Note: ⊗ indicates high match of goal with process.

Table C.6   Weighting Processes to Goals

Weight 1 to 5	Criteria	Asset Disposition	Maintenance	Contracting
4	Increase generation	3	2	5
3	Reducing expenses	3	5	4
5	Increase market share	5	3	3
	Total rate	11	10	12
	Weighted rate	46	38	47

Note: Contracting's score of 47 was calculated as follows:

(4 [weight] × 5 [increase generation score]) + (3 [weight] × 4 (reducing expenses score]) + (5 [weight] × 3 [increase market share score])

3. Match the criteria to the processes. Identify on a scale of 1 (lowest) to 5 (highest), the contribution that each core process makes to achievement of the set goals or criteria. Discuss the prioritization among the team and with the executive management to finalize the rating.
4. Calculate the total marks for each process—add the total marks assigned to each of the criteria.
5. Calculate the weighted total for each process—multiply the assigned marks by the weight applied to the goal, and then sum.

The division's weightings were agreed as shown in Table C.6. Each core process was matched to the criteria and assigned a number to represent the level of contribution made to each criterion. Contracting was selected as the primary process upon which to focus, as it received the highest rating of 47.

As long as the reasons behind the weighting of the criteria or goals and the scoring can be clearly explained, the prioritization methodology can stand up to scrutiny.

Core process selection is critical to the success of the business process improvement. Each team member must be able to explain exactly why the process was selected and the methodology for selection. Senior management needs to approve the choice before the team can progress. This ensures that any undocumented goals or criteria are brought to the foreground.

Review and Wrap-Up

Follow the standard closure method (Review and Wrap-Up) discussed in Appendix A, "Structuring Your Workshop."

Process Characteristics Workshop

Deliverable

At the end of the workshop, we will have a picture of the process, defined by the process inputs and outputs and their respective sources or customers. Prerequisites include the process workflow diagrams.

Simple Agenda

- Introduction
- Purpose of the Process
- Who Interacts
- Activities
- What Goes In
- What Comes Out
- Annotation
- SIPOC (*optional*; supplier, input, process, output, customer)
- Wrap-Up

Introduction

See Appendix A, "Structuring Your Workshop."

- I am …
- Our purpose today is to …
- Our scope today is …
- Our deliverable today is …
- Administrivia
- Today's agenda is …
- Ground Rules
- Ice Breaker

Purpose of the Process

You may develop the purpose outside the workshop and review it in the workshop for consensus. Preferably, develop a live view.

Purpose Written in Advance

- Sponsor or project manager drafts a statement of purpose.
- Mail the draft to all participants without identifying the author.

■ In the workshop, review the draft (written on a flip chart) and solicit comments from the participants until all agree with the wording. Hang the final statement on the wall.

Purpose Developed in the Workshop

■ Agree on a purpose of the organization by asking the group to state the purpose in 25 or fewer words. Start with, "The purpose of … is to … so that …" and let them finish the statement. This will be a run-on statement. Do not try to wordsmith the statement (get it perfect). Mount it on the wall.

Who Interacts

Use brainstorming for development.

■ Identify *who* (ie, people, systems, or organizations) is connected with the process.
■ To roll up the list, look at how each interacts with the process.
■ If the information both sent and received for multiple outsiders on the list is the same, then group the outsiders together at a higher level.
■ After the items are rolled up, get a definition for each item and have the documenter write each final outsider on a unique color or shaped Post-it® note.

Activities

■ After gathering initial input as to what activities are performed to support the purpose, use the plan, acquire, operate, and control life cycle to help stimulate thinking about what activities may be missing.
■ Identify in which category (plan, acquire, operate, control) each activity fits. Each activity fits into only one. Activities within a category roll up or stay separate depending on the goal of each process. Generally, you should find at least one to two planning, one to two acquiring, two or more operating, and one to two controlling activities for each process.
■ Format activity names as "verb–noun" rather than gerunds or verbals. Examples of activities are open account or report discrepancies. If necessary, repeat the naming process, creating a separate purpose statement for any new processes discovered, and then push one level deeper toward the activity level.
■ Each activity must occur only once—never the same process under multiple functions or the same activity under multiple processes.

What Comes In

- Use brainstorming to list possible inputs. Discuss each input—define, eliminate extraneous or redundant, and have the documenter write them onto small rectangles.
- To roll up the list, look at the information about each input. If the data are the same, the input is the same—even if it is coming from a different source. Roll up data elements (pieces of information about something) to the thing they define.

What Goes Out

- Use brainstorming to list possible outputs. Discuss each output—define, eliminate extraneous or redundant, and have the documenter write them onto small rectangular Post-it notes.
- To roll up the list, look at the information about each output. If the data are the same, the output is the same—even if it is coming from a different source. Break reports down to types of information—but not to individual reports. Roll up data elements (pieces of information about something) to the thing they define.

Annotation

Use a simple discussion process to build the model.

- Place the outsiders on a wall around the business shape (eg, a square with the name of the business on it). Identify which inputs and which outputs belong to each outsider by holding up one at a time. Make duplicates when an input or output is associated with more than one outsider.
- Do not draw lines from and to the outsiders—the colors of the small rectangles (eg, green is input, yellow is output) indicate the directions. Build a legend to help remember the direction.
- For any outsider that does not have an input or output—question if it belongs or if inputs or outputs are missing. Do the same for any input or output not associated with an outsider.

Review and Wrap-Up

Follow the standard closure method (Review and Wrap-Up) discussed in Appendix A, "Structuring Your Workshop."

Dreams of the Process Workshop

Deliverable

At the end of the workshop, we will have a defined vision, goals, objectives, and an action plan for the process.

Simple Agenda

- Introduction
- Vision
- Goals
- Skills and Resources
- Objectives
- Action Plan
- Responsibility Assignments
- Guardian of Change

Introduction

See Appendix A, "Structuring Your Workshop."

- Our purpose today is to …
- Our scope today is …
- Our deliverable today is …
- Administrivia
- Today's agenda is …
- Ground Rules
- Ice Breaker

Vision

Follow one of three options:

1. Develop before workshop—usually by the head of the organization—and review for consensus in the workshop.
2. Develop a draft before the workshop and modify in the workshop.
3. Use the creativity exercise—draw a picture of your business (a coat-of-arms picture is the most powerful) and extract a vision or purpose statement in the workshop.

Goals

Goals should be narrative. Use one of three methods, such as—

- Define a goal statement and then have the group use a creativity drawing exercise to draw their goals. Have each group describe their picture to the others and then capture the vision statement in narrative format on a flip chart using discussion.
- Prepare a draft vision statement (usually gathered from the senior manager of the group) and write it on a flip chart. Define a vision statement, then review the statement with the group and have them modify to meet their needs.
- Have the group develop a newspaper or magazine headline that they would like to see in a major newspaper on the date of the vision—ask, "What would the newspaper headline read on January 15, 20xx?" Have them embellish the headline with the story behind the headline. This headline and story provide the foundation for the goals.

Skills and Resources

Complete the gap analysis described earlier.

Objectives

- Describe the rules of ideation in the brainstorming process.
- Define objectives using a visual prompt.
- When the group seems to have exhausted the list, review each candidate objective carefully. Roll up the list by looking for common themes. Objectives may embrace the following:
  - Financial criteria
  - Employees
  - Customers
  - Stockholders
  - Product and product quality
  - Environment
  - How they manage the organization
- When the group exhausts the list, review each candidate carefully—aim for no more than 6 to 12 objectives.
- Review objectives and make them SMART. Do not show the SMART definition until after you have captured the raw input.
  - Specific
  - Measurable

- Adjustable and achievable (yet challenging)
- Relevant and realistic
- Time-based
■ Document the remaining objectives.

Action Plan

Complete the action items listed in the Action Plan found in Appendix A on page 251.

Responsibility Assignments

See the Responsibility Matrix described in Appendix B on page 256 for a discussion and illustration about how to make the assignments.

Guardian of Change

See the Guardian of Change described in Appendix B on page 258 for a discussion and illustration about how to conduct build the communications plan.

Review and Wrap-Up

Follow the standard closure method (Review and Wrap-Up) discussed on page 251 in Appendix A, "Structuring Your Workshop."

Strengths and Weaknesses Workshop

Deliverable

At the end of the workshop, we will have identified and defined the strengths, weaknesses, opportunities, and threats (SWOT) for the process.

Simple Agenda

■ Introduction
■ Strengths
■ Weaknesses
■ Opportunities
■ Threats
■ Assumptions
■ SWOT Analysis
■ Wrap-Up

Introduction

See Appendix A, "Structuring Your Workshop."

- I am …
- Our purpose today is to …
- Our scope today is …
- Our deliverable today is …
- Administrivia
- Today's agenda is …
- Ground Rules
- Ice Breaker

Strengths

Strengths are internal positives, especially as viewed by competitors or opposing forces. Using a brainstorming approach, identify, prioritize, and define the top six strengths, components within control that support reaching the objectives. Illustrate with examples from the organization.

Weaknesses

Weaknesses are internal negatives, especially as viewed by competitors or opposing forces. Using a brainstorming approach, identify, prioritize, and define the top six weaknesses, components within control that hinder the organization from reaching its objectives. Illustrate with examples from the organization.

Opportunities

Opportunities are external positives and beyond control, frequently trends. Using a brainstorming approach, identify, prioritize, and define the top six opportunities, components beyond control that support reaching the objectives. Illustrate with examples from the organization.

Threats

Threats are external negatives and beyond control, frequently trends. Using a brainstorming approach, identify, prioritize, and define the top six threats, components beyond control that hinder reaching the objectives. Illustrate with examples from the organization.

Assumptions

Ensure that your definitions provide ample evidence of how the strength, weakness, opportunity, or threat affects the organization. Concurrent with the activities above, capture the assumptions or constraints that must be considered when completing the analysis. Use the following headings to prompt discussion and input:

- Demographics—covers specific population groups, family composition, public-health issues
- Economics—includes finance, business, work and careers, and management
- Environment—includes resources, ecosystems, species, and habitats
- Government—includes world affairs, politics, laws, and policy
- Society—includes lifestyles, values, religion, leisure, culture, and education
- Technology—includes innovations, scientific discoveries, and their effects

If necessary, reduce each list into the top five to eight candidates and prioritize if desired, using Power Balls. The following ratings work in almost all situations:

5: high, means "will pay any price"
1: low, means "want it free; not willing to pay extra for it"
3: moderate, all the stuff in between, means "willing to pay a reasonable price" without being forced to define "reasonable"

SWOT Analysis

Look at each opportunity and threat (ie, external condition) and ask: "What should we do to take advantage of this opportunity (or defend us against this threat)?" As you agree on *what* to do, write it down. Summarize from the list and have the group identify *what* actions the group needs to take to reach their objectives.

For a more robust alternative, consult MG Rush's FAST facilitative leadership class (see Bibliography) for a quantitative method that requires a group scoring activity.

Review and Wrap-Up

Follow the standard closure method (Review and Wrap-Up) discussed in Appendix A, "Structuring Your Workshop."

Implementation Plan Workshop

Deliverable

At the end of the workshop, we will have determined the roles and responsibilities for the process implementation team members.

Simple Agenda

- Introduction
- Activities
- Priorities
- RASI (responsible, authorizes, supports, informed)
- Guardian of Change
- Wrap-Up

Introduction

See Appendix A, "Structuring Your Workshop."

- I am …
- Our purpose today is to …
- Our scope today is …
- Our deliverable today is …
- Administrivia
- Today's agenda is …
- Ground Rules
- Ice Breaker

Activities

Use a brainstorming approach to build details on the activities needed to complete the implementation.

Priorities

Using a simple method such as Power Balls, place the activities in a logical order of steps to be taken according to chronology or importance. The following ratings for Power Balls work in almost all situations:

5: high, means "will pay any price"

1: low, means "want it free; not willing to pay extra for it"

3: moderate, all the stuff in between, means "willing to pay a reasonable price" without being forced to define "reasonable"

Responsibility Assignments

See the Responsibility Matrix described in Appendix A on page 256 for a discussion and illustration about what to make the assignments.

Guardian of Change

See the Guardian of Change in Appendix B provided on page 258 for a discussion and illustration about how to build the communications plan.

Review and Wrap-Up

Follow the standard closure method (Review and Wrap-Up) discussed in Appendix A, "Structuring Your Workshop."

Wrap-Up Workshop

Deliverable

At the end of the workshop, the participants would be able to identify the successes and new learnings from the completed project. This approach can be used at any phase of the project to identify lessons learned.

Simple Agenda

- Introduction
- Objectives
- Issues
- Root Cause Analysis
- Helped and Hampered
- Wrap-Up

Introduction

See Appendix A, "Structuring Your Workshop."

- I am …
- Our purpose today is to …
- Our scope today is …
- Our deliverable today is …
- Administrivia
- Today's agenda is …
- Ground Rules
- Ice Breaker

Success Objectives

Compare results with the SMART objectives. What worked and what hampered are identified as input for later discussion.

Goals and considerations: Other results are compared with the fuzzy goals and considerations. What worked and what hampered are captured as input for later discussion.

Issues

Questions are asked about why certain actions were taken, how stakeholders reacted, why adjustments were made (or not), what assumptions developed, and other questions as appropriate. Consider the following for example:

- I did not like …
- I think that … could have been done better.
- … did not work well for the project.
- Sometimes …
- I feel that …
- If I had to do this again I would never …
- Our team never should …
- I think that … worked very well.
- I think that … was a major achievement.
- I felt proud that our team …
- Our team did well to …
- If I had to do this again, I would repeat …

Root Cause Analysis

Various methods exist to support a root cause analysis, also known as Ishikawa diagram or fishbone diagram. At the complex extreme, a Sig Sigma project might be chartered to determine the various causes, risk factors, and probabilities. At the simple extreme, take any problem and ask, "*Why* did that occur" five consecutive times. Eventually you will move from the symptom (eg, it broke) to the cause (eg, stressed it) to the root cause (eg, equipment was not properly calibrated).

What We Learned

Input from the root cause analysis stimulates discussion about options and conditions to be leveraged in subsequent projects. Assess or build a risk management plan and other next steps or actions (eg, guardian of change) by the team.

Lead a structured discussion about lessons learned by breaking up the general subject into the following specific topical areas and questions:

- Based on our experience, what do we know that is new?
- Based on our experience, what should we come to accept as true regarding ...
  - Assumptions?
  - Rules?
  - Standards?
- Based on our experience, what do we think should be adopted or created as something "new"?

Review and Wrap-Up

Follow the standard closure method (Review and Wrap-Up) discussed in Appendix A, "Structuring Your Workshop."

Appendix D: Workshop Ice Breaker and Warm-Up Activities

Batons, Jam, and Tape Activity

Purpose

At the end of the lesson, the participants will be able to analyze the non-value-added activities in the core process.

Learnings

- Definitions of non-value-added activities
- How non-value-added activities manifest themselves in the process

When to Use

- When the team is understanding the process
- When team is designing the new process

Timing

30 minutes

Resources

- Bottle of jam
- Relay baton
- Roll of transparent tape

- Note paper for each participant
- Pens for each participant

Instructions

Team works in smaller groups to discover new ways of looking at batons, jam, and tape. Facilitator challenges the participants to find as many meanings/definitions of the words as possible.

Discussion

Facilitator leads the team to identify batons as handovers, the tape as bureaucracy or red tape, and the jam as delays in the process.

Variations

Teams are asked to compose sentences using the terms *baton*, *jam*, and *tape*. The sentences should relate to the process.

Business Process Improvement Cartoon Activity

Purpose

At the end of the session, the participants will be able to demystify the things they have heard about business process improvement.

Learnings

- Establishes how business process improvement is viewed in the organization
- Identifies any doubts the team may have about the process
- Highlights possible areas/pockets of resistance

When to Use

- When the concept of business process improvement needs to be explained
- When a team is hesitant to embrace the concept and its merits
- When there is a need to unearth resistance to the concept

Timing

30 minutes

Resources

- Flip chart paper for each group
- Markers for each group
- Easel and flip chart paper for the facilitator

Instructions

Participants are paired and asked to draw a cartoon depicting what they know or have heard or have experienced with business process improvement. Teams present and explain the cartoons to the larger group. Teams can then discuss the impact of their cartoons on the larger organization and how they can mitigate the negative statements and promote the positive statements.

Discussion

Facilitator asks team:

- How do the cartoons reflect the impact of business process improvement on the larger organization?
- What is the general feeling toward business process improvement by the organization?
- What actions can be taken to mitigate the impact of the negative statements?
- What can be done to promote the positive statements about business process improvement?

Variations

Around the cooler or coffee machine—participants are given a picture of people around the water cooler and are asked to fill in the speech balloons with the conversation about business process improvement.

Carry Me Activity

Purpose

The purpose of this activity is to examine the characteristics of a process and how they can be improved.

Learnings

- That there is more than one way to achieve results
- That sometimes we think about one way only

When to Use

- During process design
- When examining existing processes

Timing

30 minutes

Resources

- Ball for each group
- Easel and flip chart paper

Instructions

Participants are split into groups of three or four. Each group is told to pass an object from the first person to the last. The group is given a practice run and then timed. The group is asked to find the fastest way to get the object from the first to the last person in the group (each group member must touch the object).

Discussion

Facilitator leads the group:

- Map the experience to the list of process characteristics
- How did the group achieve its fastest time?
- What parts of the original process were changed to achieve the fastest time?
- What in the group's thinking changed to achieve the fastest result?

Coin Toss Activity

Purpose

At the end of the lesson, the team will be able to use feedback to improve the process.

Learnings

Feedback can be a corrective or destructive tool

When to Use

- When team is interacting with stakeholders
- During design of feedback mechanism (audit) for the process

Timing

30 minutes

Resources

- Coins
- Big box
- Easel and paper

Instructions

The objective of the game is to get as many coins into the box as possible. Three blindfolded volunteers take turns to toss coins into the box. The rest of the participants observe the game with the following rules:

1. For the first participant they are to give no feedback.
2. For the second participant they are to jeer and give negative comments. No assistance is given.
3. For the third participant they are to give instructions that will assist in the coin toss and to cheer on the member's efforts.

The volunteers are not allowed into the room until it is their turn to toss. When the volunteer has completed the toss, they join the audience. The number of successful tosses that each participant made is noted.

Discussion

Each volunteer is asked how he or she felt about the observers' reactions, and the impact of their reactions on their coin toss. The groups discuss the following:

1. What the effects of feedback are on the group.
2. How they can handle the impact of negative feedback.
3. How to build feedback mechanisms that can create positive criticism for the team.

Do You Know Me? Activity

Purpose

This activity is used to identify why the team members were selected for the business process improvement project (to be used with all new teams) and for group members to be more familiar with each other.

Learnings

Skills or attributes of the group

When to Use

Whenever new groups are being formed

Timing

15 minutes

Resources

- Sticky notes for each team member
- Pens for each team member
- Box for collection of the notes

Instructions

Participants introduce themselves by name and state three facts about themselves. After the introductions, the facilitator asks the team questions based on the presentations made, such as, Who loves to dance? Who graduated 15 years ago?

Participants cannot answer questions about themselves correctly (they can suggest other names). The person with the correct answer receives an item (a sweet, a matchstick). At the end of the game the person with the most items wins.

Discussion

Facilitator asks group:

- What did we learn new about each other?
- What can we put to use in the business process improvement presentations to the wider organization?

Variations

Each participant can stand in front of the group and ask three questions. These are close-ended questions: the answer must be definite, such as, "Who graduated from xxx university"? Team members by show of hands answer the questions. The team member with the most votes wins.

Fairy Tales Activity

Purpose

At the end of the lesson, the team will determine the best advice they can give to another business process improvement team.

Learnings

- What works for the business process improvement project
- What does not work for the business process improvement project

When to Use

- When reviewing a project
- At the end of an exercise

Timing

30 minutes

Resources

- Flip chart paper for each group
- Markers for each group
- Easel

Instructions

Participants are split into groups. Each group is asked to develop a poster using a popular fairy tale to inform others of the highs and lows of the business process improvement project or of teamwork. Groups share comments with the wider team.

Discussion

Facilitator leads teams in discussion:

- Why did the team choose its specific fairly tale?
- In what ways did the team identify with the fairy tale?
- Are there any unresolved issues that the team did not deal with?
- Any challenges that are unresolved by the team are brainstormed in the larger group for solutions.

Variations

Groups are given posters of fairy tales and are asked to correlate the fairy tale to the business process improvement project.

Fear Activity

Purpose

At the end of the lesson, the participants will be able to determine which behaviors in the organization may reflect fear.

Learnings

- What people fear most
- How fear is overcome

When to Use

Whenever resistance is being experienced in a group

Timing

45 minutes

Resources

- Note paper for each member
- Pens for each member
- Flip chart paper for each group
- Markers for each group

Instructions

Participants are paired up. Each participant will draw a picture of one thing that they feared as a child, whether real or imagined. They explain the effects that the specific fear had on them as a child and how they were able to put the fear to rest as they grew older.

Discussion

Facilitator leads the sharing:

- What were the common fears in the group?
- Why were participants afraid of these things?
- How were the fears overcome?

The group then matches the documented childhood behaviors to the behaviors that are seen in the organization and are asked to consider if fear may be at the root of some of the behavior. Groups are asked to brainstorm ways to assist the organization to deal with the fear of the business process improvement.

Variations

The facilitator can distribute scary pictures and ask the team to match the pictures to behaviors that are seen in the organization.

Getting to Know You Activity

Purpose

At the end of the session, the participants will be able to demystify the things they have heard about business process improvement and to assist team members to be comfortable with each other.

Learnings

Skills or attributes of the group

When to Use

Whenever new groups are being formed

Timing

15 minutes

Resources

- Sticky notes for each team member
- Pens for each team member
- Box for collection of the notes

Instructions

Participants are given Know You cards and are asked to walk around talking to each other. During the conversation, each participant tries to get the other to confirm a fact on the card. When the fact on the card is confirmed, the card is initialed by the person to whom it relates. More than one person can sign a card. The person with the most signatures wins.

Participants will discuss the activity and their new knowledge about each other.

Discussion

Facilitator asks group:

- Did we learn anything new about each other?
- Is there anything that we can put to use in the business process improvement presentations to the wider organization?

Variations

The person(s) with the least amount of paper need to learn one thing about each team member before the end of the day.

Glass of Wine Activity

Purpose

At the end of the lesson, the participants will be able to develop a success checklist for the project.

Learnings

- Success checklist—the answers will be used to generate a success checklist and to set some goals for the process.
- Each participant has a clear vision of what a successful process looks like.

When to Use

When the team is engaged in process design for visioning the process

Timing

One hour

Instructions

Participants chat about their favorite wine and why. Facilitator plays soft music and asks participants to close their eyes and imagine that they are on a terrace overlooking the sea, the sun is setting, and they are having a glass of their favorite wine. The project is over and they are discussing the success with their significant other. What made the process an outstanding success? What are some of the things that are happening that makes the specific claim true?

Discussion

The team responses are used to generate a success checklist for the process.

Facilitator leads group to use the checklist to develop SMART (specific, measurable, achievable and adjustable, realistic and relevant, time-based) objectives for the process.

Variations

Teams can compose a column for the internal newsletter on the improved process. From the articles, the facilitator can lead the team on a discussion to generate a success list and objectives for the process.

Group Car Crash Activity

Purpose

At the end of the lesson, the participants will be able to determine how we choose the processes to be worked on.

Learnings

- That informal review as a selection technique may be inadequate
- That a scientific approach is needed to select the process for improvement

When to Use

- When selecting the process
- To justify the process selected for improvement

Timing

30 minutes

Resources

- Pictures for each team
- Flip chart paper for each group
- Markers for each group

Instructions

Participants are given four pictures of damaged cars and are asked to work in pairs to determine the rank of urgency for repairing the cars. Participants need to explain the reasons for the decisions made. Answers are shared with larger group and the criteria for selection discussed.

Discussion

Facilitator asks the group:

- How did the group select the car for improvement?
- How can we ensure that we are selecting the "correct car" for improvement?
- Recommend more scientific approaches to the selection process.

Participants are asked to relate the discussion above to the selection of processes to be worked on.

Variations

Cost estimates are given for each repair job. Participants are asked to determine which vehicle should be repaired. Facilitator leads discussion to show that the cost may not be the only factor. Performance after repairs, annual maintenance fee, and others may be considerations for which vehicle to be improved.

Group Directions Activity

Purpose

At the end of the lesson, participants will be able to describe why a workflow diagram is important.

Learnings

- Why accurate mapping is important
- Considerations for the operator to follow the mapping

When to Use

- When the team is developing workflow diagrams for the process
- When team is documenting a procedure

Timing

30 minutes

Resources

- Notes paper for each team member
- Pens for each team member
- Easel and flip chart paper

Instructions

Participants are paired and asked to draw a map showing the way to the restrooms in 30 seconds. Participants exchange directions and each person is told to follow the directions exactly as shown on the map. Team regroups in five minutes and discuss where the map took them.

Discussion

Facilitator leads the discussion:

- Why did the maps work?
- Why did the maps not work?

The reasons that the maps worked and did not work are identified and discussed. Participants establish ground rules for drawing maps. Exercise is repeated to see if the ground rules make a difference to the outcome.

Variations

A Google® map of a common location is given. Map could be directions to the office or a popular landmark. Facilitator leads team to discuss what makes the map work or any perceived difficulties that a novice operator may have with the map.

Group Resumé Activity

Purpose

To identify why the team members were selected for the business process improvement project (to be used with all new teams)

Learnings

Team members learn about each others' skills and competencies.

When to Use

- Whenever a new team is formed
- When crossing over from the business process improvement team to the process improvement team
- When new members join an existing team

Timing

30 minutes

Resources

- Flip chart paper for each subgroup
- Markers for each subgroup

- Tape to attach presentations
- Easel(s)

Instructions

Facilitator splits participants into two or three groups. Facilitator tells group that each person was selected to join the BPI team because of his or her specific skills, education, position, and so forth. Each team will create a team résumé that highlights the collective experience of the group and explains why the members were chosen to participate in the business process improvement project. The team is encouraged to boast about its accomplishments. The team can develop a name to match the résumé—for example, Stacy Know It All. No real names are to be used. Each group writes the résumés on large flip chart paper and makes a presentation to the larger groups.

Discussion

Facilitator then leads a discussion on the shared characteristics and how their talents augur well for the success of the group.

Facilitator asks the group:

- What are the shared characteristics of the groups?
- How do their characteristics contribute to the project's success?

Variations

Team can make a list of the negative characteristics they possess and discuss how their tendencies can limit the team's or project's success. Use at the end of each project phase.

Hair Dye Activity

Purpose

To identify a method for implementing a new procedure or process

Learnings

Steps taken to introduce something new

When to Use

- Before implementation
- To analyze an implementation plan or procedure

Timing

30 minutes

Resources

- Packs of hair dye
- Easel and flip chart paper

Instructions

Participants are giving the instructions from an over-the-counter hair dye product and asked to discuss the process and how the operator is advised to implement the solution. Participants are advised to think of the new process as the dye for the organization that will change the existing color of the organization. Participants are asked the lesson learned from the hair dye manufacturer.

Discussion

Facilitator leads the team to identify the suggested steps such as test a small portion, wait and see, analyze results, if happy proceed, if not happy discontinue use.

Participants are asked to list the benefit of sampling a small area of hair and the benefit of the sampling approach in their process situation.

Variations

Clothing dye can be used.

Jack-in-the-Box Activity

Purpose

To identify some of the assumptions that we make about the way that work is done and why it is done

Learnings

Participants have some level of control in their jobs

When to Use

- When defining barriers to change
- When identifying the rules or assumptions made in the organization
- When challenging teams to be creative or to think outside the box

Timing

30 minutes

Resources

- Boxes—one per participant
- Chalk
- Easel and paper

Instructions

Draw boxes on the floor for each participant. Participants stand in boxes and think of the boxes as the job or workplace that prevents them from being creative. Participants pair with people closest to them and share thoughts about how they live in a box at work. Pairs take turns suggesting how the other can step out of the box. Group shares their ideas. Participants destroy boxes afterward.

Discussion

Facilitator leads group to share ideas:

- What are some of the things that prevent us from being creative in the workplace?
- What were some of the ideas to change the roadblocks?
- How can I make a difference in the workplace or in how I do my job?

Variations

Each participant identifies four things in the organization that limit their creativity or ability to function to the fullest. As they say each thing, they draw a side of the box around them. Participants are then asked to determine four ways to remove the sides of the box so that they and be set free. The group shares the ideas and looks for commonality of thought.

Jobs Activity

Purpose

To examine the roles within the process

Learnings

- Each job requires specific skills and competencies
- Skills and competencies are transferrable across jobs

When to Use

- When specifying roles for the process
- When examining existing roles in the process

Timing

Depends on size of group

Resources

Visual prompt and paper

Instructions

Participants are given a list of job titles and are told to select two jobs that appeal to them and two jobs that they do not want to do. For each job selected they will list the strengths and weaknesses that make them ideal or less than ideal for the job. They will then examine the strengths and see how the strengths contribute to their current jobs.

Discussion

Facilitator leads groups through discussion:

- Are the jobs that appeal to you similar or different from the job that you are doing now?
- In what ways are the jobs similar or different?
- How can the existing skills be transferred to the new jobs?
- What new skills will have to be learned to be able to conduct these jobs?

Language Activity

Purpose

At the end of the session, participants will be able to identify barriers to communication.

Learnings

- Communication methods that work
- Debriefing—indicates to the group how the language is just as important as the message

When to Use

When the team is going to engage stakeholders

Timing

30 minutes

Resources

Easel and flip chart paper

Instructions

Participants work in pairs. Each participant is given a simple sentence to communicate the meaning of to his or her partner. The speaker must use a simple language that they have invented. Each person takes turns to communicate the sentence with a partner, stopping only when the partner has correctly received the message.

Discussion

Facilitator asks the group:

- How did it feel for the message not to be received?
- How did it feel not being able to understand what was said to you?
- What did you do to effectively communicate the message?
- What lessons can we take from language challenges when engaging a wider audience?

License Plates Activity

Purpose

To gauge team feelings about the business process improvement thus far, and to identify where and with whom additional team building may be needed

Learnings

- The state of the team—norming, storming, or forming
- The state of the business process improvement project

When to Use

- After the team has worked together on a few sessions
- When there is dissent among team members

Timing

30 minutes

Resources

- 3 × 6-inch (or 4 × 8-inch) paper for each team member
- Pens for each team member

Instructions

Participants work in groups to design alphanumeric license plates. At the end of the exercise, participants will have a license plate that conveys their feelings about the business process improvement and how it affects them, for example, IMCRE8V—I am creative.

Discussion

Facilitator leads participants in the discussion:

- What were some of the responses to the license plates presented?
- How can we maximize on the positive statements made?
- How can we reduce the effect of the negative statements made?
- What were the lessons learned from the exercise?

Variations

Team members are instructed to make bumper stickers. Bumper stickers are attached to their rear (backs of shirts or pants bottoms). Music is played and members are invited to walk around the room in time to the music.

Making Excuses Activity

Purpose

At the end of the lesson, participants will be able to design procedures to deal with particular shortcomings of a process.

Learnings

- Why excuses are made
- How a process can eliminate the veracity of excuses

When to Use

- When building procedures
- When examining reasons for failure of a procedure or process

Timing

15 minutes

Resources

- Flip chart paper for each group
- Markers for each group

Instructions

Team is split into groups. Each group is asked to make a list of excuses for not completing a task. Each group is encouraged to focus on a specific excuse and come up with ways to eliminate the excuse. Group repeats the process for two other excuses.

Discussion

Facilitator leads discussion:

- What is common about the excuses?
- Are there solutions for the excuses?
- How can we build the procedures to limit the use of the excuses?

Variations

Each group is asked to come up with the most ridiculous excuse (20 words), and the most ridiculous excuse wins a prize.

Measure Me Activity

Purpose

At the end of the lesson, the participants will be able to define the elements of a measuring system.

Learnings

Measuring systems that exist within the organization

When to Use

When the team is defining the measurements

Timing

30 minutes

Resources

- Note paper for each participant
- Pens for each participant

Instructions

Place a ruler or measuring tape and a pair of scales at the front of the class. Team is asked to examine the items and to think about the different uses of them and the professions that use them.

Discussion

Facilitator asks the team:

- What professions use the items?
- What are the items used for?
- Are these measuring systems and why?
- What are the characteristics of these measuring systems?

Team is asked to identify the measuring systems within the organization and their characteristics.

Variations

Facilitator can lead the team through a brainstorming exercise to generate examples of measuring systems that are common in everyday life.

Musical Composition Activity

Purpose

To look at the way that processes may emerge or form

Learnings

That a process may emerge from a chaotic situation

When to Use

- When defining the process
- When understanding how processes emerge

Timing

45 minutes

Resources

A variety of portable office equipment for each team: pens, pencils, notepads, and other office equipment

Instructions

Each participant selects an item from the box of office items. Participants are split into groups. Groups are asked to play the instruments all at once. The groups are then told to make music with the office items and compose a short tune. Each group will note their music using symbols to indicate the movement of the music, such as slow. Groups will then play their compositions for the entire team.

Discussion

Facilitator leads discussion about the activity:

- How was the tune composed?
- What are some of the strategies used to form the group?
- How can we relate the experience to process development?

Variations

Facilitator plays a piece of music and each group is told to reproduce the music and play the composition for the entire team.

Objects Activity

Purpose

To highlight the internal and external challenges that the organization may face

Learnings

- That safe situations may be unsafe
- That unsafe situations can be controlled or mitigated against

When to Use

- When analyzing a new opportunity
- When identifying a new challenge or threat to the organization

Timing

30 minutes

Resources

- Notes for each participant
- Pens for each participant
- Easel and paper
- Sharp/dangerous objects
- Safe objects

Instructions

Participants are divided into groups. Each group gets a safe object and a dangerous object. Participants write down descriptions of the safe and dangerous objects. The descriptions are shared with the group. Participants are then asked to use the descriptions and the objects to generate sentences about what they consider safe in the organization and what they consider risky. The statements can be made about anything within or external to the company.

Discussion

Facilitator then leads the discussion:

- Under what conditions can a safe object become unsafe?
- Under what conditions can an unsafe object become safe?
- Can we make any links between the activity and the SWOT analysis?

Relay Activity

Purpose

At the end of the lesson, the participants will be able to identify elements of an efficient process.

Learnings

Characteristics of an efficient and effective process

When to Use

- When the team is creating or improving a process
- When the team is identifying non-value-added activities in a process

Timing

15 minutes

Resources

- DVD of an Olympic relay race
- Easel and paper

Instructions

A video clip of an Olympic relay event is shown. Participants work in groups to describe what made the winning team different and what happened during the race. The activities and what is noticed in the relay are also discussed.

Discussion

Facilitator leads the group to the following outcomes: efficient handover, each runner holds the baton once, does something unique, has a unique purpose, but could probably run the whole race or any part of the race. The team is encouraged to design a process that looks like an Olympic relay race.

Variations

A rowing team can be used.

Relay Race Activity

Purpose

At the end of the session, the team will identify the reasons for role definition within the business process improvement team.

Learnings

- The roles of people within the team
- Characteristics of the process

When to Use

- When identifying the process characteristics
- In-process design
- Helping the group come to a mutual plan

Timing

30 minutes

Resources

Sticky notes and pens

Instructions

Participants are shown a picture of a relay team and asked to explain what happens within the relay. The role of each member on the relay team—starter, anchor, and runner—is defined.

Discussion

Facilitator leads the team in the discussion:

- How do the roles in the relay team relate to the players in the process?
- What are the inputs to the process?
- What is the purpose of the relay?
- What are the outputs?

Relate the relay race to the existing process and what makes it work or not work as effectively as a relay team. Management may start and determine the process, and staff use the process on a daily basis.

Variations

A picture of a rowing team can be used to demonstrate that if the team pulls together the stated objectives will be achieved. When pulling together does not happen, the team will not achieve the objective.

Say It Again Activity

Purpose

At the end of the lesson, the team will be able to determine why the business process improvement message needs to be clearly communicated.

Learnings

- To communicate effectively to various audiences
- Team relates how to communicate with stakeholders to ensure that the stakeholders receive the accurate message about the business process improvement

When to Use

Before any communication or interaction with stakeholders

Timing

30 minutes

Resources

None required

Instructions

Team stands in a circle. Facilitator gives the person on the right a typed message. Person then whispers the message in the other person's ear once. This is repeated around the group until the message returns to the facilitator.

Discussion

Team discusses what went wrong with the message and how to ensure that from the start to the end of the circle the message is accurately received and repeated. The game is played again using the lessons learned from the discussion.

Team relates how to communicate with stakeholders to ensure that the stakeholders receive the accurate message about the business process improvement.

Variations

Teams can be split into groups. Each group is given a sentence and asked to communicate the sentence to the other group without using words. Facilitator leads discussion on what worked and did not work for the group.

Share Your Dreams Activity

Purpose

Icebreaker

Learnings

We all have dreams.

When to Use

- When team needs to be creative
- When team seems stuck

Timing

15 minutes

Resources

- Easel
- Flip chart paper

Instructions

Facilitator writes on the flip chart paper: "If I was not a … I would have been a … " Participants are asked to fill in the blanks with a present state that they are in and what they may dream of doing.

Discussion

Facilitator leads team through discussion:

- Are what we are doing now and what we want to do mutually exclusive?
- Is there any way that we can accommodate what we want to do in our present lives?
- What can we do to achieve our dreams?

Bibliography

Ackermann, F., C. Eden, and I. Brown. 2005. *The Practice of Making Strategy: A Step-by-Step Guide*. Thousand Oaks, CA: Sage Publications.

Ambler, S. 2002. *Agile Modeling: Effective Practices for eXtreme Programming and the Unified Process*. Hoboken, NJ: John Wiley.

Andrews, D. C. and N. S. Leventhal. 1993. *Fusion: Integrating IE, CASE, and JAD—A Handbook for Reengineering the Systems Organization.* Upper Saddle River, NJ: Prentice-Hall.

Beck, K. and C. Andres. 2004. *Extreme Programming Explained: Embrace Change*. Upper Saddle River, NJ: Addison-Wesley.

Cameron, J. 1992. *The Artist's Way: A Spiritual Path to Higher Creativity*. New York, NY: G. P. Putnam's Sons/Tarcher.

Cockburn, A. 2004. *Crystal Clear: A Human-Powered Methodology for Small Teams*. Upper Saddle River, NJ: Addison-Wesley.

Dyer, J., H. Gregerson, and C. M. Christensen. 2011. *The Innovator's DNA: Mastering Five Skills of Disruptive Innovators*. Boston, MA: Harvard Business Press.

Erard, M. 2007. *Um, Slips, Stumbles, and Verbal Blunders, and What They Mean*. New York, NY: Pantheon Books.

Galbraith, J., D. Downey, and A. Kates. 2001. *Designing Dynamic Organizations: A Hands-on Guide for Leaders at All Levels*. New York, NY: AMACOM.

Goldratt, E. M. 2004. *The Goal: A Process of Ongoing Improvement*. Great Barrington, MA: North River Press.

Gordon, T. 2001. *Leadership Effectiveness Training: Proven Skills for Leading Today's Business into Tomorrow*. New York, NY: Perigee.

Hammer, M. and J. Champy. 2003. *Reengineering the Corporation: A Manifesto for Business Revolution*. New York, NY: HarperBusiness.

Hammer, M. and S. S. Stanton. 1995. *The Reengineering Revolution: A Handbook*. New York, NY: HarperBusiness.

Harrington, J. H., E. Esseling, and H. van Nimwegen. 1997. *Business Process Improvement Workbook: Documentation, Analysis, Design, and Management of Business Process Improvement*. New York, NY: McGraw-Hill.

Highsmith, J. 2004. *Agile Project Management: Creating Innovative Products*. Upper Saddle River, NJ: Pearson.

Hurson, T. 2007. *Think Better: An Innovator's Guide to Productive Thinking*. New York, NY: McGraw-Hill.

Jeston, J. and J. Nelis. 2006. *Business Process Management, Second Edition: Practical Guidelines to Successful Implementations*. Cambridge, MA: Elsevier.

Kotler, P. and F. de Bes. 2003. *Lateral Marketing: New Techniques for Finding Breakthrough Ideas*. Hoboken, NJ: John Wiley and Sons.

Lefton, R. and V. Buzzotta. *Leadership through People Skills*. (New York, NY: McGraw Hill, 2004).

Lipton, B. H. 2008. *The Biology of Belief: Unleashing the Power of Consciousness, Matter, and Miracles*. Carlsbad, CA: Hay House.

Means, J. A. and T. Adams. 2005. *Facilitating the Project Lifecycle*. San Francisco, CA: Jossey-Bass.

Metz, T. and G. Rush. 2011. *FAST+: Session Leader Reference Manual*. Oak Brook, IL: Mimeo.

Moore, G. A. 2005. *Dealing with Darwin: How Great Companies Innovate at Every Phase of Their Evolution*. New York, NY: Penguin Group.

Morgan, M., R. E. Levitt, and W. A. Malek. 2006. *Executing Your Strategy: How to Break It Down and Get It Done*. Boston, MA: Harvard Business School Press.

Naisbitt, J., 2006. *Mind Set!: Reset Your Thinking and See the Future*. New York, NY: Collins Publishing.

Nielsen, M. A. 2011. *Reinventing Discovery: The New Era of Networked Science*. Princeton, NJ: Princeton University Press.

Poppendieck, M. and T. Poppendieck. 2007. *Implementing Lean Software Development: From Concept to Cash*. Upper Saddle River, NJ: Addison-Wesley.

Sayer, N. J. and B. Williams. 2007. *Lean for Dummies*. Hoboken, NJ: Wiley Publishing.

Schwaber, K. 2004. *Agile Project Management with Scrum*. Redmond, WA: Microsoft Press.

Schwarz, R., A. Davidson, P. Carlson, and S. McKinney. 2005. *The Skilled Facilitator Fieldbook: Tips, Tools, and Tested Methods for Consultants, Facilitators, Managers, Trainers, and Coaches*. San Francisco, CA: Jossey-Bass.

Shook, J. 2008. *Managing to Learn: Using the A3 Management Process to Solve Problems, Gain Agreement, Mentor, and Lead*. Cambridge, MA: Lean Enterprise Institute.

Tabaka, J. 2006. *Collaboration Explained: Facilitation Skills for Software Project Leaders*. Upper Saddle River, NJ: Addison-Wesley.

Tenner, A. R. and I. J. DeToro. 2000. *Process Redesign: The Implementation Guide for Managers*. Upper Saddle, NJ: Prentice Hall.

Van Gundy, A. B. 1998. *101 Great Games and Activities*. San Francisco, CA: Jossey-Bass.

Watkins, J. M., B. J. Mohr, and R. Kelly. 2001. *Appreciative Inquiry: Change at the Speed of Imagination*. San Francisco, CA: Jossey-Bass.

Westcott, R. T. 2005. *The Certified Manager of Quality/Organizational Excellence Handbook*. Milwaukee, WI: ASQ Quality Press.

Whitney, D. and A. Trosten-Bloom. 2003. *The Power of Appreciative Inquiry: A Practical Guide to Positive Change*. San Francisco, CA: Berrett-Koehler Publishers.

Wilkinson, M. 2004. *The Secrets of Facilitation: The S.M.A.R.T. Guide to Getting Results with Groups*. San Francisco, CA: Jossey-Bass.

Womack, J. P. and D. T. Jones. 1991. *The Machine That Changed the World: The Story of Lean Production*. New York, NY: Harper Perennial.

Womack, J. P. and D. T. Jones. 2003. *Lean Thinking: Banish Waste and Create Wealth in Your Corporation*. New York, NY: Free Press.

Zarefsky, D. *Argumentation: 2005. The Study of Effective Reasoning*. Chantilly, VA: The Teaching Company.

Glossary

This glossary is provided as a service to the business process improvement community. The business process improvement vocabulary is a critical tool in communicating the consensual purpose, means, and results of your efforts. We have built the following vocabulary and use it ourselves. Many of the terms have been thrashed about repeatedly. We believe the following glossary provides a solid foundation for executives, managers, and other stakeholders. Instructions for linking to the glossary are at the bottom of this page. We invite you to link to this page and help establish a common vocabulary among your community, provided as a service by Morgan Madison and Company and eink Global.

For the most current glossary, navigate to the websites www.einkglobal.com and MGRush.com and download or link to the most current and up-to-date version.

Action plan: A matrix that matches actions leading to a required outcome including the *who*, the *what,* and the *when*.

Activity: A series of steps carried out in response to a business event such as receiving an invoice. Activities have definite starts and stops. Activities describe *what* needs to happen rather than *how* it may happen. Paying bills or accelerating are examples of *what*, while writing checks or pushing the gas pedal with your foot are examples of *how*. *What* items are abstract and hard to visualize, while *how* items are concrete and more easily visualized.

Alignment: Matching of goals, objectives, and vision to ensure that the achievement of any does not promote conflict in the use of resources or curtail the achievement of the others. The forming of relationships between activities and objectives to note any inconsistencies or gaps that may require a modification or addition to a plan. Mutual agreement and consensus among the project team and key stakeholders on the direction of a project, the options, and other factors. Without alignment, the change process often stalls or fails.

Assumptions: The unstated beliefs about how and why the process is designed; governs who does what in the process.

Audit: Independent and neutral test of the efficiency and effectiveness of a stated process.

Audit team: Group of people responsible for conducting the audit. May be internal or external to the process.

Benchmark: Comparative ranking of the process and its outputs, measurements, and outcome to similar processes in other organizations.

Bottleneck: Any point in the process where activities are slowed.

BPI plan: Document presented to the executive team to get approval for the BPI (ie, business process improvement) project. Includes the reason for the selected process and how the team intends to improve the process.

Business process improvement: The simplification and clarification of the way that people interact with (other) processes, people, and technology to achieve an organization's vision.

Champion: Member of the management team who is supportive of the business process improvement team and its efforts. Someone who takes a passionate interest in promoting a particular solution such as a new process or product.

Change management: The recognition that the unknown changes to the selected process will generate different levels of unease among stakeholders and the conscious implementation of mitigation strategies to resolve the issues that may evolve from their discomfort. Change management is a planned process, with a set of tools and key questions for managing the people side of change so that project goals are achieved on time and on budget, safely implemented, and accepted by stakeholders.

Communications plan: Identifies exactly how and when the business process improvement teams will interact with the target audience over the life of the project. Usually far more extensive than e-mails, the communications plan uses several channels to update, inform, and request feedback from stakeholders. The communications plan identifies the messages about the changes that need to be spread through the organization. These include both the business messages (why the organization is undertaking the changes, risks of not making the changes, etc.) and the personal messages (how the project impacts a person's day-to-day work). The channels may include e-postcards, e-magazines, updates, surveys, posters, and websites.

Concurrent activities: Activities in the timetable that can occur at the same time as other activities without compromising the outcome of each other.

Contingency: Recognition that the project budget may be inadequate to cover unexpected or unseen circumstances. Expressed as a percentage of the budget.

Core process: Process that greatly contributes to the generation of income, consumption of resources, or the amplification of goodwill. Without a core process, an organization cannot achieve its vision.

Culture: The personality and character of the organization, which governs the intangibles of the organization, the way people work, speak, dress, and behave; what is valued; and the traditions and the privileges that they enjoy. A shared set of habits, customs, knowledge, beliefs, language, and behaviors. Culture may be invisible to people who are part of it. Culture is a deep source of unstated assumptions that need to be identified and stated explicitly to fortify consensus building. Could also be the outcome of how people relate to one another.

Customer: The person, organization, or process that uses the process output.

Delay: Any point in the process where waiting and non-value-add occurs.

Dependent activities: Activities on the timetable that can be completed only when other activities have occurred.

Direct implementation: The improved process immediately replaces the previous process.

Document controller: Team member who is the custodian (maintains, distributes, and stores) of all project documentation.

Documentation plan: Identifies the document controller and how documents will be stored, retrieved, issued, transmitted, numbered, and revised during and after the life of the project.

Dream team: Team that redesigns or creates the new process.

Duplication: Any activity that is repeated during the process with the same result.

Effectiveness measurements: Measure of how effective the process is at converting inputs to outputs, the amount of activity conducted within the process, the amount of output produced, and the number of customers served.

Efficiency measurements: Identifies the minimum possible level of resources to be consumed during the process. Actual consumption is assessed against set standards as a variation or variance.

Executive sponsor: Executive manager responsible for ensuring that the project achieves the stated objective. The business process improvement team reports to the executive sponsor.

Gap analysis: Identifies how the organization can acquire the skills, competencies, and resources that are not present in the organization. May be used to set objectives.

Gatekeeper: Team member who ensures that the meetings are kept to time and that deadlines are maintained.

Goals: Stepping-stones that support the *what* of the vision. These must be aligned to the vision to make sense and add value.

Handover: A document or object is given to another person in the process, electronically or manually.

Immaterial: The outcome is not affected by a change in the parameters.

Implementation plan: Schedule of who, what, and when will implement the improved process.

Implementation report: Written report generated by the process implementation team either during or after the implementation.

Independent activities: Activities that do not depend on the completion or the outcome of other activities to be completed.

Input: Tangible object or intangible element that goes into the process to be converted or transformed into an output.

Inspection: Any approvals, checks, or balances that occur during the process. The examination or measurement of an item or activity to verify conformance to specific requirements. For example, software inspections are a disciplined approach to detect and correct defects in software artifacts and to prevent defects from surviving into operations. Software inspections are common practice in organizations committed to certain quality approaches, such as ISO 9000, Six Sigma° (Motorola), and the Capability Maturity Model° (Carnegie-Mellon University).

Lessons learned: Experiential based learning documented by the project team that may add to the organizational intelligence.

Long-term objective: An objective that will be achieved in a period taking at least two years or more.

Measurement system: The collection and analysis of data that provides a continuous assessment of the performance of the process.

Materiality: The extent to which an outcome is affected by a change in parameters.

Medium-term objective: An objective that will be achieved in less than two years but more than one year.

Non-value-added activities: Activities that do not directly contribute to the conversion of inputs to outputs. Typically, non-value-added activities can be removed from the process without changing the quality of the output.

Objective: A desired position reached or achieved by some activity by some time. Objectives are measurable restatements of goals. They provide specific, measurable, adjustable, relevant, and time-based targets for a group.

Opportunity: Trend or condition external to the organization or process that can guide efforts to help achieving vision, goals, or objectives.

Opportunity register: Documentation of external or internal situations that the team can use to positively champion the progress of the business process improvement.

Outcome measurements: Measures of the ability of the process to meet the customers' needs.

Output: The tangible object or intangible element that the customer receives at the end of the process.

Output measurements: Measures of how effective the process is at converting inputs to outputs, the amount of activity conducted within the process, the amount of output produced, and the number of customers served. (Same as effectiveness measurement.)

Outreach member: Team member responsible for communication with the process stakeholders.

Primary activity: Activity that is essential to the entire process. The outcome is compromised if the outcome of primary activity is inaccurate.

Procedure: Documentation of the systematic activities that take the user from the beginning to the end of a process. Reveals the *what, when,* and *who* of the process.

Process: A collection of sequential activities that convert inputs to outputs.

Process characteristics: Common features of all processes.

Process examination team: Team responsible for documentation of the as-is process and attaining executive approval for the project.

Process implementation team: Team responsible for implementing the new process and ensuring that it works. Also responsible for documenting the procedures for the process.

Process management team: Team responsible for the first phase of the project. The team is responsible to get management buy-in for the project and for selection of the process to be improved.

Process owner: The person in the organization who has a vested interest in the process. The process owner loses most when the process fails and gains most when the process succeeds.

Project budget: The resources—services and materials—with the associated costs that are needed for the completion of the business process improvement, phased over the life of the project.

Project team: A multifunctional group of individuals chartered to plan and execute a project. Groups of people who have accepted responsibility for the determination of the project scope, the execution, and completion of the project and the implementation of the results. At different phases of the project, the team members change to reflect the needs of the particular phase of the project.

Project timetable: A list of the activities needed to complete the project, matched to the time they are expected to occur.

Process measurements: Identifies the minimum possible level of resources to be consumed during the process. Actual consumption is assessed against set standards as a variation or variance. (Same as efficiency measurements.)

Redundant activity: Any activity that is repeated to decrease the likelihood of errors.

Report analysis: Identification of all the reports generated from independent databases other than the main database or operating system. Provides the reasons that the reports exist and provides solutions to generate the reports from the main operating system or database.

Resistance: The level of nonacceptance the stakeholder evidences for the proposed change. The more pain or the less power that the change brings, the greater the stakeholder resistance.

Rework: Activity that ensues when work is returned to an earlier point of the process to be corrected or otherwise.

Risk register: Assessment of the impact that external and internal situations may have on the project outcome and the probability that situations will occur. Identification of the mitigating strategies and the likelihood that the implementation will lessen the impact.

Rule: Mandatory beliefs about what must be done in the process. Usually undocumented, they are accepted by everyone in the process as the way things must be done and by whom during the process.

Sample: A small quantity of the population that is thought to represent the whole.

Sampling risk: The risk that the sample may not be representative of the whole population.

Scribe: Team member who records the findings during project meetings.

Secondary activity: Minor tasks that may contribute to the completion of the process but are not essential to the successful completion.

Sequential activities: Activities that can happen only after other activities are completed. They may need the outputs of other activities to begin.

Short-term objective: An objective that will be achieved in less than one year.

Skills analysis: Identifies the skills, competencies, and resources that exist or do not exist in the organization. Results can be used to complete a gap analysis.

SMART objectives: Objectives that include elements that make them specific, measurable, achievable (or adjustable), realistic (or relevant), and time-based.

Source: The person, system, or process that feeds the inputs into the selected process.

Stakeholder(s): Individuals and groups that have a vested interest in a project or are impacted in some way. Key stakeholders have influence on project decisions but are not formally on the project team. Internal or external people, groups, and systems that interact with the organization or process.

Stakeholder analysis: Examination of how each proposed process change will affect stakeholders and their interaction with the process. Can be done at group or individual level.

Stakeholder group: A group of stakeholders who interact with the process or organization in the same manner.

Stakeholder interest: Determination of the motives and needs of each stakeholder that allows anticipation of how the stakeholder will interact with the process and support the project or not.

Stakeholder strategy plan: Blueprint of how the business process improvement team intends to interact with stakeholders. Focuses on how the business process improvement team can use stakeholders' interests to further the project.

Strength: Condition internal to the organization that can accelerate the achievement of vision, goals, and objectives.

Team leader: Responsible for the project team, has a vested interest in the project outcome.

Team: The collection of people from various functional areas who come together to complete the business process improvement project.

Team charter: Document that outlines the responsibility of the business process improvement team and its members during the project.

Team member: Participant with one of the business process improvement teams.

Threat: Trend or conditions external to the organization that that may hamper or limit the achievement of its vision, goals, or objectives.

Value-added activities: Activities that directly contribute to the conversion of inputs to the desired outputs. These activities must be present to guarantee a quality output.

Vision: The organization's dream, where it is headed, how it sees itself when it is running at full steam, without constraints, what the business process improvement strives to attain on a daily basis. This is a clear and compelling image of the desired results in sufficient detail that it can be recognized as complete when accomplished. This sets the overall direction for a business. Objectives support the vision. A vision is intended for planning and communication, and thus a vision should be purposefully articulated to bridge the present and future; it should serve as a critical impetus for change; it should be brief, memorable, and sufficiently complete to direct effort.

Vision statement: Written statement that conveys the reason why the business process improvement exists. A vision is intended for planning and communication, and thus a vision should be purposefully articulated to bridge the present and future; it should serve as a critical impetus for change; it should be brief, memorable, and sufficiently complete to direct effort.

Weakness: Condition internal to the organization that may limit or prevent the achievement of vision, goals, or objectives.

Workflow: The diagrammatic representation of a process.

Workflow diagram: A diagram that represents the process workflow.

Index